Come, Come,
Yet Again Come

*"Come, come, whoever you are;
wanderer, worshipper, lover of learning,
it does not matter.
Ours is not a caravan of despair.
Come, even if you have broken your vow
a thousand times.
Come, come, yet again come."*

Come, Come, Yet Again Come

Responses to Questions

OSHO

New Age Books

ISBN: 81-7822-154-3

First Edition: Delhi, 2003

© 1981 Osho International Foundation
© All revision 1953-2003 Osho International Foundation
All rights reserved.

Osho is a registered trademark of Osho International Foundation, used under license.

For more information: www.osho.com
A comprehensive multilingual web site featuring Osho's meditations, books and tapes and an online tour of the meditation resort at Osho Commune International.

Published by
NEW AGE BOOKS
A-44 Naraina Phase I
New Delhi-110 028 (INDIA)
Email: nab@vsnl.in
Website: www.newagebooksindia.com

Printed in India
at Shri Jainendra Press
A-45 Naraina Phase-I, New Delhi-110 028

Preface

You have heard many people, you have read many people; but hearing me or reading me is a totally different experience, for the simple reason that I am not a speaker, an orator, a lecturer.

Your questions may be the same, but my answers cannot be the same for two reasons. First, I have forgotten your questions and my answers—I cannot repeat, I am not a gramophone record. Secondly, your questions may be the same, but the questioners are different—and I answer the questioner, not the question.

Naturally, words will be repeated. Somebody has counted that I have answered fifteen thousand questions, and I am not a learned man; my vocabulary is very limited. But because I am not answering the question, even though the words may be the same, the answer has a different nuance every time. Not that I am making an effort not to repeat myself...I don't remember at all, I have never read any of my books.

Each time when I am answering you, I am never prepared for it. I don't know myself what is going to be my next sentence. It is not ordinary speaking; it is a communion, not only communication. I have nothing to communicate. I am not trying to convince you about something—because if I am trying to convince you, then the only way is to repeat the same thing again and again and again so it becomes a conditioning in your mind.

My words are not important. What is important is your silent listening. What is important is that my words are not coming from the mind, but from my deepest silence. Although they cannot contain silence, when they come from the deepest silence something of that silence surrounds them. They cannot contain it, but something of the silence surrounds them. It is as if you have taken a bath in a lake; you cannot contain the lake, but when you come out of it, something of the lake—the freshness, the coolness—comes with you. The lake is left behind, but some quality of the lake is carried with you.

You are listening in silence; I am speaking in silence. My words reach to you with some freshness, with some fragrance; and because you are silent, that fragrance, that silence, deepens your silence—makes it fragrant.

It is very difficult for intellectuals to understand what is happening. It is a very non-intellectual, heart-to-heart communion. Words are only excuses.

I would love to sit silently with you, but then you cannot be silent. If I am silent, then your mind will go on: yakkety-yak, yakkety-yak. Just to save you from trouble, I have to speak, and because I am speaking, your mind becomes engaged in listening. It forgets its own yakkety-yak, or postpones it.

It is certainly a miracle. And these are authentic miracles, not miracles like Jesus walking on the water.

I have heard a story: Two rabbis and one bishop were very great friends. All three had gone fishing on the same lake where Jesus used to walk—Lake Galilee.

The bishop was an American; those two rabbis were local Jews. Talking about Jesus, one rabbi said, "You Christians make too much of small things. Here, everybody knows how to walk on water."

The bishop said, "Everybody...? You can walk on water?"

The rabbi said, "Of course," and he stepped over the side of the boat and walked on water.

The bishop could not believe his eyes.... He is a Jew, he does not even believe in Christ! These are the people who crucified Jesus. This is absolutely unfair of God—that even rabbis should be allowed to do miracles.

The first rabbi came back. The bishop asked the second rabbi, "Can you also walk?"

He said, "Everybody can walk. You have unnecessarily made too much fuss about Jesus—that he walked on water. In Israel, everybody walks on water."

The bishop said, "This is a new thing; I have never heard of it. Just show me that you can also walk on water." And the second rabbi stepped out of the boat and walked on water. The bishop looked with unblinking eyes—he even forgot to breathe.

And the second rabbi came back, and both of them said, "Now, you are a follower of Jesus; you can try. Do you trust Jesus?"

The bishop said, "Absolutely."

Then they said, "You can try."

So the bishop stepped out on his side–this was the other side of the boat—and started drowning. One rabbi said, "What do you think, should we tell that American idiot where the stones are?"

Local people know where the rocks are. These are not miracles. The real miracle happens almost invisibly. Your being silent here...just listening to the birds: tweet, toot, toot—it is a miracle.

OSHO
The Rebellious Spirit
Chapter 14

Contents

Preface .... *v*

1. Whoever Knocks is a Welcome Guest 1
2. From the Body to the Soul 21
3. A Flute on the Lips of God 37
4. You are the Question 53
5. Let Sannyas Happen 69
6. A Thousand and One Ways to Laugh 85
7. Aes Dhammo Sanantano 101
8. Silence and Song Meet 117
9. The Very Alphabet of Love 135
10. Everybody Can Laugh 147
11. The Suchness of Things 161
12. From Italy to Nirvana 183
13. Of Course the Grass Grows by Itself 197
14. The Forgotten But Not the Lost 215
15. No Question Means the Answer 233

    Appendix 249

CHAPTER 1

Whoever Knocks is a Welcome Guest

The first question

I am a sinner. Can I also become your sannyasin?

Yes, absolutely yes! In fact, only a sinner can become a sannyasin. Those who think themselves saints, holier-than-thou, they are the closed people, they are the dead people. They have become incapable of living, incapable of celebrating.

Sannyas is celebration of life, and sin is natural: natural in the sense that you are unconscious—what else can you do? In unconsciousness, sin is bound to happen. Sin simply means that you don't know what you are doing, you are unaware, so whatsoever you do goes wrong. But to recognize that "I am a sinner" is the beginning of a great pilgrimage. To recognize that "I am a sinner" is the beginning of real virtue. To see that "I am ignorant" is the first glimpse of wisdom.

The real problem arises with people who are full of knowledge. All that knowledge is borrowed; hence, rubbish. The people who think they are virtuous because they have created a certain character around themselves are the people lost to God. Your so-called saints are the farthest away, because God is life, and your saints have renounced life. In renouncing life they have renounced God too.

God is the hidden core of *this* life. This life is just the outermost part, the circumference; God is the center of it all. To renounce the circumference, to escape from it, is to renounce the center automatically. You will not find God anywhere. The farther away you go from life, the farther away you will be from God. One has to dive into life, and of course when you are unconscious you will miss the target many times.

The original Hebrew word for sin is very beautiful. By translating it as "sin", Christians have missed the very message of Jesus. The original Hebrew word for sin is so totally different from your idea of sin that it will be a surprise to you. The root word means forgetfulness; it has nothing to do with what you are doing. The whole thing is whether you are doing it with conscious being or out of unconsciousness. Are you doing it with a self-remembering or have you completely forgotten yourself?

Any action coming out of unconsciousness is sin. The action may look virtuous, but it cannot be. You may create a beautiful facade, a character, a certain virtuousness; you may speak the truth, you may avoid lies; you may try to be moral, and so on and so forth. But if all this is coming from unconsciousness, it is all sin.

It is because of this that Jesus has a tremendously significant saying. He says, "If your right eye causes you to sin, take it out and throw it away. It is much better for you to lose a part of your body than to have your whole body thrown into hell."

Now, if you don't understand the real meaning of sin, you are bound to misinterpret the whole statement and Jesus will look too harsh, too hard, too violent. Saying, "If your right eye causes you to sin, take it out and throw it away," does not look like a statement of Jesus. A man of profound love and compassion — he cannot say it, he cannot be so violent. But this is how Christians have interpreted him.

What he means is: whatsoever causes you to forget yourself, even if it is your right eye... That is just to emphasize the fact. It is simply a way of talking, an emphasis: "If your right eye causes you to forget yourself, then take it out and throw it away." He is not saying anything which has to be taken literally; it is a metaphor. He is saying that it is better to be blind than to be forgetful of yourself, because the blind man who remembers himself is not blind, he has the real eye. And the man who has eyes, if he has forgotten himself, what is the use of having eyes? He cannot see himself—what *else* can he see?

Your question is beautiful. You say, "I am a sinner..." Everybody is! To be born in this world means to be a sinner. But remember my emphasis: it means to forget oneself.

That's the whole purpose of the world: to give you an opportunity to forget yourself. Why? — so that you can remember. But you will ask— and your question will look logical — "If we already remembered before, then why this unnecessary torture that we have to forget ourselves and *then* remember again? What is the point of this whole exercise? It seems to be an exercise of utter futility!" It is not; there is great significance in it.

The fish in the ocean is born in the ocean, lives in the ocean, but knows nothing about the ocean — unless you take the fish out of the ocean. Then, suddenly, a recognition arises in the fish. Only when you lose something do you remember. Only in that contrast does remembering happen. Then let the fish go back to the ocean. It is the same fish, it is the same ocean, the same situation—yet everything is different. Now the fish knows that the ocean is her life, her very being. Before, she was in the ocean but unaware; now, she is in the ocean but aware. And that's the great difference, the difference that makes the difference.

We have lived in God, we all come from the original source of existence, but we have to be thrown out into the world so that we can start searching for God again, searching for the ocean — thirsty, hungry, starving, longing. And the day we find it again there is great rejoicing. And it is not anything new.

The day Buddha became enlightened he laughed and he said to himself, "This is very strange! What I have gained is not an achievement at all, it is only a recognition. I had it always, but I was unaware of it."

The only difference between a sinner and a sage is that the sinner is full of forgetfulness, and the sage is full of remembering. And between these two is that hocus-pocus being called the saint. He does not know anything, he does not remember anything. He has heard other sages or may have read the scriptures, and he repeats those scriptures like a parrot—not only repeats but practices also. He tries to behave like a sage. But any effort to behave like a sage shows only one thing: that you are not a sage yet.

The sage lives simply, spontaneously; there is no question of effort at all. He lives life just as you breathe. He is very ordinary; there is nothing special about a sage. But the saint is very special, because the saint is trying to *do* something. And of course he is making a great effort, because it is not his own understanding. So he is continuously torturing himself to behave rightly, violently forcing himself to behave rightly. Naturally, he expects much respect from you. He can go on doing all this masochism, this self-torture, if you give him respect. Just think: if the so-called respect given to the saints disappears, out of one hundred of your saints, ninety-nine point nine percent will immediately disappear. They are living only for the ego.

It is good that you realize that you are a sinner. This is the beginning of something tremendously significant. You can be a sage; all that you have to avoid is being a saint! That is the trouble: the saint is the false coin which looks exactly like the real coin; in fact, it looks more real than the real one. It has to, because it has to deceive people. Avoid being a saint.

That's what my sannyas is: living your ordinary life with only one addition, that of awareness — and the sinner will become a sage. The sinner becomes a sage through awareness; the sinner becomes a saint through cultivating a character.

I don't teach you character, I teach you consciousness. Hence, I am not at all interested that you are a sinner and that you have been doing all kinds of sins—that is irrelevant. It is accepted that in your unconsciousness what else can you do?

I accept you with total love, respect.

Many times I have been told, particularly by the so-called saints, "You go on giving sannyas to everybody—this is not right. Sannyas should be given only to people of character!"

It is as if you go to a physician and he says, "My condition for giving you medicine is that I give it to you only when you are healthy. Come to me when you are healthy. I never give medicines to people who are ill, I never waste my medicines on ill people! First become healthy and then come to me." You can understand the absurdity of that.

If I say to somebody, "First go and become *worthy* of sannyas, then come to me," that means that if he can become worthy of sannyas by his own effort, then why cannot he become a sannyasin by himself? What is the need for him to come to *me*? He needs help, and anybody who *asks* for help should be given help, and it should be given unconditionally.

There is a beautiful statement of Mevlana Jalaluddin Rumi, one of the greatest Sufi masters ever. Take it to your heart.

> *Come, come, whoever you are;*
> *wanderer, worshipper, lover of learning...*
> *It does not matter. Ours is not a caravan of despair.*
> *Come, even if you have broken your vow a thousand times.*
> *Come, come, yet again come.*

Come, come, whoever you are... sinner, unconscious, living a life which is not glorious, divine, meaningful; living a life which has no poetry, no joy, a life of hell... Whosoever you are, Mevlana says, "Come, I am ready to receive you. Be my guest!"

The master is a host; he refuses nobody. True masters never refuse anybody. They cannot. If *they* start refusing people, then there is no hope. If you go under a tree, a shady tree—tired of your journey and the burning sun on your head—and the tree refuses you, it does not give you refuge, it does not shelter you... It does not happen at all. The tree is always ready to give you shelter, its shadow, its fruits, its flowers, its fragrance.

A great Tibetan story is...

Once there lived a master who never initiated anybody. His fame slowly became very well known all over the country, even beyond the boundaries of the country. And people would come and fall at his feet and ask to be initiated. But his conditions were such that nobody was able to fulfill them, so nobody was ever thought worthy—nobody deserved initiation.

He had only a servant, not even a disciple. One day when he was ill and on his deathbed, he called his servant and told him, "Go to the marketplace, and whosoever wants to be initiated, bring them all. I am going to initiate!"

The servant was shocked. He said, "Are you talking in a delirium or something? Your whole life you insisted on certain qualities—unless those were fulfilled you would not initiate— and nobody has ever been able to fulfill your conditions. Now you are telling me to go to the marketplace and tell people that anybody who wants to be initiated should come? What about the conditions? What about the prerequisites? What about the essential readiness? What about the groundwork?"

The master said, "Don't waste my time anymore, because this is my last day on the earth. Simply go! Do what I am saying, don't argue. You are my servant—simply follow the order. Go and find anybody who wants to come!"

The servant went, puzzled. He could not believe his own ears, could not believe his own eyes. But because the master had ordered, and he was just a servant, he had to follow. He went into the marketplace very unwillingly. He shouted in the marketplace. Nobody believed him; they thought he had gone mad. He said, "I am not saying it, he himself has told me! I also think that he has gone mad, now you are thinking that I have gone mad. I am simply a servant. He must have gone mad! He is dying, he has lost all his senses. But give it a try you are not going to lose anything."

A few people, just out of curiosity, a few people who had nothing to do... It was a holiday, so they said, "Okay, we are coming. Let us see what happens!" Somebody had quarreled with his wife and had nowhere to go, so he said, "I am coming." A gambler and a drunkard who were just on the road, simply followed seeing this whole bunch of people, not knowing where they were going.

So this strange crowd reached the master's place, and he started initiating them one by one. The first man he initiated was the drunkard. Of course he was so drunk that he could not even think that the master was mad —he did not even realize that he was being initiated! He was not aware at all what was happening. When the master said, "Do you want to be initiated?" he simply nodded his head.

The servant could not believe it. He said, "What are you doing? This man is completely drunk, he is an alcoholic, and you are giving him initiation! And there is a thief in the crowd, and one man has come because he is unemployed and he thought at least this way he would find some employment — at least he could become a saint and people would feed him. And there are a few people who have come because it is a holiday. A few others have come just out of curiosity: 'Let us see what is happening.' The man next to the drunkard has come here only because his wife has thrown him out and closed the doors. He was standing outside, and he said, 'Okay, so I am coming also!' These are not seekers and searchers — they are not religious at all! What are you doing? Your whole life you were waiting for worthy people, people who are deserving!"

The master said, "Listen, the truth is — now I can tell you — I was not a master at all! Just this morning I have realized myself, but I could not tell anybody that I was not a master. So rather than telling the truth, I always tried to make some impossible demands which could not be fulfilled. In that way I saved my ego. But today I have come to know who I am, and now I know that everybody is capable of knowing because everybody is basically the same. Even this drunkard is no more unconscious than anybody else. Everybody is unconscious, and unconscious people need initiation; they need the help of those who have become conscious. The conscious person can function as a catalytic agent."

Mevlana is right: *Come, come, whoever you are; wanderer, worshipper, lover of learning... it does not matter.* The master is ready; it does not matter who comes to him. Whoever knocks on his door is a welcome guest.

Ours is not a caravan of despair. Remember this beautiful statement: "Ours is not a caravan of despair." I can also say this. Ours is not a caravan of despair, it is a celebration — it is the celebration of life.

People become religious out of misery, and the person who becomes religious out of misery becomes religious for the wrong reasons. And if the very beginning is wrong, the end cannot be right.

Become religious out of joy, out of the experience of beauty that surrounds you, out of the immense gift of life that God has given to you. Become religious out of gratitude, thankfulness. Your temples, your churches, your mosques and *gurudwaras* are full of miserable people. They have turned your temples also into hells. They are there because they are in agony. They don't know God, they have no interest in God; they are not concerned with truth; there is no inquiry. They are just there to be consoled, comforted. Hence they seek anybody who can give them cheap beliefs to patch up their lives, to hide their wounds, to cover up their misery. They are there in search of some false satisfaction.

Ours is not a caravan of despair. It is a temple of joy, of song, of dance, of music, of creativity, of love and life.

You are welcome, join the caravan.

> *Come, even if you have broken your vow*
> *a thousand times.*

It does not matter. You may have broken all the rules – the rules of conduct, the rules of morality. In fact, anybody who has any guts is bound to break those rules. Only people who are without guts, who have no spine to their being can follow the priests and the politicians, the demagogues, the people who have vested interests in the establishment. But if you have any intelligence then you will be a rebel. And the rebel will be called a sinner, and the obedient fool will be called a saint.

This starts happening from the very childhood. The obedient child is praised by the parents, obviously — for the simple reason that he is not a pain in their necks. He is so dull, so dead that whatsoever they say he does. He is an imitator; he is a carbon copy, and the parents' egos feel very nourished by the child. He follows them, he believes in them, he adores them.

But the intelligent child will not be respected by the parents. They will always feel some trouble with the intelligent child, because he will ask questions which they can't answer because they don't know themselves. He will ask such things as will be embarrassing to them. He will create situations in which they will see their impotence. They will not be able to control him — and everybody is interested in controlling everybody else; nobody wants to give freedom. They will not be able to enslave the child; he will resist all efforts to enslave him, he will give them a good fight. In fact, he is the child to be loved, to be respected, because he has some life, he has some soul. But he will be condemned.

Intelligence is condemned, imitativeness is respected. Original faces are distorted and masks are painted, beautifully decorated. The true, the authentic, is denied, and the false, the inauthentic, is raised as high as possible. And the same thing goes on happening in the schools, colleges, universities. The whole of society is a repetition of the same thing on a larger scale.

Only very stupid people become your presidents, your prime ministers. You will not tolerate intelligent people, you will not give power to intelligent people, because you will be afraid of them. You will always want some stupid people to dominate you, because there will always be a certain affinity between you and the stupid. There will be a certain understanding, a communication.

Jesus is bound to be crucified, and Mother Teresa of Calcutta is going to win the Nobel Prize. Socrates is going to be poisoned and killed, but not the so-called professors of philosophy in the universities; they are very respectable people. Socrates was not respectable. If he had been respectable, then Athens would not have behaved in such an ugly way. He was condemned like a criminal, but the professors of philosophy who are teaching Socrates are very respected people; they all have respectability. They write great treatises on Socrates, and nobody poisons them.

One of my professors wrote his thesis on the philosophy of Socrates, and he got a DLitt in it. He was very happy, and all his students gave him a party. I was also present. I asked him one thing: "Socrates was given poison and you are given a DLitt. There must be something wrong with your treatise! It cannot be Socratic, that much is certain. I have not looked into your treatise, and I am not going to look into it at all — I am not going to waste my time! One thing is certain: something is absolutely un-Socratic about it; otherwise, why should the society, the university, give you recognition?"

Whoever Knocks is a Welcome Guest 9

He could not answer me, but he became an enemy. He started avoiding me, and I started haunting him! Wherever we would meet alone — sometimes walking on the road to the university, or going for a morning walk, or in the night—I would always look out for him and say, "Hello, Socrates!" He would become so angry!

One day he told me, "Why are you after me? What wrong have I done to you?"

I said, "You have not done anything wrong to me, I am simply trying to make the point clear to you that writing a treatise on Socrates is one thing, and to *be* a Socrates is totally another. If you were a Socrates you would have been crucified, you would have been stoned to death. The same university would have condemned you; you would have been expelled from this university."

And finally, *he* was not expelled from the university, I was expelled. And when I was expelled, I went to him and told him, "Look! I am not even a professor, I have not written a treatise on Socrates, and they have expelled me!"

And the reasons they gave me were: "You ask embarrassing questions of the professors. You disturb their classes. You don't allow them to finish their syllabus and you go on persisting with one question for months at a time."

And I said, "How can I drop the question unless it is answered? If it is not answered, then what are months? — even a whole life has to be devoted to it!"

And they said, "You may be right, but people have come here to get their degrees. They are not interested in truth, nor are the professors interested in truth. Go and find some other place."

And then no other university was ready to accept me, because I had become notorious! One university accepted me on the condition that I would never ask any question. Now, what kind of universities are these? So when the vice-chancellor said to me, "You have to put it in writing for me that you will not ask the professors any questions," I said, "I can do that, but then you have to understand one thing: that I will not attend the classes. But you have to give me permission to appear in the examination, because I will not be fulfilling the percentage of attendance required — seventy-five percent. It is impossible."

He said, "Why? Why can't you attend the classes?"

I said, "If I attend the classes, then I will not be able to resist the temptation to ask questions! Then I will ask questions. Either allow me to ask questions or give me the attendance mark; otherwise, what will be the point of my being there?"

He said, "Okay, we will give you the attendance mark."

So I never attended the classes — it was against the rules, but they gave me a ninety percent attendance mark. I never went to any class, because one thing was certain, that once I saw a professor then I didn't care what I had given in writing—I *had* to ask the questions!

My father used to tell me wherever he would take me with him, "Keep silent, don't ask any question; otherwise, please don't come with me."

I would promise him that I would not ask the question, and I would ask the question. And he would come home very heated—"You promised...!"

I said, "What can I do? I completely forget! When I see stupid people talking about great things, I cannot resist —I simply forget. It is not that I want to hurt you or anything, but what can I do? That man was talking about the soul being immortal, and he knows nothing. I simply asked him, 'If I kill you, will you be angry or not? If the soul is immortal, allow me to kill you! At least allow me to slap you – what to say about killing! The soul is immortal!' And he was saying, 'I am not the body.' 'So perfectly okay—I slap the body, and you are not the body!' And he became angry, and you are also becoming angry. I was not asking anything wrong, I was simply asking a question that *he* had raised!"

People go on talking nonsense, but this whole society exists for the lowest, for the mediocre.

I agree with Mevlana— *mevlana* means the master. Jalaluddin Rumi was called Mevlana by his disciples out of great love. Mevlana says:

> *Come, even if you have broken your vow*
> *a thousand times.*

Intelligent people are bound to break all their vows many times, because life goes on changing, situations go on changing. And the vow is taken under pressure — maybe the fear of hell, the greed for heaven, respectability in society... It is not coming from your innermost core. When something comes from your own inner being, it is never broken. But then it is never a vow, it is a simple phenomenon like breathing.

Come, come, yet again come!

If you want to be a sannyasin, you are welcome. Everybody is welcome, without any conditions. You do not have to fulfill any requirements. Just the longing to be in deep contact with me is enough, more than enough. Just the desire to be close to me, to be intimate with me is enough. That's what sannyas is all about.

And drop this idea of being a sinner, because that must be creating some guilt in you. That guilt is one of the oldest tricks of the priests for dominating people. They create guilt in you. They give you such stupid ideas that you cannot fulfill them. Then guilt arises, and once the guilt has arisen, you are trapped.

Guilt is the trade secret of all the so-called, established religions. Create guilt in people, make them feel bad about themselves. Don't let them be respectful of their own lives; let them feel condemned. Let them feel, deep down, that they are ugly, that they are **not** of any worth, that they are dust, and then of course they will be ready to be guided by any fool. They will be more than ready to become dependent, in the hope that "somebody will lead us to the ultimate light." These are the people who have been exploiting you for centuries.

The time has come when a great rebellion is needed against all established religions. Religiousness is needed in the world but no more religions—no more Hindus, no more Christians, no more Mohammedans — just pure religious people, people who have great respect for themselves.

And remember, only a person who has respect for himself can respect others, because life is the same. If you are too hard upon yourself you will be more hard on others, obviously. You will magnify their sins; you have to, just to give yourself consolation that you are not the only sinner, there are greater sinners than you. That will be your only consolation in life: that you need not worry, you are just a small sinner, there are great sinners.

That's why people go on creating rumors about everybody else. And people believe rumors very easily. If somebody says something ugly, derogatory about a person, you immediately believe it. But if somebody praises him, you don't believe it, you ask for proofs. You never ask for proofs about derogatory remarks and rumors. You are very willing to believe them for the simple reason that you *want* to believe that "everybody is far worse than I am." That's the only way to feel good, a little bit good, about yourself.

The priests have given you only two alternatives. Either you follow the impossible rules that they impose; then you feel paralyzed, crippled, imprisoned. Or, if you want to live a life of freedom and you want to be natural, guilt arises. In both ways you are being exploited.

I am here to free you from all exploitation.

Freedom is the taste of sannyas, the fragrance of sannyas. My sannyasins are not trying to cultivate any character, they are trying a totally different phenomenon: they are raising their consciousness. And then I leave everybody free to live according to his own light.

The second question

> I have come to a dead end. I see the impotence of the mind and feel all action is useless. Does the mind totally die only in samadhi? Please say something about mind and action in witnessing.

You say, "I have come to a dead end"—but I don't feel it so. Not yet, because when you really come to a dead end, a transformation immediately happens. You are coming closer to it, of that much I am certain. The dead end is not far away, but you have not come to it yet. Your whole question proves it.

You are coming closer, you are feeling intuitively that it is not far away—but it has not been reached yet. Still, there is hope. Still, deep down, you are dreaming that this is not going to be the dead end; hence the question arises.

You say, "I see the impotence of the mind..." You have not seen it yet, you only think you have. Seeing and thinking are totally different, but one can get mixed up very easily. Thinking can pretend to be seeing. You are not seeing the impotence of the mind; otherwise even this question would not arise. If the mind is really impotent, what can it ask? What can it think about? It simply falls from you, it withers away.

But the shadow is on you, and that's a good sign. The day is not far away when you *will* see the impotence of the mind—and then immediately the transformation. Then, immediately, a sudden enlightening experience. All questions disappear, all answers disappear, because when the mind is seen, *really* seen as impotent, what is there to ask and what is there to find? The mind simply evaporates. Then life is left, pure life, unhindered, undistorted by the mind.

Then you will not say that you feel all action useless. If you see the impotence of the mind, the mind disappears but action becomes for the first time tremendously beautiful. There is no question of utility at all. Life has no utility in itself. What is the use of a roseflower? — but still it goes on growing, still it goes on opening, still it goes on releasing its fragrance. What is the use of it? What is the use of the sun rising every day? Is there any use for the sun itself? What is the use of the starry night?

The word "use" is part of the paraphernalia of the mind. Mind always thinks in terms of utility. The mind is a Jew; it always thinks in terms of purpose, profit, utility. When the mind disappears, action does not disappear, activity disappears—and there is a great difference between the two. Activity has utility; action is pure joy, pure beauty. You act not because something has to be achieved, you act because action is a dance, is a song. You act because you are so full of energy.

Have you watched a child running on the seabeach? You ask him, "Why are you running? What is the purpose of your running? What are you going to gain out of it?" Have you watched the child collecting seashells on the beach? You ask him, "What is the utility of it all? You can use your time in a more utilitarian way. Why waste your time?"

The child is not concerned about utility at all, he is enjoying his energy. He is so full of energy, so bubbling with energy that it is a sheer dance— any excuse will do. These are just excuses— seashells, pebbles, colored stones. These are just excuses— the sun, the beautiful beach... just excuses to run and to jump and to shout with joy. There is no utility at all.

"Energy is delight"— that is a statement made by William Blake, one of the most mystical poets of the West. Energy IS delight. When there is great energy, what are you going to do with it? It is bound to explode.

Action comes out of energy, out of delight. Activity is businesslike. Action is poetry. Activity creates a bondage because it is result oriented: you are doing it not for its own sake, you are doing it for some goal. There is a motive, and then there is frustration. Out of a hundred cases, ninety-nine times you will not achieve the goal, so ninety-nine times you will be in misery, frustration. You did not enjoy the activity itself, you were waiting for the result. Now the result has come, and ninety-nine times out of a hundred there is frustration. And don't hope for the remaining one percent, because when you achieve the goal, there is frustration also. The goal is achieved, but suddenly you realize that all the dreams you have been dreaming about the goal are not fulfilled.

You have achieved the money, but where is the joy that you have always been hoping for when the money was there? You have that great marble palace, but you are the same poor man—the same emptiness inside, the same hollowness. You used to live in a hut, now you start living in a palace—but the *same* person. You were miserable in the hut, and you will be even more miserable in the palace, because the palace has more space and of course when there is more space you will be more miserable. What else can you do with that space? All that you know is how to be miserable.

So you see poor people and you see rich people. The only difference is that the poor people are still hoping. There is hope, hence poor people are not so frustrated. Rich people have lost all their hopes; they are more frustrated. The poor person can still dream— he can still go on counting in his mind how great a bank balance he will have next year and the year after. Soon the day will come when he will be rich and he will have a car and a good house and a good wife, and the children will be going to good schools. But what can the rich man dream? All that he can dream about he has already, and nothing is happening out of it. The money is there, but he is as empty as ever.

There are two kinds of poor people: the poor poor and the rich poor. And remember, the second category is far worse.

Activity means there is a goal; activity is only a means to that end. Action means that the means and the end are together in it. That's the difference between action and activity.

Activity will become useless, but then action arises and action has a totally different dimension. You act for the sheer joy of acting. For example, I am speaking to you—it is not activity, hence I am not concerned with the result at all. It is a pure act. I enjoy communicating with you, I enjoy communing with you. I am grateful to you that you allow me. If you don't allow me, I will have to talk to the trees or to the rocks, or I will have to talk to myself! I am obliged to you; you need not be obliged to me. It is a pure act. There is something in me that wants to relate. There is no goal orientation—I am not expecting anything from you. If something happens, good; if nothing happens, even better! If you become enlightened, good; if you don't become enlightened, far out! –for the simple reason that if you all become enlightened, who am I going to talk to? So please, delay your enlightenment as long as you can—this much of a favor you have to do for me! It is a simple act. No motive, no future in it— just the present.

Hence I am not trying to create a system of thought—I cannot, because to create a system of thought you have to be motivated. Then you have to link everything in a certain logical order. I can enjoy fragments.

When P.D. Ouspensky wrote his first book on Gurdjieff, he gave it the title *In Search Of The Miraculous*. He was a man of a philosophic bent, a great mathematician, logician and philosopher. When he showed the book to George Gurdjieff, his master, Gurdjieff just looked here and there for a few minutes and then he said, "Give it a subtitle too: *Fragments Of A Teaching*."

He was a little puzzled, because he had tried to make a whole system and Gurdjieff was suggesting an extra title. "The main title, *In Search Of The Miraculous*," Gurdjieff said, "is okay, but it needs the subtitle, *Fragments Of A Teaching*—in fact, *Fragments Of An Unknown Teaching*."

Ouspensky asked, "Why?"

Gurdjieff said, "Because I cannot create a system of thought – these are all fragments."

And you can see it happening here. You can collect all my thoughts, but they will be only fragments – fragments but not a system. To create a system, you need to be goal oriented. You have to follow a certain structure, and you have to go on like an arrow towards a target.

That is not possible either for a man like me or Gurdjieff. We cannot follow any goal. Our every act is complete in itself, entire in itself. It has no relationship with the past and no relationship with the future. It is total. If I die this very moment, there will be no desire in me even to have completed the sentence.

Action is an end unto itself; it has no utility. When the mind is seen to be impotent, the mind disappears. In that very seeing, the mind disappears. And, of course, with it all utilitarian activities will also disappear, because mind is the cause of goal orientation. It contains all your motives. It contains your past and the future; it does not contain the present at all. And when there is no mind, all that is left is pure present. You act moment to moment, and each moment is enough unto itself. Hence the beauty of the statements of Jesus, Buddha, Lao Tzu, because each statement is in itself perfect, it needs nothing. You can take any statement from anywhere, and you can meditate over it and it will give you the taste of *tao, dhamma*—truth.

Buddha used to say again and again that the taste of the sea is the same. You can taste it from anywhere, from any shore – the taste is the same. This shore or that makes no difference. Each statement of a buddha has the taste of truth. But it is not concerned with utility...

You are feeling in an intuitive way that something is coming closer of which you are afraid: "the dead end." Everybody becomes afraid, and out of fear the question has arisen. You ask, "I have come to a dead end. I see the impotence of the mind and feel all action useless. Does the mind totally die only in *samadhi*?"

Just the reverse is the case: when the mind dies totally, what is left is samadhi. So I cannot say that the mind dies totally only in samadhi; that will be putting things upside down. The mind dies first, and then what is left is called samadhi. That state of no-mind is called samadhi.

But the death of the mind frightens, scares one. That's what you are feeling: the shadow of death. It is not *your* death, it is the death of the mind which is not you. But for many lives we have lived identified with the mind, so when the death of the mind comes closer it feels as if *we* are going to die. It is not a dead end for *you*, it is certainly a dead end for the mind. That too has not come yet, but the mind is freaking out, because once it has come, then there is no way out for the mind. If it can escape just before the dead end, then there is a possibility of surviving...hence the question.

You say: "Please say something about mind and action in witnessing." In witnessing, mind remains only as a biocomputer, a mechanism, but separate from you; you are no longer identified with it. When you want any memory you can use the mind just as you can put on your tape recorder. Mind is *really* a tape recorder. But it is not continuously on, not twenty-four hours on. When needed, the witness, the man of meditation, the man of awareness, is capable of putting the mind on or off. He puts it on when there is some need.

If I am talking to you, I have to put the mind on; otherwise language will not be possible. No-mind is silent, there is no language; only mind can supply the language. I have to use the mind to relate with your mind; that's the only way to relate with your mind, so I put it on.

When I go back and sit in the car, I put it off. Before Heeren turns the ignition on, I turn *my* ignition off! In my room I don't need my mind. When my secretary comes with the letters, or with some work, I say to her, "Hello!" And inside I say, "Hello, mind. My secretary has come!" Otherwise there is no need for the mind.

When you are witnessing, the mind remains, but not constantly working. Your identity is broken. You are the watcher; the mind is the watched. It is a beautiful mechanism, one of the most beautiful mechanisms that nature has given to you. So you can use it when needed for factual memory – for phone numbers, for addresses, for names, for faces... It is a good tool, but that's all it is. It need not sit upon you continuously twenty-four hours a day. Even while you are sleeping, it is sitting on your chest torturing you, giving you nightmares. All kinds of relevant and irrelevant thoughts go on and on.

It does two harms. One: you lose your purity of witnessing, you don't remain a mirror. Your mirror becomes so covered with the dust of thoughts that you start becoming closed to existence, you cannot reflect existence. The full moon is there, but your mirror does not reflect it. How many people are there who see the full moon? Even if they see it, they don't *see*—their seeing is not of any value. They don't rejoice, they don't dance. How many people are there who see the flowers? Just now the birds are singing, but how many people are there who are aware of the birds and the wind passing through the trees?

When the mind is no longer hovering over you continuously, you become aware of infinite beauty, of truth, of the celebration that goes on and on in existence. But the mind is there, put aside— you can put it on when needed.

And when activity ceases, action is born. Action means response; activity means reaction. When you are in action, it means the mind is put aside and your consciousness is in a direct contact with existence; hence the response is immediate. Then whatsoever you do is not ready-made. It is not a ready-made answer given by the mind; you are responding to the reality as it is. Then there is beauty, because your action is true to the situation.

But millions of people in the world are simply living through ready-made answers. They are already carrying the answer; they don't listen, they don't see the situation confronting them. They are more interested in the answer that they are carrying within themselves than in the question itself, and they go on living their answer again and again. That's why their life becomes a boredom, a repetitive boredom, a drag. It is no longer a dance, it cannot be a dance.

Action is a dance; activity is a drag. Activity is always untrue to the situation; action is always true to the situation. And activity is always inadequate because it carries an answer from the past, and life goes on changing every moment, so whatsoever you bring from the past is never adequate, it always falls short. So whatsoever you do, there is frustration; you feel that you have not been able to cope with reality. You always feel something is missing, you always feel your reaction was not exactly as it should have been. And the reason is that you have simply repeated, parrot-like, a ready-made answer, cheap but untrue – untrue because the situation is new.

The mind will be there but with a new status, with a new functioning. It will be under your control: you will be the master, not the mind. You will use it when it is needed; you will not use it when it is not needed. It cannot insist that you have to listen to it, that you have to go on listening to it. Even if you are sleeping, it goes on knocking on your doors; it does not allow you even to have a beautiful sleep.

The second loss is that because the mind is working twenty-four hours a day, from the cradle to the grave, it becomes mediocre, it becomes stupid. It never has enough energy, it becomes very weak; hence the impotence. If the mind has time to rest, it will again become rejuvenated, it will again be fresh.

The mind of a buddha is always fresh, it is always young. It is always responding with such freshness, with such newness that it seems unbelievable. Your questions may be the same, but the answers of a buddha always have a new nuance to them, a new flavor, a new fragrance. You can go on listening to the buddha for years, and still you will remain enchanted. Even if he repeats something it is never the same—the context is different, the color is different, the meaning is different.

The mind will be there, more alive, more potent, more restful, younger, fresher— not your master but a good servant, an obedient servant. Activity will disappear totally; there will arise action.

Action means there is no goal to it. Just as the poets say "poetry for poetry's sake" or "art for art's sake," the same is the situation with the mystic. His action is for action's sake; there is no other goal to it. He enjoys it just like a small child, innocently he enjoys it.

Witnessing is the miracle that changes everything in your life. Then the dead end is only a new beginning, a death and a birth—the death of the old, a total death; a discontinuity with the old, and the arrival of something absolutely unknown, the arrival of the new. It is a resurrection — a crucifixion and a resurrection. But the resurrection is possible only after crucifixion.

The dead end is going to come, but it is the beginning also. And you will see the beginning immediately, when the dead end has come. If you are just thinking about it, that it is coming, it is coming...the mind can even say, "It has come—beware, escape! While there is time, run away!" Then you will miss the other side of it. You will see only the cross, you will miss the resurrection.

You are thinking the mind is impotent. Your thinking is on the right track, but thinking will not help, *seeing* is needed. Become a witness so that you can see that the mind is impotent. *Feel* that activities are useless, but not action. Action continues. Buddha lived for forty-two years after his enlightenment. Action continued, activities disappeared.

The last question

Please, a few jokes to take back to England.

I am perfectly willing, but you'd better go to France or to Italy or to America. Taking jokes to England is absolutely futile! They will think you are mad. Take something serious for those people, something gloomy like their climate, with no sun shining, all clouds. Take an umbrella with you! And if you don't know how to be really English, meet Proper Sagar – take a few lessons from him. He is so proper that even though he has been living here for seven years, I have not been able to destroy his Englishman.

Ordinarily I never feel hopeless, but when I look at Proper Sagar sometimes I suspect that maybe with Sagar I have to feel hopeless. He is such a perfect English gentleman! First look at him...! As for the jokes, a story about Jesus' birth...

After Jesus was born, Joseph went with Mary to visit the in-laws.

"We live in Nazareth now," said Mary. "The baby was born in Bethlehem just a few days ago, in a farmer's barn because we couldn't find a room!"

"You mean with all the livestock?" exclaimed Mary's mother.

"That's right," replied Mary, "and just as he was born, three old men appeared."

"Three drunks," explained Joseph.

"And three shepherds," continued Mary.

"And they got drunk, too!" explained Joseph.

"You mean, you all got drunk?" said Mary's father, shocked.

"That's right!" said Joseph.

Joseph must have been a drunkard. Jesus himself remained a

drunkard his whole life. Those three wise men from the East...and Joseph says, "There were three drunkards, three drunks."

An American and a Frenchman are discussing how many lovemaking positions there are. After much talk, they decide to enumerate them.

The American begins by saying that there are one hundred positions. In the first one, the woman lies on her back and the man rests on top of her.

"Voila!" cries the Frenchman. "That makes one hundred and one!"

One can always miss the obvious!
And the last...

The Vatican announced that the pope was to visit one of the few Catholic churches in Poland. The local priest arranged for all the strong believers from his community to clean and make the place tidy. The church was blessed to have a special relic from the time of Christ: a bunch of St. Peter's pubic hairs. One of the helpers, thinking it was rubbish, threw it away.

When the priest did a last minute check of the precious relic before the pope's arrival, he was shocked to find that the "holy remembrance" had disappeared. Desperate, he reached beneath his robe and grabbed a few of his own to place in the box.

The priest wa9s guiding the pope through the church. When they arrived at the box containing the relic, he said, "And this, Your Holiness, is our most holy gift from God!"

"Ugh!" groaned the pope when he smelt it. "You can still tell our Peter was a fisherman!"

Enough for today.

CHAPTER 2

From the Body to the Soul

The first question

Jesus says, "Seek and you will find." Does a desireless search exist?

Jesus was in a very unfortunate situation: he had learned all the secrets in the East and he was introducing something that had never existed in the Jewish tradition before—that was his crime. The orthodox, the traditional, the conventional mind could not understand him.

Lao Tzu was far more fortunate— he had the right people to talk to. Buddha was blessed—he could say things in as subtle a way as possible. In that sense Jesus was hoping against hope. It was a great challenge and he took the risk—he sacrificed his life. But he was misunderstood: it was bound to happen, it was inevitable. Whenever you introduce a new truth, you have to suffer for it, but it is a joy to suffer in the service of truth.

Jesus could not even say the whole truth—that would have been too much. So whatsoever statements have come down in the name of Jesus are only half the story; the other half has never been told. Jesus could not say it because of the Jews he was surrounded with, and Christians have been clinging to those half-truths for two thousand years.

For example, this statement is only a half-truth: "Seek and ye shall find." The other half, which has been said by Lao Tzu, is far more important; without it the first half becomes not only meaningless but dangerous. Lao Tzu says, "Do not seek and you will find. Do not seek and you have found it already." Both statements will look contradictory to each other; they are not.

The beginning of the pilgrimage starts with searching, seeking, inquiring; there is no other way to begin. Unless you inquire what is the meaning of life, unless you go in search of the essential core of existence, you will never move, you will not even take the first step. Hence, the search has to begin. But if you continue searching forever and ever, if your search never comes to an end, you will remain in the mind. It is the mind which searches.

Search is also a subtle desire. Even the inquiry into knowing is ambitious. The very desire to achieve something—money, power, prestige, meditation, God, whatsoever it is, any desire, any ambition—leads you into the future; it distracts you from the present. And the present is the only reality, the only truth there is.

The person who never begins the search will remain unconscious; the person who always remains in the search will go crazy. The search has to begin so that you become a little more alert, a little more observant, vigilant, aware. And then the search has to be dropped so that you become silent, so that the mind disappears, so that the future evaporates and you are simply herenow, neither seeking nor searching. In that stillness of no-search, truth is found.

And Lao Tzu is right when he says, "Seek and ye shall miss. Seek not and find immediately." But his statement is the second part of the journey. Jesus was speaking to the beginners; he is like a primary school teacher. Lao Tzu is talking to the adepts, to those who have come a long way; he is talking to the initiates. He is talking to people who can understand the joy of not searching, the stillness, the tranquillity, the calmness of simply being—no ambition, no desire, no future, no time, no mind.

Jesus' statement is only half of the truth, and the beginning half. It is good for those who have not started the journey. It is meaningless, and not only that but harmful, for those who have started the journey and who are coming to realize the utter futility of all search.

The truth is within you, and every search means going out, going somewhere else, leaving your home. When you drop searching you will come back home naturally, spontaneously; you will settle at the very core of your being.

You also ask, "Does a desireless search exist?"

No. All search is a manifestation of desire. But there is something like a state of consciousness which can be called non-searching, non-seeking, a state of total rest. In that total rest is samadhi. In that absolute tranquillity is realization.

Sylvia Moses has asked a similar question... She says, "For many years

From the Body to the Soul

I have been wondering what the difference is between spirituality and religiousness. Until now I have been unsuccessful in obtaining an answer. Can you tell me?"

Sylvia, the statement of Jesus, "Seek and ye shall find, ask and it shall be given to you, knock and the doors shall be opened unto you," contains religiousness. Lao Tzu's statement: "Seek not and find immediately," or Rabiya al-Adabiya's statement to Hassan...

Hassan was a Sufi seeker; Rabiya was a Sufi master. Everyday Rabiya used to pass through the marketplace, and she would see Hassan kneeling down in front of the mosque and praying to God with raised hands: "My Lord, how long have I to ask you? Open thy doors so that I can enter!"

Rabiya had heard this prayer thousands of times. One day she came up to Hassan, shook him out of his prayer and shouted at him, "Stop all this nonsense. The doors are always open! Why don't you enter?"

And it was a great revelation to Hassan. Suddenly, he realized what he had been asking: "Lord, open thy doors so that I can enter!" And Rabiya was saying, "The doors are always open, God has never closed them. If you want to enter, enter, but don't go on playing with this stupid prayer again and again. Don't waste your time and don't waste his time! If you want to enter, enter; otherwise go home! I don't want to see you sitting here in front of the mosque again!"

Hassan was shocked, bewildered. But it was the right moment, because when a person like Rabiya says something to somebody it is always at the right moment—when the person is ready to understand. He understood, he followed Rabiya. He touched her feet and thanked her, and told her, "You are right. I was just being a fool! I wasted my life!"

Rabiya said, "Stop! Don't talk nonsense again! It has not been a wastage. If you had not prayed all these years here you would not have understood me. It has helped. It has not helped God to open the doors because the doors are open, but it has helped you to understand my statement that the doors are open for you to enter. I cannot say this thing to anybody else in this town; only you were ripe. The spring has come only to you, that's why the flower has blossomed."

Sylvia, religiousness means the circumference, and spirituality means the center. Religiousness has something of spirituality, but only something— a vague radiation, something like a reflection in the lake of the starry night, of the full moon. Spirituality is the real thing; religiousness is just a by-product.

And one of the greatest misfortunes that has happened to humanity is that people are being told to be religious not spiritual. Hence, they start decorating their circumference, they cultivate character. Character is your circumference. By painting your circumference, the center is not changed. But if you change the center, the circumference automatically goes through a transformation.

Change the center—that is spirituality. Spirituality is an inner revolution. It certainly affects your behavior, but only as a by-product. Because you are more alert, more aware, so naturally your action is different, your behavior has a different quality, a different flavor, a different beauty. But vice versa does not... If your body is healthy then your lips are red, but you can paint them with lipstick and they will look red—and ugly. A woman with lipstick is the ugliest woman possible. I sometimes wonder who she is trying to deceive! Her whole face is saying something else, her whole body is saying something else, and her lips are so red... Such redness does not happen naturally; they are painted. But there are fools in the world—she will find some fool to kiss those painted lips too!

I cannot believe it!—just try tasting lipstick and you will understand what I mean when I say I cannot believe it! And layers and layers of lipstick, old, rotten!

People are living with painted faces, wearing masks. These people are called religious. Christians, Hindus, Mohammedans, Jainas—these are religious people. Buddha, Jesus, Zarathustra, Krishna, Lao Tzu—these people are spiritual.

Spirituality belongs to your essential being, and religiousness only to the outermost: actions, behavior, morality. Religiousness is formal; going to the church every Sunday is a social affair. The church is nothing but a kind of club, a Rotary Club, a Lions Club – and there are many clubs. The church is also a club, but with religious pretensions.

The spiritual person belongs to no creed, to no dogma. He cannot belong to any church, Hindu, Christian, Mohammedan...it is impossible for him to belong to any.

Spirituality is one; religions are many.
My insistence here is on inner transformation.
I don't teach you religion, I teach you spirituality.
I can understand, Sylvia, why you were unable to find any answer.

You must have been asking the religious people—the Christians, the bishops, the popes, the priests, or the rabbis. They will give you answers because they are supposed to know. They know nothing; they are just supposed to know.

"Rabbi," asked Little Saul one day, "why do coachmen have brown, white, red or black beards, but never green ones?"

"I have to ponder on this," replied the rabbi.

"Rabbi," asked Little Saul again, "why do you always chain the horse with its tail towards the carriage instead of its head?"

"I have to think about this," replied the rabbi.

Next day the rabbi saw Little Saul and told him, "I have found the solution to both your questions: if the beard of a coachman were green and you put the horse with its head towards the carriage, the horse might think the beard was grass and eat it!"

The rabbis, the priests, the bishops—they are supposed to know everything. You can ask any question, sensible or not so sensible, making some sense or making no sense at all, but they will answer. It is their business to answer all kinds of stupid questions.

You must have been asking these people, Sylvia, that's why you have not been successful in obtaining an answer. They don't have the answer. Only a Jesus can answer your question, or a Buddha or a Kabir or a Nanak—somebody who knows life from his innermost being, who has come to know the eternal in himself.

Spirituality belongs to the eternal, and religion belongs to the temporal. Religion belongs to people's behavior. It is really what Pavlov, Skinner, Delgado and others call a conditioning of the behavior. The child is brought up by Christians—then he is conditioned in one way, he becomes a Christian. Or he is brought up by Hindus—he is conditioned in another way, he becomes a Hindu. His conditioning is an imprisonment; he will remain a Hindu. He will think like a Hindu or a Christian his whole life. And those thoughts are not his own, they have been put into his head by others – by the vested interests, by the establishment, by the state, by the church. They have their own interests: they want to dominate you. And the best way to dominate you is to condition you from the very beginning so deeply that you start thinking that this conditioning is what you are.

You are not a Christian, or a Hindu, or a Mohammedan. You are born as a spiritual being and then you become a victim of your parents, teachers and priests. And of course these parents, these teachers and these priests go on telling you, "Respect your parents, respect your teachers, respect your priests." If you don't respect them you will fall into hell; if you respect them, then all the pleasures of heaven are yours. This is a simple psychological strategy to make you afraid and to make you greedy. These are the two things people are ruled by: fear and greed. And the spiritual person is one who is free of both.

Just a few days ago I talked about one friend, Ajai Krishna Lakanpal. He wanted to take sannyas one month ago, but he wrote to me saying, "I am ready to take sannyas today if you say so; otherwise, I will feel happier taking sannyas on the twenty-fifth of October, on my birthday. I want to ask my mother. I know she will allow it, she will not prevent me."

So I said, "Okay, ask your mother." And his mother has not prevented him, she has permitted him to take sannyas. Of course she said, "I will not feel very happy, but if you are feeling good about it you can take sannyas."

Now he has written to me: "My mother will not feel happy, that's why I cannot take sannyas." First it was the permission of the mother; now the permission is there but the mother will not feel happy.

Just a few days ago I discussed it, and he became very angry. He wrote an angry letter to me. A few points which he has written are worth considering—it shows how people are being conditioned. The first thing he was angry about was that I told you he is forty-five years old. He was angry because he is only thirty-six. It does not matter—forty-five or thirty-six, how does it matter? But the anger is caused by something else; this is just an excuse to find some fault.

I was informed wrongly, so now I am putting it right. Ajai Krishna, you are not forty-five, you are twenty-seven... forty-five plus twenty-seven divided by two, and you will be thirty-six— exactly thirty-six!

And again he goes on rationalizing. He says, "My old master, Kamu Baba, has said, 'Never hurt the feelings of your parents. If you hurt the feelings of your parents, then no master can ever help you.'"

True. But are you sure, Ajai Krishna, that you are not hurting the feelings of your parents?

He himself writes in his letter: "My father died and I feel guilty because I am an alcoholic and I did not listen to him. I continued to drink too much, and he died. And now I feel guilty that I was not up to his standards."

Did you not remember your Kamu Baba's statement? Now, do you think, Ajai Krishna, your mother is happy with your alcoholism? Are you not hurting your mother by drinking too much? But that problem does not arise. The father has died, the son feels guilty and still he continues to drink—maybe a little more so that he does not feel guilty. The mother is old, sixty-eight, or maybe seventy-eight— because again it is my secretary who has informed me! Is your mother very happy with your alcoholism? Are you not hurting her? Do you think alcohol can help when you hurt your mother? A master cannot help, that is true—Kamu Baba must be right. But can alcohol help?

And not only that, he quotes the Koran. He says, "In the Koran it is said, 'Don't hurt your parents. To be surrendered to your parents, to sit at their feet, is to be in paradise.'"

And do you think, Ajai Krishna, that the Koran says to go on drinking as much as you want? The Koran also says that if you drink you will fall into hell! So you choose only that part of the Koran which helps you to do what you want to do.

He also quotes Jewish scriptures, that they too say to respect your parents. But they are all against alcohol. If you really respect your mother, then give one proof: stop drinking. If you really want to make her happy, stop drinking. That will be proof; otherwise this is sheer playing with words, rationalization. Neither are you interested in Kamu Baba, nor are you interested in your father, nor are you interested in your mother. Your whole interest is: you are afraid of sannyas.

And the last thing which he says in his letter is: "It is not true that I am afraid of sannyas. It is because of compassion for my mother." And by being an alcoholic you are being very compassionate to your mother...?

But all the religions down the ages have been teaching you to respect your parents. Why? Why do the religions teach that? It is a subtle strategy of exploitation. Your religion has been given to you by your parents, and if you go against your religion, they will be hurt.

If a Hindu declares, "I am simply a human being, no longer a Hindu," the parents will be hurt. So the parents have also taught him to respect them and believe in whatsoever they have said—they cannot be wrong. As if your parents are enlightened people! As if your parents know what they are doing! Their parents did the same thing to them, they have done it to you, and you will do it to your children. This is how diseases go on being transferred from one generation to another generation.

Of course the priests will say, "Respect your parents," because there is a conspiracy. The conspiracy is that all their interests are involved together in keeping hold of you.

To be my sannyasin means to be a rebel. I am not saying to hurt the feelings of your parents, I am saying to be yourself. Be lovingly yourself, be respectfully yourself. There is no need to go out of your way to hurt your parents, but if they don't allow you to be yourself then it is their responsibility. If they feel hurt, that is their responsibility, not yours. Don't harm them, but don't harm yourself either, because your first responsibility is towards your own self; everything else is secondary.

But man's mind is very cunning: he will hide his cowardice in the beautiful word "compassion"; he will rationalize everything.

Sylvia, your religions are nothing but the rationalizations of fear, of greed. They are conspiracies against you by the establishment, by the people who are ruling you politically, religiously, philosophically, in every way—by the people who have reduced humanity to a great concentration camp.

And you must have asked these people, "What is the difference between spirituality and religiousness?" They cannot say—they don't know themselves.

Spirituality is rebellion; religiousness is orthodoxy. Spirituality is individuality; religiousness is just remaining part of the crowd psychology. Religiousness keeps you a sheep, and spirituality is a lion's roar.

The second question

I have heard that your sannyasins celebrate death.

You have heard rightly! My sannyasins celebrate everything. Celebration is the foundation of my sannyas—not renunciation but rejoicing; rejoicing in all the beauties, all the joys, all that life offers, because this whole life is a gift of God.

The old religions have taught you to renounce life. They are all life negative; their whole approach is pessimistic. They are all against life and its joys. To me, life and God are synonymous. In fact, life is a far better word than God itself, because God is only a philosophical term, while life is real, existential. The word "God" exists only in scriptures; it is a word, a mere word. Life is within you and without you – in the trees, in the clouds, in the stars. This whole existence is a dance of life.

I teach love for life.

I teach the art of living your life totally, of being drunk with the divine *through* life. I am not an escapist. All your old religions have been teaching you escapism—they were all in a certain sense hip. The word "hippie" has to be understood. It simply means one who escapes from the battle of life, who shows his hips...! All your old religions are hippie! They have shown their hips. They could not accept the challenge of life, they could not confront and encounter life. They were cowards; they escaped to the mountains, to the monasteries.

But even if you escape to the mountains and to the monasteries, how can you leave yourself behind? You are part of life. Life pulsates in your blood, life breathes in you, life is your very being! Where can you escape? And all those efforts to escape, considered correctly, are suicidal. Your monks, your nuns, your mahatmas, your so-called saints, were all suicidal people; they were trying gradual suicide. Not only were they suicidal, they were cowards too—cowards because they could not even commit suicide in a single blow. They were committing suicide gradually, in installments; by and by, slowly they were dying. And we have respected these unhealthy people, these unwholesome people, these insane people. They were against God because they were against life.

I am in tremendous love with life, hence I teach celebration. Everything has to be celebrated, everything has to be lived, loved. To me nothing is mundane and nothing is sacred. To me all is sacred, from the lowest rung of the ladder to the highest rung. It is the same ladder: from the body to the soul, from the physical to the spiritual, from sex to *samadhi*—everything is divine!

An old neo-sannyasin told an actor playing Hamlet that he himself had once played the part.

"What was your interpretation of the role?" asked the actor. "Did Hamlet really make love to Ophelia?"

"I don't know if Hamlet did," replied the sannyasin, "but I certainly did!"

Celebration has to be total, only then can you be multidimensionally rich. And to be multidimensionally rich is the only thing we can offer to God.

If there is a God, and someday you have to face him, he will ask you only one question: "Have you lived your life totally or not?"— because this opportunity is given to you to live, not to renounce.

Paul, my sannyasins celebrate death too, because to me death is not the end of life but the very crescendo of life, the very climax. It is the ultimate of life. If you have lived rightly, if you have lived moment to moment totally, if you have squeezed out the whole juice of life, your death will be the ultimate orgasm.

The sexual orgasm is nothing compared to the orgasm that death brings, but it brings it only to the person who knows the art of being total. The sexual orgasm is a very faint thing compared to the orgasm that death brings. What happens in sexual orgasm? For a moment you forget that you are a body, for a moment two lovers become merged into one unity, into one organic union. For a moment they are not separate entities; they have melted into each other like two clouds which have become one.

But it is only for a single moment, then they are again separate. Hence all sexual orgasms bring in their wake a kind of depression, because you fall from the height. You reached a crescendo, and for only a fragment of a moment you remained on the peak and then the peak disappeared. And when you fall from that height, you fall into the depth of depression.

This is one of the contradictions of sex: it gives you the greatest pleasure and also the greatest agony. It gives you ecstasy and agony – both. And each time you reach an orgasmic state, you know that soon it will disappear. Then there is disillusionment, disappointment.

Death gives you the ultimate in orgasmic joy: the body is left behind forever and your being becomes one with the whole. It is immeasurable. If to become one with a single person gives you so much joy, just think how much joy will happen in becoming one with the infinite! But it does not happen to everybody who dies, because the people who have not lived rightly cannot die rightly either. The people who have lived in deep unconsciousness will die in deep unconsciousness. Death will give you only that which you have lived all your life; it is the essence of your whole life.

If your life was of meditativeness, awareness, witnessing, then you will be able to witness death too. If your whole life you remained cool, centered in different situations, death will give you the ultimate challenge, the ultimate test. And if you can remain centered, calm and cool and watching, then you will not die an unconscious death, your death will bring you to the ultimate peak of consciousness. And then, certainly, it *has* to be celebrated.

So whenever one of my sannyasins dies, we celebrate, we dance, we sing. We give him a good farewell.

A midget had died and left a widow. Friends came to pay their condolences and look at the body lying in an upstairs room of the house. After one friend came down he was asked by the widow whether he had shut the door of the room where the body lay.

"No," said the visitor, "I didn't think it was necessary."

"Then I'd better go upstairs and shut it," replied the widow. "The cat has had him downstairs twice already. You know, my cat is a neo-sannyasin and he wants to celebrate the occasion!"

Little Pierino goes camping with his parents. A little while after, at the end of a day doing many things, they bed down for the evening. Pierino cries, "Mummy, I can't sleep. There is a dead ant on my belly!"

"Shhh, Pierino," says his mother, "be a good boy, just go to sleep — it is nothing to worry about."

After a few minutes Pierino's voice is heard again, "Mummy, Mummy, I can't go to sleep—I've got a dead ant on my belly!"

"Pierino," scolds his mother, "come on now, don't tell me that a small dead ant stops you from sleeping!"

"Well," replies Pierino, "it is not the dead ant really, it is all his orange sannyasin friends that have come to celebrate his death!"

Yes, my sannyasins celebrate death because they celebrate life. And death is not against life; it does not end life, it only brings life to a beautiful peak. Life continues even after death. It was there before birth, it is going to continue after death. Life is not confined to the small space that exists between birth and death; on the contrary, births and deaths are small episodes in the eternity of life.

We celebrate everything. Celebration is our way to receive all the gifts from God. Life is his gift, death is his gift; the body is his gift, the soul is his gift. We celebrate everything. We love the body, we love the soul. We are materialist spiritualists. Nothing like this has ever happened in the world. This is a new experiment, a new beginning, and it has a great future.

In the past there have been materialists who denied the soul, and there have been spiritualists who denied the body. Both were agreed on one point: that only one can be accepted, either the body or the soul. They were either/or people. They were not ready to accept the whole as it is; they were choosers.

My sannyasins live in choiceless awareness. We are not choosers; we simply accept whatsoever is the case. The materialists—the Charvakas in India and the Epicureans in Greece—denied the soul. They said, "There is no soul. The soul is just imagination. The soul is illusion." And the spiritualists—Shankaracharya in India and Berkeley in Europe—these people said that matter is illusory, maya. The body does not exist really, it is only your imagination. It is a dream, made of the same stuff as dreams are made of; you are a soul. But both are agreeing on one point: that they cannot accept reality as it is, they have to choose.

It is as if one electrician chooses the positive pole and another electrician chooses the negative pole, and each denies the other pole. There will be no electricity, no light in the world.

That's what has happened: the spiritualist has not been able to transform the world, the materialist has failed also—because the world exists with polar opposites. Without polarity there is no world at all. The day is needed as much as the night; the body is needed as much as the soul; the world is needed as much as God. There can be no circumference without a center and there can be no center without a circumference. This is a simple fact.

My sannyas is the acceptance of that which is. We are not choosers. Who are we to choose? And what difference is our choice going to make? You can choose whatsoever you like, but whatsoever you don't like is going to remain there. Just by not choosing it, it is not going to disappear. And because you have not chosen it, you will remain half, lopsided.

The East has remained lopsided because of so-called spirituality. It has remained poor, unscientific – without any technology, without industry. It has become lousy, lazy, lethargic; it has lost all joy in existence because "this is all a dream, why bother about it?" It is hungry, ill, poor, but "this is all illusion. You are simply dreaming that you are poor, you are not really poor. You are simply dreaming that you are starving, you are not starving."

And the West has chosen materialism, so there is great technology, beautiful houses, better roads, better cars, better airplanes, but man is very empty and meaningless. Without spirituality there is no center; man falls apart. The Western man is half; the Eastern man is half.

My effort here is to create the whole man. To me the whole man is the only holy man. The East and the West have to meet; they have to become complementaries, not antagonists. But this is possible only if we change the whole philosophical background. Hence I teach a very contradictory philosophy. Spiritual materialism is the name that I give to my philosophy.

I want you to be materialists and spiritualists simultaneously, in a balanced way. I would love society to have all the facilities, all the comforts and conveniences that science and technology can provide, and I would also love people to have a great awareness inside them so that they can enjoy whatsoever science provides. I would like everybody to be a buddha, but at the same time I would also like the world to become more and more comfortable, more and more loving, more and more beautiful.

We can transform this world into a paradise, but then we have to stop choosing. We have simply to accept the whole as it is, with all its contradictions. Those contradictions are contradictions only because of our logical obsession; otherwise they are complementaries. Life and death—both are beautiful.

The last question

What does it mean when a woman says she is afraid of a man?

If you had asked me what it means when a man says that he is afraid of a woman, I would have answered you very accurately. But your question is such that it is almost unanswerable. It is very difficult to say what it means when a woman says she is afraid of a man – the woman says one thing and means another thing! She may simply be making you feel at ease—"Don't be afraid, I myself am afraid of you!" She must see that you are trembling! She must be aware of your fear.

Everyman is afraid of the woman—he has to be. From the very beginning he is in the hands of a woman, the mother, and the fear is created from those very early days. Your first impression of a woman is that of a mother, and the mother has made you immensely afraid. And you have seen that not only were you afraid, but your father was also afraid of your mother. Outside the house he was like a lion, and whenever he came home he started wagging his tail!

You have seen this. Children are very perceptive; they go on looking at what is happening. They understand perfectly well who is really the master of the house. They are afraid of the mother, the father is afraid of the mother, everybody seems to be afraid of the mother, and naturally they become accustomed to the fear.

And then man is capable of tackling any problem intellectually. He is afraid of the woman because her ways of tackling a problem are very intuitive, instinctive. No woman is intellectual—intelligent of course, but not intellectual. Man's intelligence is of one kind, and hers, the woman's intelligence, is of a totally different kind. Man's intelligence is the essence of his intellect, and woman's intelligence arises out of her intuitiveness. There is no meeting ground – there is no possibility of it. They are polar opposites, that's why they are attracted to each other. Because they cannot understand each other there is mystery between them; that mystery is of great appeal.

A frustrated man was staring hopelessly down the platform at the departing train. "If you hadn't taken so long getting ready," he accused his wife, "we would have caught it."

"Yes," she replied, "and if you hadn't hurried me we wouldn't have so long to wait for the next one!"

"Is this supposed to be art? Why on earth did they hang this picture here?" one woman asked another in an art gallery.

"Maybe they couldn't find the painter," the other replied.

A beautiful blonde filled in the job application.

The personnel director looked it over, then said, "Miss Johnson, under 'Experience' could you be a little more specific than just 'Oh, boy!'?"

A girl in a whorehouse of a red-light district told the madam one day that she was quitting.

"You can't do that," protested the madam, "you're the best girl I've got. Why, I've seen you go upstairs thirty and more times a night."

"That's right," the girl agreed. "That's why I'm quitting. My feet are killing me, and it's on account of those damn stairs!"

It is very difficult for me to answer your question. You will have to ask your woman yourself.

Schumann, the postman, was retiring. On his last day, as usual, he delivered to Mrs. Katz, who invited him in for a fine breakfast.

When he finished and was about to leave, she beckoned him into the bedroom where they made love for an hour. When he was getting ready to leave, she handed him an envelope with a dollar bill in it.

Schumann was overwhelmed. "Look, Mrs. Katz," he said finally, "I've been delivering your mail for the past twenty years and you have never so much as offered me a cup of coffee. So why today did all this happen?"

"Well," she said, "I told my husband Sol that you were retiring today and he said, 'Fuck him! Give him a buck!' – the breakfast was my idea!"

Enough for today.

CHAPTER 3

A Flute on the Lips of God

The first question

This poem is by Robert Graves:

*Those who dare give nothing
are left with less than nothing;
Dear Heart, you give me everything,
which leaves you more than everything—
though those who dare give nothing
might judge it left you nothing.
Giving you everything,
I too, who once had nothing,
am left with more than everything
as gifts for those with nothing
who need, if not our everything,
at least a loving something.*

What is the source of your infinite spring of giving?

The source is always the same. We are just like rays of the same sun. The source of existence is what we call God; it is better to call it the ultimate source. From there everything comes, and to there everything returns.

But the man who starts thinking himself separate from the source is bound to become miserly. Not knowing that he is part of the source, he becomes very small, afraid to give. Then his mathematics is: if you give you will have less; if you go on giving, one day you will be a beggar.

Not knowing about the infinite source is the cause of our miserliness. And to be a miser is to be in misery, because the person who cannot give becomes incapable of receiving. The person who cannot give becomes closed—he is afraid to give. He has to be very cautious to keep his windows and doors closed, tightly closed, so nothing escapes from him. But these are the same doors from where things come. If you keep your doors closed, the sunrays will not reach you, the wind will not come to you; you will not be able to see the stars and the flowers, and the fragrance will not float into your being. The miserly person is bound to be in misery—he is cut off. He lives as if he were a tree without roots, ungrounded, uprooted. His life is nothing but a process of slow dying; he does not know anything of abundant life.

Jesus says to his disciples, "Come, follow me and I will give you abundant life." What does he mean by abundant life? He simply means that if your ego can be surrendered, if you can drop the idea of being separate from existence, in that very dropping you become open—open to give, open to receive. And the ultimate miracle is: the more you give, the more you receive; the more you give, the more you become worthy of receiving.

It is like a well. You can lock up the well, you can cover it up in fear—maybe in the coming year there are not going to be any rains. It is better, advisable, to preserve the water in your well, to prevent your neighbors, to prevent everybody from drinking or taking water from your well. You can keep the well closed, but when the time of need arises you will be surprised: the well water will no longer be worth drinking, it will have become poisoned. And, moreover, the well will have lost its springs.

If you go on drawing water from the well, the springs go on feeding it. The more you draw the water, the bigger the springs which go on opening up. Your well is just a small window in the ocean, a faraway window; it is connected with the ocean. If you create a vacuum in the well, if you go on emptying it, then the waters will be rushing in from all sides to fill it up. Nature abhors a vacuum—physically, spiritually, on every dimension and plane.

Be empty, and you will be surprised: the emptier you are, the more full you will be. Hence, by giving you don't have less; by giving you have more. By giving you don't become a beggar; by giving you become an emperor.

A Flute on the Lips of God

Gautam the Buddha came to visit Vaishali, one of the big, beautiful capitals of those days. The king of Vaishali was very egoistic: he was not willing to go to receive Buddha in his capital.

His chief minister was an old man his father's age. He had looked after the king's affairs for his whole life since he was just a child, because when the king was a child his father had died. He was almost like a father to him, and the king had great respect for the old man. The old man said, "If you don't go to receive Buddha, then take my resignation!"

The king was puzzled, he could not believe it. Why this insistence? He said, "Why should a king go to receive a beggar?"

The old man laughed and he said, "It is just the opposite! You are the beggar and he is the king, and the beggar has to go to receive the king. He is the king because he has given; he is the king because he goes on giving. The more he has given the more he has. Either see the point or here is my resignation, because I cannot serve a fool!"

The king understood the point. He went, he fell at the feet of Buddha and he said, "Excuse me, forgive me! I had always thought that you were just a beggar; now I can see that I am a beggar because I go on clinging to whatsoever small things I have got. By not clinging you have declared your real power, your mastery."

Clinging shows that you are not really the master but a slave.

The king asked Buddha, "Bless me, so that one day I can also become an emperor like you."

This poem by Robert Graves is beautiful. Poets come far closer to the truth than the philosophers, the theologians, the priests, the scholars, the so-called learned people. Poets are a little bit crazy; that's why they can have a few glimpses of the beyond. They are not logical; hence they can comprehend something which is bigger than logic. Theologians, philosophers, scholars – they are just fools hiding their foolishness. And it is because of these so-called learned people that the world has become so poor physically, spiritually, in every way.

Just the other day I was reading a news item from Pakistan. It says that great scholars of morality are nowadays busy banishing the word *ishq*, love, from prose and poetry prescribed for university students in Pakistan.

Ishq is far more significant than the word "love." Love is only one of the dimensions of ishq. "Love" means of the world. "Ishq" has two aspects: either it can be an ordinary love, the love between a man and a woman, or it can be a love between man and existence.

Banishing the word, the very word "ishq," from all prose and poetry prescribed for the university courses is such a foolish idea. And these are the great scholars of morality! I was puzzled because if you banish the word "ishq", then particularly in the language that is spoken in Pakistan—that is the official language of Pakistan, Urdu—there will not be anything left at all, because the whole of Urdu poetry and prose is centered on the word "ishq". All the great poets, from Mir and Ghalib to Iqbal, will have to be banished. In fact, no other language of the world has such beautiful poetry as Urdu. Urdu is tremendously expressive. In just two small lines, Urdu can say more than any other language can manage to say in a whole page. It is very telegraphic, and it is full of love.

Banish the word "love" and you banish all the great poets, all the great mystics. You will have to banish all the Sufis because they talk about love. And they are not only banishing poetry and prose devoted to love, even the word love, "ishq," has to be removed—even the mention of the word!

These are the fools who have been dominating humanity for centuries. They would like to destroy even the possibility of love. There is a certain logic in it, because humanity up to now has existed in a very insane way. It has continuously been preparing for war. There are only two periods in history: either people are fighting—that is war time, hot war—or people are preparing for the war that is going to happen sooner or later. You can call it peace time, but it is not peace time at all; it is only a gap between two wars. It is needed because unless you prepare, how are you going to fight? It is cold war.

The whole of human history up to now can be divided into two periods: hot war and cold war. And because man has been continuously fighting, destroying, murdering, there is no possibility of growing roses of love. We have to make factories for war; we have to create soldiers, not lovers.

My sannyasins are lovers, not soldiers. They herald a new beginning. To me, love is synonymous with God. These words of Graves are tremendously significant:

> *Those who dare give nothing*
> *are left with less than nothing...*

They look a little crazy because they are illogical, they are unmathematical—but they are absolutely true. They transcend ordinary economics and its laws; they indicate a meta-economics.

> *Those who dare give nothing*
> *are left with less than nothing...*

Beware! While the time is there, give, give as much as you can, give whatsoever you can. Sing a song, share a joke, dance! Give whatsoever you can give. It costs you nothing, but it will bring you more and more joys.

Existence goes on repaying you tremendously. Whatsoever you give to existence, it returns a thousandfold; it comes back to you. You give one flower, and a thousand flowers shower on you. Don't be clingers. If you really want to be rich, if you want to have an enriched inner world, then learn the art of giving.

> *Those who dare give nothing*
> *are left with less than nothing;*
> *Dear Heart, you give me everything,*
> *which leaves you more than everything—*
> *though those who dare give nothing*
> *might judge it left you nothing.*

> *Giving you everything,*
> *I too, who once had nothing,*
> *am left with more than everything*
> *as gifts for those with nothing*
> *who need, if not our everything,*
> *at least a loving something.*

I don't have any other source than you have, but you are not ready to accept that source; it goes against your ego. You want to be an island unto yourself, and that is your misery, that is your poverty. Your soul will remain undernourished. You will not know how beautiful existence is, how blissful every moment can be, what an ecstasy it is just to breathe and to be.

Give, give for giving's sake. Share for sharing's sake. Don't ask anything in return, because then it becomes a business – and love is not a business. In fact, there is no need to be worried whether anything returns or not, because the very giving is such an ecstasy that who cares whether anything returns or not? Be obliged to the person who receives anything from you. Don't think that he has to be obliged to you. That is wrong, that is absolutely wrong. That is still clinging to the miser's mind.

You can be as vast as God himself, but your vastness is possible only if you start giving. And it is not a question of what you give; just a smile or just a gesture of love is enough. It costs nothing to be loving, to be kind, and still it brings you a great harvest—thousands of flowers start blossoming in your being.

You ask me, "What is the source of your infinite spring of giving?"

I am not the source, I am not at all, because the more you are, the less is the flow from the source; the less you are, the more the flow from the source.

When *you* are not at all, then you are just a hollow bamboo which becomes a flute on the lips of God. Then the song starts flowing. And to sing the song of God, to allow God to sing a song through you, is the greatest joy of life.

The second question

> You often tell us that we lost our awareness of our buddha-nature because of conditioning processes of every kind. This far, I can imagine, but if mankind originally had this awareness, how did we lose it in the beginning? How did conditioning start originally? And if existence is just a flowing, why is it important that many people become enlightened? Why do you make the effort, or don't you make any? And is your being here, and everything, also just a flowing?

To know is one thing and to imagine is totally different. Imagination can deceive you, it can go on giving you false coins. But remember: All that glitters is not gold. Imagination can give you very glittering coins, but they will not be real gold. You will have to know, and my knowing cannot be of any help to you. The moment I share my knowing with you, only imagination will be triggered in you; you will start imagining.

There is no need to ask me why it happened originally; you can go to the origin within yourself and see why it happens. It is not a question of going into the past, going back to Adam and Eve; you have to go within yourself, because it is happening every moment. You are at the source, at the very origin of things, and still you are conditioned. And if you can watch the process within yourself, you will have known the whole of history. Then you will be able to understand the story, the biblical story, which is really beautiful and significant, of how Adam and Eve became conditioned.

It was God the Father who started the whole nonsense...

In the Garden of Eden there were millions of trees, and he pointed out two trees in particular – the fruits from these trees were not to be eaten. One was the Tree of Knowledge, and the other was the Tree of Immortal Life. My feeling is that if God had not prohibited it, Adam and Eve would never have been able to find those two trees in that tremendously vast garden. But because he pointedly said to them, "Don't eat the fruit from these two trees," naturally they became obsessed. It must have started their fantasies. They must have started dreaming about those two trees. They must have started thinking, "Why has God prohibited us? There must be something in it."

I was a small child and my father told me, "Listen, you are mixing with a few people who smoke cigarettes — don't ever start smoking!"

I said, "You have started me on it! I have never thought about it; in fact I have always thought how foolish these people are. Rather than breathing the pure air, they waste money and breathe smoke! Taking the smoke in and out looks very stupid!"

Things like that have always looked stupid to me. From my very childhood I have never taken part in any game—volleyball, football...because I cannot imagine what the point is! You throw the ball from here to the other side; they throw the ball back to this side. You can have two balls and both go home! What is the point of it? And people are perspiring— and not only the players, but the others who have gathered to watch...!

So I told my father, "I was never interested, but now, because you tell me not to smoke I am going to! Why are you preventing me? If there is nothing in it, can't you trust my intelligence? And if *you* can't trust my intelligence, why should I trust your intelligence? It has to be a mutual understanding. You are not trusting my intelligence— you are telling me not to smoke. If it is foolish I am not going to do it myself; if it is not foolish then nobody can prevent me. And how long can you prevent me? In what ways can you prevent me?"

And he understood the point. He was a rare man in many ways. He brought home a packet of cigarettes, handed it over to me and he said, "You experiment, you be finished with it! I have understood your point."

And I tried and I was finished. Tears started coming to my eyes, I started coughing, and I could not understand why people should do such stupid things and torture themselves. Since then, whenever I see anybody smoking, I think he must be an ascetic, a great saint doing some penance!

But Adam and Eve were treated by God the Father as every father treats every child. No father trusts the intelligence of the child. And in fact, the child has more intelligence than the father because the father has lived, experienced many things. His mirror has become covered with many experiences, with much knowledge. His clarity is no longer the same as that of the child. The child is utterly perceptive, he can see immediately; there is nothing to hinder him. The father's intelligence is covered with much dust.

But the father on his side feels afraid. He thinks the child is still a child who does not know what to do, what not to do. He may go astray. Out of his concern, he prevents— and that's how conditioning begins.

The biblical story is significant. It is not an historical story because the world never began in that sense, it has always been there. There is no beginning and no end. The whole idea of beginning and end is absurd; the world is eternal. But the story is significant, and it is repeated in each child's life. It is a psychological story, not historical, of tremendous importance. Every father, every mother is doing the same.

I have come across thousands of parables, but there is no parable comparable to this story. The father was anxious that Adam and Eve should not become interested in two things: one was the Tree of Knowledge... because the moment you become knowledgeable you lose your intelligence.

That's my whole teaching: unburden yourself of knowledge so that you can again discover the purity of your intelligence. Wisdom is freedom from knowledge. And God wanted Adam to be wise, not knowledgeable. He wanted him to be intelligent, not an intellectual. Hence he prohibited him: "Don't eat from the Tree of Knowledge."

This is significant; it shows the father's concern, his love, but it also shows that he does not trust the child's own perceptiveness. No father ever trusts, no mother ever trusts, howsoever old the son may be.

Makima's mother, Shunyo, is old. She must be over sixty-five, and *her* mother who is ninety goes on writing letters to her: "You are still a fool! What are you doing there? Come home! Have you gone crazy or something? I have always known that you would do something like this!"

Now, the ninety-year-old mother giving messages to the seventy-year-old daughter...! But one can see the point because the distance is the same – twenty years' distance. When Shunyo was one year old, the mother must have been twenty-one years old; now she is seventy, and the mother is ninety. When she will be ninety, if the mother is still alive she will be one hundred and ten – the difference will remain the same! And the mother will always go on thinking in those terms – that she is a fool, she does not know anything. Now what is she doing with these orange people and meditating and wearing orange clothes? She has gone crazy! The mother wants to protect her.

The Father was concerned for Adam and Eve, and his concern is significant: "Don't become knowledgeable." It is a tremendously meaningful story, because if you become knowledgeable you will lose your intelligence. Intellectuals have no intelligence at all.

I have come across thousands of intellectuals, the so-called intelligentsia, and they are the most stupid people you can ever come across. You will find farmers, gardeners, carpenters, who are far more intelligent than professors, theologians, scholars. They are full of rubbish! Of course, they have read much and they can repeat all that they have read; they have great information, but information is not wisdom. Information can be collected by a computer, and far more efficiently, but a computer is never wise. I don't think there will come a time when you will come across a computer who has become a buddha! It is not going to happen ever. Yes, a computer can become an Albert Einstein, certainly, there is no doubt about it. And he will function far better than Albert Einstein, because it will be just a mechanical thing.

Mathematics is mechanical, but love is not mechanical. No computer is going to fall in love, no computer is going to experience beauty, no computer is going to understand truth. Yes, facts it can accumulate...

God wanted Adam and Eve not to become computers; hence he told them, "Beware of this tree." But his telling them not to eat from this Tree of Knowledge became a temptation.

That's how conditioning begins: with should-nots, with all good intentions—but the ultimate result is harmful. Even God committed the same mistake; he had to commit it if he was to be a father. And he is the supreme father, hence he committed the supreme mistake!

And the poor serpent is unnecessarily dragged into the story. It has nothing to do with the serpent. How can the serpent seduce Adam and Eve to eat the fruit from the Tree of Knowledge? God had already done the basic work; he had already triggered their desires for knowledge. The serpent only convinced them about their own suspicions.

The serpent told them something very significant. He told them, "God has prohibited you from eating of this tree because he is afraid if you become knowledgeable you will be just as great as he is. So he wants to eat the fruit of this tree himself and he does not want you to eat from the same tree, so you will remain always inferior and lower."

Now the ego is set on fire! And the logic seems to be very relevant. Adam and Eve are convinced that this must be the cause. Knowledge cannot be a bad thing—how can knowledge be bad? God must have been afraid; that's why he has prohibited it.

And the serpent told them, "He has also prohibited you from eating from a second tree, because if you eat from it you will also become immortal just like God. Then there will be no difference between you and God; you will be equal."

Adam and Eve ate from the Tree of Knowledge and were thrown out of the Garden of Eden. They were not given the chance to eat from the other tree. But why had God prohibited them from eating from the other tree? There is also some significance on his side. God wanted them to live in the immediate, because that is true life—to live now and here. The moment you start thinking of immortality, you enter into the world of the future, you enter into the world of time. You lose contact with the real moment, you lose your grounding in the now; that's how mind is created.

These are the two ways in which the mind is created. These are the two parents—father and mother. They give birth to the mind. One is the desire for the future—the desire, the ultimate desire, to become deathless so that the future is absolutely certain. And the other is the desire to accumulate knowledge. These two desires function as father and mother for the mind. The mind is the child of these two desires meeting; the mind is a by-product.

God was basically right. He wanted Adam and Eve to live in the present, because reality is always present. But he was wrong psychologically. To tell them not to eat from the Tree of Immortality made them suspicious, and the suspicion was exploited by the serpent. Of course, they were thrown out before they could eat from the second tree, but since then man has been searching for immortality. And the search still goes on.

Science is still working continuously to find a way to prolong life—to make it longer and longer and longer, and then ultimately to make life immortal. And now science says that the body has no need to die; maybe they have come very close to the Tree of Knowledge and to the Tree of Immortality. Science says the body can go on renewing itself. If it can renew itself for seventy years, why not seven hundred years? Or if some parts become useless, then they can be replaced.

Sooner or later science is going to replace many of your parts. Then it will be very simple. If something goes wrong, you go to the workshop and your parts can be replaced. Your heart is not functioning well—you go to the garage and a plastic heart can be implanted in you. Slowly, slowly, all the parts will become plastic, because plastic is the most immortal thing in existence. It goes on living and living. You cannot destroy plastic. There is no natural process for plastic to dissolve into the earth. That is creating a problem for ecologists, because so many plastic bottles and jugs and toys are gathering under the earth, in the riverbeds, in the ocean. There is a danger that because plastic is never reabsorbed by the earth like everything else, it creates a hindrance to the natural rhythm and cycle of nature. Sooner or later there will be so much plastic that it will hinder all natural processes. Plastic is very immortal!

But just think of a man who slowly, slowly becomes plastic: his head goes cuckoo, it is changed; his heart is not functioning well, it is changed; his hands, his legs...slowly, slowly all is changed. Nothing is left of the old man, just the name, the label.

Once I saw Mulla Nasruddin with a very beautiful umbrella, and I asked him, "Nasruddin, when did you purchase it?"

He said, "I have not purchased it, it is very old, twenty years old."

So I said, "It is a miracle – twenty years old! It looks so fresh and so new! How did you manage that for twenty years?"

He said, "I am absolutely certain it is twenty years old. Of course, it got changed at least two hundred times. Just the other day, when I was coming out of the mosque, it got changed again— but it is twenty years old."

Man can be changed, and still the label will remain the same. Man is coming closer and closer to discovering the secret of immortality. Scientists say that if we can reprogram the basic cell out of which man grows, then everything is possible. When your mother's and your father's basic cells meet and you are created, many things are determined at that moment. For example, what kind of body you will have, what kind of hair you will have, how long you will live. Those two cells meeting and merging decide it; they are programmed. Their meeting becomes a new program: you will live seventy years, eighty years... If that program can be changed— for example if they can be told that you will live seven hundred years— just a little change, in some hormones, in some chemicals, that will do the miracle. And it is very close. My feeling is that within this century we will be able to discover the secret.

Since Adam was thrown out of the garden he has been working, looking, searching, for some way to find the secret of immortality. In the past, alchemists were doing the same—trying to find the way, some alchemical way, for man to be immortal. And now science is trying to do the same. The obsession is still there.

You ask me, Corry, "How did conditioning start originally?" It starts with every child, because the parents would like the child to be just a carbon copy of them. Their ego would like the child to represent them— their philosophy, their religion, their ideology, their politics, their nationality, their race, everything. The child has to be the carrier, the vehicle, the medium of all their ambitions and desires, of all their frustrations, failures. They are hoping, "We will die but part of us will live in the child"— so program the child in such a way that "what we have not been able to achieve, he will achieve."

A Flute on the Lips of God

They are trying to enforce their ambitions on the child; that's how conditioning begins. They are not allowing the child to be himself. No parent ever allows the child to be himself; it has not happened up to now. That's why humanity is living in such misery: because no child is allowed to be himself. How can he be happy? Happiness happens only when you are authentically yourself.

And don't ask me how it happened in the very beginning, because there has been no beginning. Whenever a child is born there is a beginning; otherwise existence has continued forever and forever.

And you also ask, "And if existence is just a flowing, why is it important that many people become enlightened?" That's why: existence is just a flowing, and many people are not flowing.

Only the buddhas know how to flow. The enlightened person knows how to flow, how to be in tune with existence, how to relax, how to let go. The others are fighting, not flowing; they are pushing the river. And you are taught to fight, to compete, to struggle, to achieve, to be ambitious; to be this, to be that, to become a president or a prime minister. You are told from the very beginning until you come back from the university that you have to become this – and others are deciding it. Nobody is bothered about your intrinsic nature.

It is as if marigolds are being educated in the university and told, "Become roses." They will go berserk! They cannot become roses; that is not possible. At the most they can pretend —they can pretend that they are roses, they can put up masks. They will become deceivers, hypocrites, but deep down they will know, "We are marigolds"—and they will hate that they are marigolds. But that's what they are. They cannot become roses because that is not in their nature, and they cannot allow their marigolds to dance in the sun because that is against their education.

You have created a real problem; now the person will always remain schizophrenic. If he tries to be a rose he will know that he is just a hypocrite. If he tries to be a marigold he will know that he is falling short of the ambitions of his parents, teachers, professors, priests, politicians. He will feel guilty. You will not allow him to rest in any way; either he will feel guilty or he will feel unnatural. In both ways he will remain tense, anxiety ridden, full of anguish. The same energy that might have become a dance, a song, an ecstasy, has become poisoned. It is now only anguish and nothing else, an agony and nothing else.

Enlightenment does not mean any ambition. If it is an ambition, then again you will start fighting for it. Enlightenment simply means being in a state of let-go. Enlightenment simply means undoing what the society has done to you. What your parents have imposed upon you, throw it away; what the society has conditioned you to be, put it aside. Reassert your being. Love yourself and respect yourself, and try to be just yourself.

Socrates says, "Know thyself." That is not possible. First *be* thyself; otherwise how will you know? If you try right now to know yourself you will not be able to; you will know somebody else who you are not but you are supposed to be. You will know only that which you are supposed to be; you will not know yourself.

Hence I say to you, first *be* thyself. And the miracle is, if you *are* just yourself, knowing is not difficult at all; that is very simple. Being oneself, one knows automatically who one is.

Enlightenment is not a desire, is not a goal, is not an ambition. It is a dropping of all goals, a dropping of all desires, a dropping of all ambitions. It is just being natural. That's what is meant by flowing.

You ask, "And if existence is just a flowing" —yes it is— "why is it important that many people become enlightened?"

It is important because people are not natural—they have not been allowed to be natural. Your parents are sitting on your shoulders, they are guiding you. May be they are dead, but still their voices are alive in you. Try to do something against your father, and you will immediately hear his voice saying: "Don't do this, you are offending me!" Try to do something which your mother has put inside you, and immediately you will hear your mama's voice—immediately! Whether she is alive or not, that's not the question; it's now inbuilt in you. It is there like a gramophone record; it will immediately start playing. It will immediately say, "Stop! Think of your dead mother! She never wanted you to do this. Be respectful at least to your dead mother! You were never respectful while she was alive, but at least now one should be respectful towards the dead."

This is bondage. But everybody is living in bondage, because everybody who brought you up wanted to have power over you, to enjoy the mastery over you. And children are the most helpless people in the world, the most exploited class. It is not the proletariat who are the most exploited class, it is not women who are the most exploited class. It is the children who are the most exploited class—and so helpless. The proletariat can revolt—they have revolted in Russia, in China and in other communist countries. The women all over the world are making efforts to revolt, but it is impossible to imagine how children will revolt. They are so helplessly dependent on their parents, they cannot think of any revolt. And unless revolution happens in them all other revolutions are going to be superficial. The basic conditioning, the basic imprisonment is created in childhood when the child is so helpless that he has to accept whatsoever conditions you put upon him just to survive.

Corry, enlightenment simply means putting aside all that has been imposed upon you forcibly. It is coming back to your nature; it is a second birth. Jesus says, "Unless you are born again you shall not enter into my kingdom of God." That's what he means.

In the East, particularly in India, the person who comes to know existence is called *dwij*. Dwij means twice born, one who has attained the second birth. The first birth is destroyed by others; now you can have a second birth and it will not be destroyed by others because now you are on your feet, strong enough to survive.

You ask me, "Why do you make the effort, or don't you make any? And is your being here, and everything, also just flowing?"

I am not making any effort at all. It is not an effort, it is not work, it is just play. I am enjoying it—it is a beautiful drama. These orange people, this Buddha Hall—this is just a stage and all my sannyasins are just actors. It is just a play. It is rooted in playfulness. I am not doing anything. I am the laziest person you can find in the world. That's why I say I am the lazy man's guide to enlightenment!

The third question

You say that one needs a master in order to become enlightened, yet you are enlightened and you have had no master. How can this be?

I am just crazy! I was just fooling around with the idea of enlightenment and went a little too far!

An unhappy elderly woman was pushing a baby in a pram down the street when she encountered an acquaintance.

"Whose baby is it, Mrs. Johnson?" asked the other. "I know it is not yours."

"It is, my dear," said Mrs. Johnson; "it is my husband. He was fooling around with a rejuvenation remedy and he went too far!"

The last question

Why are there so many Jews here?

Why not? The last time they missed Jesus; this time they don't want to miss! It is so simple. And they are very intelligent people: once they missed—and they really missed!—and now they feel very sorry because if they had been with Jesus they would have been doing the greatest business in the world! They feel very jealous of the Vatican. They cannot believe how these dumb Italians defeated them! It was basically their right. This time they don't want to miss. They have arrived.

A Jewish father and his son are standing in front of a cathedral.
"Father, what is this house with the high steeple?"
"Son, you should know this. It is a church."
"What is a church?"
"Well, the Christians say that God lives there."
"But, Father, isn't God living in Heaven?"
"Yes, son, you're right. But this is where he does his business."

They are really some of the most intelligent people on the earth; hence they can see what is going to happen.

During the second world war, a German officer went into Moishe Finkelstein's grocery shop to buy some matches.

"Matches!" he ordered.

Finkelstein passed him some matches.

I want the tips on the left side instead of the right!" the officer demanded.

Finkelstein acted as though he was finding another box of matches, but instead he gave the officer back the same box of matches, reversed.

Satisfied, the officer left the shop. Once outside, he said to his friend, "Fucking Jews— always trying to fool you!"

Enough for today.

CHAPTER 4

You are the Question

The first question

There are no answers.

Yes, there are no answers, because there are no questions either. Life is not a problem. Had it been a problem there would have been no need for religion—philosophy would have solved it, science would have found all the answers. Because life is not a problem it cannot be reduced to a question or to many questions. No question is really relevant to life.

Life is a quest not a question, a mystery not a problem, and the difference is vast. The problem has to be solved, can be solved, must be solved, but the mystery is insoluble; it has to be lived, experienced. The question has to be solved so that it disappears; encountering a mystery, you have to dissolve in it. The mystery remains, you disappear. It is a totally different phenomenon. In philosophy the problem disappears, but *you* remain; in religion the mystery remains, you disappear, you evaporate.

The ego is very much interested in questions and very much afraid of the mystery. The questions arise out of the ego. It plays with the questions, tries to find out answers— and each answer in its own turn brings more questions. It is an unending process; that's why philosophy has not come to any conclusion. Five thousand years of philosophizing, and not even a single conclusion! It is proof enough that philosophy is an exercise in sheer futility; its claims are very bombastic.

In India we have a proverb that you dig the whole mountain and in the end you find only one rat— but philosophy has not even been able to find the rat. It has been trying, and with great effort, to find some way out of the questions, but it gets more and more lost in the jungle. Now there are more philosophical problems than there were before, and they will go on increasing because the moment you assert a single answer it immediately explodes into many questions. It solves nothing, it simply gives you more work to do.

Religion takes life from a totally different vision. Its intrinsic quality is to be mysterious, and a mystery is that which cannot be reduced into the game of questions and answers. You have to be utterly silent to experience it, you have to be a no-mind to experience it. It can be experienced, but the experience cannot be put into words; it remains inexpressible.

Hence, Buddha has no answer. Not that he never answered questions—he answered questions for forty-two years just to be polite to you. But if you look deeply into his answers you will find that rather than answering he is simply seducing you towards silence. The answers are not answers but strategies to bring you to a point of deep understanding that nothing can be solved. The moment you understand that nothing can be solved, your mind simply dies. The mind can live on only with questions, problems, puzzles, riddles. The moment there is nothing to be solved, the whole function of the mind is destroyed. The very earth underneath its feet has been taken away. Questions are nourishment for the mind.

I have been answering you, but none of my answers is an answer. It is simply a way of bringing you to that ultimate jump from mind to no-mind, from thoughts to no-thought, from questioning to living. And when you start living the mystery, I call it a quest. Then it becomes a totally different phenomenon—you are not standing outside it. When it is a question, you are standing outside. You tackle the question, you look from all sides, you search all the aspects, all the possibilities; you dissect it, you look in, you try to find some clue; you propose some hypothesis, you experiment. The question is there outside you, on the table, but you are not part of it.

In a quest *you* are the question; there is no division between you and the question. The quest means you are diving deep within yourself. In a real quest there is only one question: "Who am I?" All else fades away, and finally even "Who am I?" starts dissolving. Then a great mystery descends on you; you are surrounded by miracles. The whole of life is transformed; it becomes translucent. Then it is a song, a dance, a celebration.

This is the whole approach of religion. Religion is anti-philosophical, and philosophy is basically anti-religious. There can be no religious philosophy, and there can be no philosophical religion.

You are right when you say, "There are no answers."

But before that, remember, there are no questions either.

The second question

What is sannyas?

Sannyas is a crazy way of living life. The ordinary way is very sane, mathematical, calculated, cautious. The way of sannyas is non-calculative, beyond mathematics, beyond cunningness, cleverness. It is not cautious at all; it is knowingly moving into danger.

Friedrich Nietzsche says, "Live dangerously." He had it written on his table in golden letters: "Live dangerously"—but he never lived dangerously! In fact, a person who is not living dangerously needs to be reminded of the fact again and again everyday. On his table, when he comes to work— "Live dangerously." If you are living it, there is no need to be reminded.

Friedrich Nietzsche lived in a very cowardly way. He had great ideas—just as all philosophers have—but they were mere ideas. The life and the ideas of philosophers are polar opposites: they say one thing; they do exactly the opposite. There is no rhythm in their being; they are going in all directions simultaneously.

But those two words, "Live dangerously," are significant. Sannyas is a way to live your life in total danger. What do I mean when I say sannyas is living dangerously? It means living moment to moment without any past. The past makes your life convenient, comfortable, because the past is known; you are familiar with it, you are very efficient with it. But life is never past, it is always present. The past is that which is no more, and life is that which is. Life is always now, here, and all your knowledge comes from the past. Trying to live the present through the past is the way of the coward; it is the calculated way. People call it sanity, but it is very superficial and never adequate. There is no rapport with the present.

That's why millions of people are so utterly fed up with life. Life is such a gift, and people are fed up with it. It is very strange and amazing.

Why should people be so fed up with life? The reason is not life itself; the reason is they are carrying the mountainous load of the past: all their experiences, knowledge, information—what others have told them. They have accumulated great junk and they are carrying that junk. And the load is so heavy, and their eyes are covered with so much dust, that they cannot see the beauty of the present. And whatsoever they do see is something other than the reality.

The rural preacher ended his long, dull sermon by requesting the board of deacons to remain for a few minutes after the service. In the group which stayed on was a stranger.

"Pardon me, sir," said the minister politely, "but I asked that only the board remain."

"That's why I stayed on," retorted the man. "I was never more bored in my life!"

Your religions are boring you, your philosophies are boring you, your scriptures are boring you. Thousands of years of the past are the cause of your boredom. You cannot dance— you are chained to the past, you are imprisoned in the past.

Sannyas means escaping from that prison. The prison may be of Hinduism or Mohammedanism or Christianity or Judaism or Jainism—it does not matter what the name of the prison is. On the earth there are three hundred religions; that means three hundred kinds of religious prisons. And there are thousands of ideologies; they are also prisons within prisons. And there are sects and subsects... You must have seen Chinese boxes—boxes within boxes within boxes. You open one box, then another; you open that and then another; you go on opening and you always find a smaller box within. Each prison has more prisons inside it. Ultimately you are left only in a dark cell.

Sannyas is rebellion against all slavery; it is living life in absolute freedom. To live life in absolute freedom, without traditions, without conventions, without religions, without philosophies, without ideologies—political, social, and others—to live unburdened is sannyas. But it will look crazy to the whole world. Freedom looks crazy because everybody is living an imprisoned life. To prisoners, the person who escapes from the prison looks crazy, because for them prison is comfortable, convenient, secure, safe.

A Hungarian secret police colonel was inspecting a strip of the border.

"Too many people have been slipping across at this point," he informed the guards. "I have been ordered to test your security precautions."

After deploying the guards at strategic points, the colonel began creeping on all fours toward the barbed wire.

"Can you see me now?" he called out. When they cried back "Yes," he started again. On the third attempt he slipped under the fence.

"Can you see me now?" he called back.

"No, Comrade Colonel," was the answer.

"Then you will never see me again!" the officer shouted as he hastened on his way to freedom.

Sannyas is an escape from the prison—Catholic or communist, it does not matter; it is an escape into the open. To live moment to moment is a crazy way, a poetic way, the way of the lover. People are living lives of prose—clear-cut but mundane, superficial. Anything which is very clear-cut is bound to be superficial. Life is mystery, and the only way to commune with it is through poetry, not prose.

The prose style of life is the ordinary lifestyle.

The poetic style of life is sannyas.

It is bound to be a little bit crazy— all poets are crazy, all painters are crazy, all dancers are crazy, all musicians are crazy. All that is great on this earth has something of madness in it.

Zorba the Greek says to his boss, "Boss, everything is right in you, only one thing is missing—a little bit of madness!"

And I agree with Zorba. Sannyas gives you a little bit of madness, but that little bit of madness brings rainbows to your life. Multidimensional is that little bit of madness. It opens many doors which have remained closed for thousands of years. It allows the sun and the rain and the wind to come in. It gives you a chance to whisper with the clouds and the stars. It is a way of falling in love with existence. To live without falling in love with this tremendously beautiful existence is very stupid, ridiculous. That is missing the whole opportunity of being, of being alive, of being intensely alive, passionately alive.

Sannyas is a risk! The people who cannot take any risk cannot be sannyasins. Hence, the people who are Hindu sannyasins are not real sannyasins; they are still clinging to the safety of the Hindu tradition.

The *Vedas* and the *Bhagavadgita* and the *Ramayana*—the whole past gives them the feeling that they are on the right track: "How can so many people be wrong?" They are following like sheep — a large crowd of sheep, ancient, very ancient, prehistoric! The more ancient a tradition is, the safer it looks.

The person who cannot risk, deals with life in a businesslike way—tries to cheat life, exploit life. He tries to give less and get more, because that is the way of profit.

The sannyasin does not care at all about getting anything back from life; he simply gives in sheer trust, and he receives a millionfold. But that's another matter; that is not his consideration at all. The man who is trying to exploit life will not get much out of it, and whatsoever he does get will remain inessential. He will remain a beggar and he will die a beggar. He will never know what it means to be an emperor.

The sannyasin knows what it means to be an emperor, because he simply gives; he enjoys giving, he loves sharing. And the miracle of life is: the more you give the more you have. When you give totally, the whole sky descends on you, the whole beyond becomes your within.

Sannyas is hope—hope against all hope. People have lost all hope; they are living hopelessly. They are living simply because they are cowards and cannot commit suicide.

The existentialist philosophers are right when they say that the most important philosophical problem is suicide: to live or not to live, to be or not to be. If this is life that ordinary people are living, then it does not seem to be worth living at all. What is the point of getting up every morning and going through the same empty gestures you have gone through thousands of times? The same breakfast, the same nagging wife, the same ugly husband; the same suspicions, the same possessiveness, the same jealousy, the same anger, the same ambition; rushing to the office, the same boss— everything is the same, a constant repetition.

And again coming back home and sitting in front of that idiot box called the television, and looking at the same story, the same triangles —two women and one man or two men and one woman—the same story, the same triangle! And you already know the conclusion; in fact, you can write the whole story yourself. But what else to do? Playing cards, listening to the radio, reading the newspaper—it is almost the same. And then to bed again, and the same nightmares... Nothing seems to be of any significance, and you have done it all, and many times.

The existentialists are raising a significant question: Why go on living? The only reason seems to be that people are afraid of dying, they are cowardly. They are living hopelessly because at least they have not chosen to live. Death has to be chosen, and they cannot take any decision on their own.

Sannyas is choosing your life and also choosing your death. Sannyas means becoming decisive, conscious, deliberate.

No matter how bad the news might be, there was one man who had a stock comment: "Ah well, it might have been worse."

One day a friend said to him, "I have had an experience to which you can't apply your favorite clichÈ. I dreamed the other night that I died, went to hell, and was doomed to everlasting torment."

"Ah well, it might have been worse," said the optimist.
"How in hell could it have been worse?" cried the other.
The optimist replied, "It might have been true!"

The way of sannyas is the way of tremendous hope, trust. Life is basically good, beautiful, divine, so if we are missing then something is wrong with us, not with life itself. Life is so beautiful that it makes even death beautiful.

Sannyas is not a way of doing anything, it is a way of being. It changes your inner world and, of course, your outer world changes with it, but that is secondary. It changes your center, it changes your awareness, and then your behavior, your actions. Whatsoever you do has a new quality to it, a grace that descends from the beyond— a song said or unsaid, sung or unsung, but it is there within your heart, a dance, the quality of dance to your feet...

Hence, I say it is a crazy way of living, but that's the only way to live life rightly. A poetic way, the way of the lover—but only love knows.

Logic is blind, love has eyes.

Only love can see the ultimate truth that surrounds you within and without.

The third question

What do I want?

Nobody knows exactly because nobody is even aware of who he is. The question of wanting is secondary; the basic question is: Who are you? Out of that, things can be settled—what your desires, your wants, your ambitions will be.

If you are an ego then of course you want money, power, prestige. Then your life will have a political structure. You will be in constant struggle with other people, you will be competitive—ambition means competition. You will be continuously at others' throats and they will be continuously at your throat. Then life becomes what Charles Darwin says: the survival of the fittest. In fact, his use of the word "fittest" is not right. What he really means by the fittest is the most cunning, the most animal-like, the most stubborn, the most stupid, the most ugly. Charles Darwin will not say that Buddha is the fittest or Jesus is the fittest or Socrates is the fittest. These people were killed so easily, and the people who killed them survived. Jesus could not survive. Certainly, according to Darwin, Jesus is not the fittest person. Pontius Pilate is far more fit, more on the right track. Socrates is not the fittest, but the people who poisoned him, who condemned him to death are. His use of the word "fittest" is very unfortunate.

If you are living in the ego then your life will be a struggle; it will be violent, aggressive. You will create misery for others and misery for yourself too, because the life of conflict cannot be anything else. So it all depends on you, who you are. If you are the ego, still thinking of yourself in terms of the ego, then you will have a certain stinking quality. Or if you have come to understand that you are not the ego, then your life will have a fragrance. If you don't know yourself, you are living out of unconsciousness, and a life of unconsciousness can only be one of misunderstanding. You may listen to Buddha, you may listen to me, you may listen to Jesus, but you will interpret according to your own unconsciousness—you will misinterpret.

Christianity is the misinterpretation of Jesus; so is Buddhism the misinterpretation of Buddha, and so is Jainism the misinterpretation of Mahavira. All these religions are misinterpretations, distortions, because the people who follow Buddha, Mahavira, Krishna, are ordinary people without any awareness. Whatsoever they do, they will save the letter and kill the spirit.

A philosopher was walking around a park and noticed a man who was sitting in the lotus posture, eyes open, looking at the ground. The philosopher saw that the man was totally absorbed in his gazing downwards. After watching him for a long time, the philosopher could no longer resist and went over to the strange fellow asking, "What are you looking for? What are you doing?"

The man answered without shifting his gaze, "I am following the Zen tradition of sitting silently doing nothing and then the spring comes and the grass grows by itself. I am watching the grass growing, and it is not growing at all!"

There is no need to watch the grass growing – but that's what always happens. Jesus says one thing, people hear it, but they hear only the words and they give to those words *their* meaning.

A mother took her small son to the psychiatrist and for at least three hours told the psychiatrist the whole story of her son. The psychiatrist was getting tired, fed up, but the woman was so absorbed in the telling that she was not even giving the psychiatrist an opportunity to prevent her. One sentence followed another with no gap.

Finally the psychiatrist had to say, "Please, now stop! Let me ask the son something!"

And he asked the son, "Your mother is complaining that you don't listen to whatsoever she says to you. Have you difficulty in hearing?"

The son said, "No, I have no difficulty hearing—my ears are perfectly okay—but as far as listening is concerned, now you can judge for yourself. Can you listen to my mother? Hear I can; I have to. I have even been watching you—you were fidgeting. One has to hear, but listening—at least I am free to listen or not. Whether I listen or not, that is up to me. If she is shouting at me, hearing it is natural, but listening is a totally different matter."

You have heard, but you have not listened, and all kinds of distortions have gathered around. And people go on repeating those words without any idea of what they are repeating.

You ask me, "What do I want?" I should ask you rather than you asking me, because it depends where you are. If you are identified with the body, then your wants will be different; then food and sex will be your only wants, your only desires. These two are animal desires, the lowest. I am not condemning them by calling them the lowest, I am not evaluating them. Remember, I am just stating a fact: the lowest rung of the ladder. But if you are identified with the mind, your desires will be different: music, dance, poetry, and then there are thousands of things...

The body is very limited; it has a simple polarity: food and sex. It moves like a pendulum between these two, food and sex; it has nothing more to it. But if you are identified with the mind, then mind has many dimensions. You can be interested in philosophy, you can be interested in science, you can be interested in religion – you can be interested in as many things as you can imagine.

If you are identified with the heart, then your desires will be of a still higher nature, higher than the mind. You will become more aesthetic, more sensitive, more alert, more loving. The mind is aggressive, the heart is receptive. The mind is male, the heart is female. The mind is logic, the heart is love.

So it depends where you are stuck: at the body, at the mind, at the heart. These are the three most important places from which one can function. But there is also the fourth in you; in the East it is called *turiya*. Turiya simply means the fourth, the transcendental. If you are aware of your transcendentalness, then all desires disappear. Then one simply IS with no desire at all, with nothing to be asked, to be fulfilled. There is no future and no past. Then one lives just in the moment, utterly contented, fulfilled. In the fourth, your one-thousand-petaled lotus opens up; you become divine.

You are asking me, "What do I want?" That simply shows you don't even know where you are, where you are stuck. You will have to inquire within yourself— and it is not very difficult. If it is food and sex that takes up the major part of you, then that is where you are identified; if it is something concerned with thinking, then it is the mind; if it is concerned with feeling, then it is the heart. And, of course, it cannot be the fourth; otherwise the question would not have arisen at all!

So rather than answering you I would like to ask you where you are. Inquire!

Three pigs entered a bar. The first pig ordered a drink and then asked the way to the bathroom. The second pig ordered a drink and also asked the bartender the way to the bathroom. Then the third pig came up to the bar and ordered a drink.

"Don't *you* want to know where the bathroom is?" sneered the bartender.

"No!" replied the little pig. "I am the one that goes, 'Wee, wee, wee...all the way home!'"

I should ask you, "Where are you? What kind of identification? Where are you stuck?" Only then can things be clear – and it is not difficult. But it happens again and again that people ask beautiful questions, particularly Indians. They may be stuck at their sex center, but they will ask about *samadhi*. They will ask, "What is *nirvikalpa samadhi*, where all thoughts disappear, that thoughtless consciousness? What is it? What is *nirbeej samadhi*, the seedless, where even the seeds for any future are completely burnt? What is that ultimate state when one need not return to the earth, to the womb, to life again?" These are just foolish questions they are asking; they are not their questions. They are not at all concerned with their real situation. They are asking beautiful questions, metaphysical, esoteric, to show that they are higher quality beings; that they are scholarly, that they know the scriptures, that they are seekers; that they are not ordinary people, they are extraordinary, religious. That is driving the Indians into more and more of a mess.

It is always good to ask something which is relevant to you rather than to ask something which is of no concern to you. People ask me whether God exists or not, and they don't even know whether they exist or not!

Just the other day, Divakar Bharti, another Indian, asked me, "Why am I here?"

Divakar, are you really here? Ask yourself, are you really here? I don't think that you are here. Physically of course you are here, but spiritually, *really*, you are not here. Unless you drop that idea of being Indian, of being a Hindu, you cannot be here, you cannot be part of *my* commune. You have carried all kinds of nonsense inside you and you are still clinging to it.

It is always good to ask realistic questions, because then it can be of some help to you. If you are suffering from the common cold and you go to the physician and you ask about cancer, because a man like you – how can he suffer from such an ordinary thing as the common cold...? Every ordinary person suffers from the common cold, that's why it is called the common cold. But you are such an uncommon person—you are not any Tom, Harry or Dick. You are so special, you have to suffer from something very special, so you ask a question about cancer. And if the physician helps you in curing the cancer you will get into more trouble— that treatment is not going to fit you at all. It will create more complications in you because those medicines can kill you, because there is nothing for them to work upon; there is no cancer in you and they cannot be of any use for the common cold.

In fact, for the common cold there is no medicine. If you take medicine, the common cold goes within seven days; if you don't take any, it goes within one week! In fact, it is so common that medical science has not bothered about it at all. Who cares about such small things? People are concerned about going to the moon, and about such small matters as the common cold or a leaking fountain pen, who bothers? The fountain pen still leaks! People have reached the moon and they have not yet been able to make a one-hundred-percent-guaranteed fountain pen which is not going to leak!

Just look inside yourself. Where exactly is your problem?

A general visiting a field hospital asks one of the bed-ridden soldiers, "What is wrong with you?"

"Sir," replies the soldier, "I've got boils."

"What treatment do you get?"

"They swab me down with iodine tincture, sir."

"And that helps?" asks the general.

"Yes, sir!" replies the soldier.

Then the general goes to the soldier in the next bed and finds out that this guy has hemorrhoids. He too gets swabbed down with iodine; it helps, and he does not have any other wishes. The general then asks the third soldier, "What is wrong with you?"

"Sir, I've got swollen tonsils. I get swabbed down with iodine, and yes, it helps."

"Anything you would like?" asks the concerned general.

Yes, sir!" replied the soldier. "I'd like to be the first to be swabbed down."

First you have to see your situation, where you are; only then can you say what you want. If you are being swabbed down with iodine tincture after these two fellows—one who has got boils and one who has got hemorrhoids—and you are suffering only from swollen tonsils, then the problem is clear!

Inquire, look for the exact place where you are. As far as I am concerned, all desire is a sheer wastage, all wanting is wrong. But if you are identified with the body I cannot say that to you because that will be too far away from you. If you are identified with the body I will say: move a little towards higher desires, the desires of the mind, and then a little higher, the desires of the heart, and then ultimately to the state of desirelessness. No desire can ever be fulfilled. This is the difference between the scientific approach and the religious approach. Science tries to fulfill your desires and of course science has succeeded in doing many things, but man remains in the same misery. Religion tries to wake you up to that great understanding from where you can see that all desires are intrinsically unfulfillable.

One has to go beyond all desires; only then is there contentment. Contentment is not at the end of a desire, contentment is not by fulfilling the desire, because the desire cannot be fulfilled. By the time you come to the fulfillment of your desire, you will find a thousand and one other desires have arisen. Each desire branches out into many new desires. And again and again it will happen, and your whole life will be wasted.

Those who have known, those who have seen—the buddhas, the awakened ones—have all agreed on one point. It is not a philosophical thing, it is factual, the fact of the inner world: that contentment is when all desires have been dropped. It is with the absence of the desires that contentment arises within you—in the absence. In fact, the very absence of desires *is* contentment, *is* fulfillment, fruition, flowering.

Move from lower desires to higher desires, from gross desires to more subtle desires, then to the subtlest, because from the subtlest the jump into no-desire, into desirelessness, is easy. Desirelessness is *nirvana*.

Nirvana has two meanings. It is one of the most beautiful words; any language can be proud of this word. It has two meanings, but those two meanings are like two sides of the same coin. One meaning is cessation of the ego, and the other meaning is cessation of all desires. It happens simultaneously. The ego and the desires are intrinsically together, they are inseparably together. The moment ego dies, desires disappear, or vice versa: the moment desires are transcended, ego is transcended. And to be desireless, to be egoless, is to know the ultimate bliss, is to know the eternal ecstasy.

That's what sannyas is all about: the quest for the eternal ecstasy that begins but never ends.

The fourth question

What is courage?

Courage means going into the unknown in spite of all the fears. Courage does not mean fearlessness. Fearlessness happens if you go on being courageous and more courageous. That is the ultimate experience of courage—fearlessness; that is the fragrance when the courage has become absolute. But in the beginning there is not much difference between the coward and the courageous person. The only difference is, the coward listens to his fears and follows them, and the courageous person puts them aside and goes ahead. The courageous person goes into the unknown in spite of all the fears. He knows the fears, the fears are there.

When you go into the uncharted sea, like Columbus did, there is fear, immense fear, because one never knows what is going to happen and you are leaving the shore of safety. You were perfectly okay, in a way; only one thing was missing—adventure. Going into the unknown gives you a thrill. The heart starts pulsating again; again you are alive, fully alive. Every fiber of your being is alive because you have accepted the challenge of the unknown.

To accept the challenge of the unknown in spite of all fears, is courage. The fears are there, but if you go on accepting the challenge again and again, slowly, slowly those fears disappear. The experience of the joy that the unknown brings, the great ecstasy that starts happening with the unknown, makes you strong enough, gives you a certain integrity, makes your intelligence sharp. For the first time you start feeling that life is not just a boredom but an adventure. Then slowly, slowly fears disappear; then you are always seeking and searching for some adventure.

But basically courage is risking the known for the unknown, the familiar for the unfamiliar, the comfortable for the uncomfortable arduous pilgrimage to some unknown destination. One never knows whether one will be able to make it or not. It is gambling, but only the gamblers know what life is.

An African delegation to Moscow was being treated to all aspects of Russian culture. One of the secret service agents was telling an African how to play Russian roulette with a six-shooter handgun with only one bullet in the chamber.

"You put it to your head," he said, "and pull the trigger."

The African was not impressed. "African roulette is much more fearsome!" he said.

"Impossible!" exclaimed the Russian, "Please explain."

"There are six naked women," said the African, "and each one will give you a blowjob—you just choose any one."

"That needs no courage," sneered the Russian.

"Aha!" exclaimed the African. "But one of them is a cannibal!"

Enough for today.

CHAPTER 5

Let Sannyas Happen

The first question

Every time I hear you praising capitalism I get angry. You say sannyas means to get rid of all conditioning and to escape out of every cage whether it is religious, philosophical or political. But isn't capitalism a cage too? Why can't we live a creative life in wealth and freedom without any "isms"?

Capitalism is not an "ism" at all; just don't get too obsessed by the word. Sometimes words become too important to us and we tend to forget the reality.

Capitalism is not an ideology; it is not imposed on the society, it is a natural growth. It is not like communism, or fascism, or socialism—these are ideologies; they have to be imposed. Capitalism has come on its own. In fact, the word "capitalism" has been given by the anti-capitalist thinkers: the communists, the socialists and others. Capitalism is a state of freedom; that's exactly why I am in support of it. It allows you all kinds of freedoms. Communism will not allow you all kinds of freedoms; communism will give you only one ideology to believe in—there is no question of choice.

I am reminded of Henry Ford...

When he made his first model, those cars were only made in one color—black. And he himself used to take the customers round his showroom; he would go around with them and show them the cars. He used to say to people, "You are free to choose any color, provided it is black!"

That's exactly the attitude of communism: you are free to choose any ideology, any philosophy, any religion, provided it is communism.

In a communist society there is no hope for a multidimensional humanity to grow; it can allow only a certain type to grow: it is linear. You cannot conceive that in a communist pattern even Karl Marx would be possible; he would not be allowed. You cannot conceive a Jesus, a Buddha, a Krishna, or a Lao Tzu being born in a communist society; they would be destroyed at the very beginning.

Before the Russian revolution, Russia produced the greatest novelists in the world. Before the revolution, Russia passed through an immense period of creativity; it was almost an explosion. Nowhere else, in no other time, were so many great artists born together: Leo Tolstoy, Fyodor Dostoevsky, Anton Chekhov, Maxim Gorky, Turgenev, and many more. What happened to all that creativity after the Russian revolution? Not a single Tolstoy, not a single Dostoevsky, not a single Maxim Gorky has appeared. It is impossible, because the government directs you about what to write, what not to write. The bureaucracy dictates everything. You cannot paint according to your own heart, you cannot sing the song that you want to sing; you have to dance to the tune that the government plays. Naturally, only mediocre people have been happy in Russia. Untalented people will find it very good, but talented people, who are the salt of the earth, will be retarded.

Only one outlet is there, to go into politics, and that too is not easy. Once you are in power it is very difficult for anybody else to replace you. Joseph Stalin remained in power longer than any other person, and he was hated by the people from their very guts, but nobody was able to say anything. He killed more people than Genghis Khan, Tamerlane, Nadirshah; even Adolf Hitler comes second to him. And he killed very methodically. It is estimated that he must have killed several million people at least, with no guilt.

The day he died and Krushchev came into power, Krushchev started saying things against him. Even his dead body was removed from the Kremlin, from the place where it had been ceremoniously placed. It was dragged from the grave in a very insulting way and removed to a faraway place which nobody visits.

Krushchev had always served Stalin as a servant, and when he started saying things against him... In one of the meetings of communist workers he was talking against Stalin, and a worker shouted from the back row, "Where were you when he was alive? Why didn't you say these things when he was alive?"

For a moment there was a very uneasy silence. Even Krushchev could not find any words. Then he asked, "Can I ask one thing, sir? Can you stand up, comrade? Who has asked this question?" And Krushchev laughed and he said, "Now you know! That's my answer!"

Communism is an "ism"; capitalism is not an "ism." Capitalism is simply a natural phenomenon that has come on its own. There are no capitalist philosophers, there is no capitalist party, there is no capitalist economy which has been enforced on people; it is a growth.

But you seem to be too attached to the word. Rather than looking at the reality you have become distracted by the word "capitalism." It simply means a state of *laissez-faire*, a state of freedom where one is allowed to be himself. Capitalism is not an "ism" but a natural state of society which is capable of producing capital, which is capable of producing wealth.

Now for sixty years or more communism has existed in Russia. Still, communism existing in Russia has not been able to make it a rich society; it is a poor country. Of course they go on competing as far as war technology is concerned, but the people are poor. America is far richer; in fact, it is the richest society that has ever existed on the earth. Even the poorest man in America is in a far better situation than any Russian, for the simple reason that people are allowed to produce wealth if they choose to. If they choose not to produce wealth, if they want to be painters, poets, they are allowed— that is their freedom, that is their birthright. In communism you don't have any birthright.

And remember, equality is a very unpsychological idea. People are not equal. Albert Einstein, Karl Marx, Gautam Buddha, Jesus, Mohammed, Ghalib— can you consider that these people are equal? The society consists of thousands of types; it is beautiful because of the variety. Communism destroys variety. It makes people in a certain pattern, it gives them a certain structure. The whole society becomes like an army: everybody is regimented, everybody is following a certain ideal.

Don't be too obsessed with the simple word "capitalism." But we live in words the very word, the mention of the word, can create anger in you. That simply shows anger is there. And it is a natural phenomenon, particularly when you are the disciple of a master— deep down you are angry at him. There are reasons for it, because surrendering is going against your ego, and the ego is always ready to take revenge—any excuse will do.

Judas betrayed Jesus. Do you think he simply betrayed Jesus because of thirty silver coins? That is not the case. Judas would not have betrayed him for only thirty silver coins. He had lived for a long time with Jesus, had loved him, worshipped him, was surrendered to him. Then what came over him? And he felt immensely guilty: the day Jesus was crucified...within twenty-four hours Judas committed suicide out of sheer guilt. What had he done? He could not survive, he could not live— the guilt was too heavy.

But nobody has looked into the psychology of Judas. So many people have researched deeply into the psychology of Jesus, but nobody has bothered to look into the psychology of Judas, which is worth studying because masters are few and disciples are many, and their psychology should be understood. And it is not the first case...

Gautam Buddha was betrayed by his own cousin-brother who was a disciple; Devadatta was his name. Mahavira was betrayed by his own son-in-law who was his disciple. It is almost an inevitable phenomenon that each master has been betrayed by somebody who was very close. Why? There must be some hidden reason. Don't just condemn Judas; Judas is only one of the examples.

To surrender to a master creates anger. Unwillingly you have to surrender, finding no other way. You have tried every possible way to be on your own, but the more efforts you have made, the deeper you have gone into the mess. So ultimately, as a last resort, you surrender. But the unwillingness is there. You would have been far more happy if there had been no need to surrender. But because there is nothing else to do— you have done everything and it has all failed— you need somebody's help and support, you need somebody's guidance. And in spiritual matters, guidance is possible only if you trust, if you surrender, if you put your ego aside. So you put it aside, but very unwillingly, reluctantly, and it waits for its own time to take revenge. So any small excuse becomes a very big thing.

Now the word "capitalism" is torturing you. If you understand me, what you are saying is exactly what I mean by capitalism.

You say: "Why can't we live a creative life in wealth and freedom without any 'isms'?"

That's exactly what capitalism is! Drop the word "ism," find something else. I am not much concerned with words. I am not a linguist, not a grammarian.

Noah Webster, the lexicographer, was in his office making love to his secretary, when Mrs. Webster walked in.

"Noah!" she gasped. "I am surprised!"

Quickly pulling his trousers up, he replied, "Not so, my dear. You are shocked, I am surprised!"

The grammarian, the lexicographer, the linguist, is continuously thinking of words. He is right! He says, "No, you are shocked— you are using the wrong word—I am surprised!" But it is not a question of words at all.

Don't get too obsessed with words; otherwise you will be getting angry again and again. If you want to be angry, that's another matter; then you can find any excuse. And you will find a thousand and one—I can provide you with as many excuses as possible!

"You say sannyas means to get rid of all conditioning..." Yes, and it includes the obsession with words too. And you say, "to escape out of every cage..." True.

Capitalism is the only state where you are not forced to live in a cage, you are free. But capitalism is in a very dangerous state, for the simple reason that there are only a few people who are capable of creating wealth, and they create great jealousy in others. Those who cannot create wealth become jealous— and there are more of them.

Just think: if society were ruled by poets, people would be angry at poetry, because only a few people are capable of creating poetry —a Shakespeare, a Milton, a Kalidas, a Rabindranath... Only very few people are able to create poetry, and they would be the rulers. What about the ninety-nine point nine percent of people who are absolutely unpoetic? They would become very angry. Or if the society were ruled by musicians, then what about those who cannot produce music, who are not creative in that dimension? Then Beethoven, Mozart, Wagner...a few people would be able to dominate; they would be at the top. And what about the others? The millions would feel angry. The same is true with capitalism: very few people are capable of creating wealth; it is a dimension of creativity. Not everybody is a Ford or a Morgan or a Rockefeller. This is bound to be so.

But to understand your jealousy and to get rid of it is sannyas. To understand your jealousy will help you tremendously to find your dimension of creativity. Everybody is born with a certain potential, but it is not the same and it is good that it is not the same.

If everybody was a Shakespeare, literature would lose all joy. If everybody was a Jesus, carrying his own cross, the whole scene would look very crazy! And those Jesuses would go on carrying their crosses, and who would crucify them? They would not find anyone to crucify them! It would be a very, very long and tedious journey to nowhere. They would die natural deaths, carrying their crosses unnecessarily. It is good that everybody is not a Jesus, not a Buddha...

Everybody has to be himself, and capitalism simply gives you the possibility to be yourself. Certainly you will have to prove your mettle, you will have to work; you will have to create, you will have to bring your total energy to a focus. But only then will you be able to shine forth.

Capitalism is basically individualism, it is not a social structure. It is more than that; it is just democracy and freedom. But when you allow everybody to be himself, certainly you will feel very jealous, because you can only be one thing and there will be many people who can be many other things. Somebody will be a poet, somebody will be a sculptor, somebody will be a novelist, somebody will be a musician, a dancer, an architect, a scientist...and maybe you are just a boxer. But there is no need to be worried—you can be the greatest boxer in the world! One has to look within oneself and discover one's potential.

Capitalism gives you the freedom to be yourself; that's why I support it. My support has reasons behind it. I am not supporting it as an economical phenomenon; there is much more involved in my support. And to my understanding, capitalism will bring a socialism of its own kind as a by-product, because when people have created too much wealth, what are they going to do with it? What will you do with the wealth when you have created it?

Albert Einstein discovers the theory of relativity, the secret of atomic energy; then it becomes part of the whole society, then sooner or later everybody is going to be benefited by it. A few people will create wealth, but they will reveal the secrets of how to create wealth. Sooner or later this whole society will be benefited by it.

A real socialism will come out of capitalism as a by-product. When too much wealth is created, people will not be so greedy; the greed arises only because the wealth is very scarce. And you can see it very clearly—you can see it here. The poor person is very greedy, the rich person is not so greedy. The people who are coming from the West are less greedy than the people who are living in India. The Indians *talk* about no-greed, greedlessness, but they are the most greedy people in the world. They have to be—they are so poor, they have to cling.

It happens almost everyday: some Western sannyasin will turn up at the office and will say, "I would like to donate ten lakh rupees, but I don't want my name to be mentioned because this is not such a big thing." But no Indian turns up even with ten rupees! If you want ten rupees from Indians you have to go to them and persuade them. Then too it will be very difficult for them. They will give you ten rupees only if you convince them: "You will be getting a thousandfold more in the other world." Then they will give; otherwise not. Unless they are convinced and you prove through the scriptures that they will get a thousandfold, exactly a thousandfold more; unless it is a business proposal... And it is a really good business! You give ten rupees here, and you get a thousandfold more there! Where can you get that much interest? It is almost like winning a lottery! Then it is worth risking ten rupees.

I had to stop Indians completely. I have told my office people, "Don't accept from Indians, because we don't want money with any conditions." They bring their conditions also – they are donating ten rupees, but they will bring their conditions. And these conditions have to be fulfiiled: "Osho should not say this; Osho should say this." Just because they are donating ten rupees they want to control everything —how sannyasins should behave, how they should move around in the society. Just because of their ten rupees all the sannyasins have to follow a certain moral code decided by them.

You can see it easily: the West has created enough wealth; the greed is disappearing. But in the East, the greed has gone on increasing more and more. In fact, because there is so much greed, people talk about greedlessness. The saints go on teaching people, "Don't be greedy," because they know they are greedy; otherwise, why would they teach that? It would be stupid to talk that way.

I have seen the most ancient scriptures. They all talk about greedlessness, nonattachment; they all talk about nonviolence, no stealing, no adultery. Look on everybody's wife as your mother or sister or daughter, as the case may be...the most ancient scriptures! All these rules of conduct prove only one thing: that man has always been just the opposite; otherwise, why so much fuss about committing adultery? The most ancient scriptures talk about it: "Don't commit adultery." People must have been committing adultery! Either the people were committing adultery or these people who were writing the scriptures were crazy!

People must have been very greedy, because all the Jaina scriptures, almost on every page, talk about greedlessness, as if that was the only obsession of the people. "Renounce," they all say; "gold is dust." If gold is dust, why renounce it? Nobody renounces dust! Even those scriptures don't say, "Renounce dust because dust is just gold and nothing else, so renounce it. Don't touch dust because it is just gold." But they all talk about renouncing gold, and in the same breath they go on saying it is dust. They are contradicting themselves. And the people they are talking to must have been very greedy, must have been clutching at gold.

And the people who are talking, at the same time as they say to people, "Renounce gold," they say, "Donate gold to the temples." Donate dust to the temples...? Donate the dust of the whole world to the temples—will that make any sense? But, "Donate gold..." And that too, Jaina monks in their scriptures say, "Donate only to Jaina temples." Donating dust only to Jaina temples? Why not to Hindu temples too? Why not to Buddhist temples too? And the Buddhists go on saying the same: "Donate only to the Buddhist temples, because they are *true* temples." What difference does it make whether the temple is true or untrue? You are only donating dust! Even if you donate to the untrue temple, what is wrong with it?

Brahmins say, "Only donate to the brahmins." Jainas say, "Only donate to the Jaina monks." And Buddhists say, "Only donate to the Buddhist monks." All others are charlatans; *they* are the true people. That shows their real intention.

Remember, a society is possible which will not be greedy, but that is possible not through socialism; it is possible only through the growth of capitalism, through the growth of freedom. Talented people have to be given absolute freedom to create whatsoever they can—poetry, wealth, music. Whatsoever they can create let them create, and their creativity will raise the society to higher levels.

Capitalism is pure freedom. Of course, everybody is not capable of creating wealth, hence it creates jealousy. But we should not be dominated by jealousy, we should not be dominated by those who are uncreative. If we are dominated by the uncreative, by the jealous, then we will destroy all the talented people. And they are the real people, they are the people who raise humanity to higher levels.

Humanity owes all its growth to very few people, not to the masses—not at all. The masses have been the hindrance; they are like rocks preventing the growth of society. Society has been benefited only by a few scientists, a few mystics, a few creators; the others have been just hindering in every possible way. And these others constitute the majority, and of course they are jealous. But nobody says directly, "I am jealous." They will talk about equality, socialism, communism...beautiful words to hide something ugly.

Whenever I say something, meditate over it. Being angry is not going to help. Anger simply shows that something in you is hurt, some wound is there. Maybe you have come believing in socialism, communism, and all that kind of nonsense. There are many sannyasins who have belonged to political ideologies in their past. When they come to me it becomes difficult for them to drop all their rubbish—but you have to drop all your rubbish.

It is easy for you when I say, "Don't be a Christian," because in fact you are not a Christian at all. When I say, "Don't be a Mohammedan or a Hindu," who is a Mohammedan, who is a Hindu? These are only formalities. But when I say, "Don't be a communist or a socialist," then it hurts more, because particularly the new generation is very much addicted to the communist ideology.

Capitalism is not an ideology at all, that's why I prefer it.

The second question

> I am seventy-five years old. I want to become a sannyasin, but I don't know why I am hesitating.

I think you should wait a little more! Let death come first, then I can initiate you into sannyas...because when death has already happened, there will be no hesitation: you will not be there at all. Seventy-five years old and still hesitating? One leg is already in the grave! Ninety-nine percent is almost dead. Only one percent can become a sannyasin now, and even then you are hesitating. It almost always happens with old people.

The people who followed Jesus were all young, almost all of them his own age. The people who followed Buddha were his age or nearabout. The same was true with Mahavira. The older a person becomes, the more cautious he becomes, and one can understand why. He has lived in the world with so many deceptive people all around. He has been deceived again and again, he has been cheated, so he becomes very cautious, hesitant. He clings to the familiar and becomes afraid of the unknown.

But sometimes it happens that your very cautiousness can be the most destructive thing in your life, because to be very cautious means to die before your death. It is a well-known psychological fact that people die nearabout thirty years of age. Of course, they live on afterwards, and they actually die nearabout seventy or eighty. So what are these fifty years? It is a kind of posthumous existence.

The gay couple were strolling down a Paris street. One kept saying to the other, "Watch out, dearie, don't step in the doggie-doo! Watch out dearie, don't step in the doggie-doo. Oh shit! I just stepped in the doggie-doo!"

Making the other cautious, he has forgotten completely about himself!

You are becoming too wary, too cautious, and soon you will fall in the doggie-doo! And then it will be too late – it is already late. It is evening time, the sun is setting. Don't waste time.

An old man of ninety-seven and his wife of ninety-two were appearing before the judge because they wanted a divorce.

The judge was very surprised. "You're so old," he said. "Why do you want to separate now, after all these years of being together?"

The old man did not answer. But after some minutes his wife said very shyly, "Your honor, we wanted to wait till all our children died."

Now, what are you waiting for – all the children to die first? Now, what is the point of waiting? You have waited enough! And remember, death will not ask you, it will not even inform you, it will not even knock on your doors. It simply comes, and before you have recognized it you are finished.

Before death happens, let sannyas happen, because sannyas in fact has two functions. For you now it can fulfill only one function. It has two functions: the first is the art of life and the second is the art of dying. The first you have missed – next time you are around don't miss it! But the second is still possible; you can learn the art of dying. You can die peacefully, silently, blissfully, surrendered to God. And in fact, the second part is far more important than the first part, because the first ultimately leads to the second. The art of life is only a preparation for the art of death.

If one can dance, sing and celebrate one's own death, if one can die in deep consciousness, with no complaint, with no grudge, but in immense gratitude towards God, one has fulfilled one's mission in life.

The third question

Are all desires insane?

Yes, all desires are insane. Desire as such is insane because desire means living in the future, and the future does not exist at all. What exists is the present.

To live in the present is the only sanity there is, but to live in the present you have to drop all desiring. Desire takes you away from now and here. Desire means fantasizing about the tomorrow. Desire means: "If this happens, if I can manage this, then I will live." You are sacrificing the present for the future, and the present is and the future is not. Sacrificing that which is, for that which is not, is insanity, sheer insanity.

A high-pressure salesman for a milking-machine company seemed unable to convince a farmer to buy his appliance.

"There's no use talking," persisted the farmer, "I've only got one cow to milk."

"But this machine will save you time in milking even one cow," he insisted. "Look! It is just about milking time now. Let's go to the barn and I'll show you."

In the barn the salesman set up his machine and began the demonstration, carrying on meanwhile his persuasive flow of talk. The old man began to take a keen interest in the proceedings as he beheld the wondrous efficiency of the milker.

"Well, mister," the farmer conceded at last, "I admit it's wonderful. I'd like mighty well to have it, but I've got no money and no way of borrowing any."

He paused and looked longingly at the shining machine. "I tell you, though, what I'm willing to do," he went on, "I'll let you take the cow as the first payment."

That's what you all are doing—sacrificing the present for the future, sacrificing that which you have for that which you have not yet and may not have ever. The tomorrow never comes. All that comes is always today, and you can become addicted to sacrificing the today for the tomorrow. Then you will go on doing the same thing your whole life—always sacrificing the now for something which is not.

This is how people are living. That's why their life remains a desert with no oasis; nothing flowers, nothing blossoms, no fragrance, no festivity. People look so sad, with such long faces. The whole earth seems to have suddenly turned very religious. Everybody looks like a saint— so dead, so serious, so sad, that if the old saints come back to the earth they will be very much puzzled: "What has happened? Has the whole world become saintly?" Of course, they will find a few exceptions— my sannyasins! And they will think that my sannyasins are crazy. That's what the whole world thinks about my sannyasins because they are still enjoying, living, loving, dancing, singing.

Just the other day I received a letter from an old woman—I loved her letter. Her son was a sannyasin and he died just two weeks ago in a car accident. She writes to me: "I am grateful to you, because just before he died he came to see me after many, many days, and he was so happy. I have never seen him so happy— he was almost dancing. And he was so loving to me... I have never seen him so loving. There has never been such a communion between me and him. There was always something like a wall separating us, but the day he came to see me, all barriers dropped. Although he died and I will never be able to see him again, I am immensely happy and grateful to you that you had made him laugh and sing and enjoy and you had helped him to drop his seriousness. He died joyously."

It is from a mother. It is very difficult for a mother to accept the death of her son. But she could accept even the death, although she knows nothing of sannyas and she has never been here. But the one thing she understood was that something very essential had changed in the life of her son. She is not at all sad about his death. She is happy that before he died he had attained something; he had not lived in vain.

Desires are crazy. They make you sad in two ways: if they are not fulfilled you will be sad, frustrated; if they are fulfilled you will be sad and frustrated—in fact, more so, because when your desires are fulfilled, then you suddenly recognize that you have been chasing shadows, illusions. You have been trying to catch hold of a rainbow, and all that you find is that your hands are wet, that's all!

People go on asking for the impossible; in fact, the more impossible a thing is, the more attractive it appears because it gives a challenge to your ego. The ego is not interested in the easy, it is interested in the difficult, and if it is impossible it is immensely interested. The ego exists only through the difficult and the impossible. That's why the ego is not interested in God, because God is the most simple phenomenon in the world. You don't have to do anything to achieve God, because he is already inside. You don't have to do a thing. You have just to sit silently and watch and look in, and you will find him. It is so easy; that's why the ego is not interested in it at all. The ego is interested in climbing Everest. And what are you going to find there? What did Edmund Hillary find on Everest? Nobody asks him; there was nothing to find.

I have just heard one story...

When he reached the peak of Everest, Edmund Hillary was feeling very great to be the first man to reach there. Then he suddenly saw an Indian monk squatting on the ground. He was very shocked— somebody had already reached there before him! He was so shocked he could not even say, "Hi! How are you?"

Before he could say anything, the Indian monk said, "How much for the watch?"

And people are going to the moon! And what do you think there is on the moon? Nothing at all! They go on bringing back a few rocks. You could have gathered those rocks here, anywhere; there was no need to go so far away!

One story I have heard...

When the Americans reached the moon for the first time they were very puzzled, because from the other side of the moon there was such a noise. So they went to see what was happening, and there were at least ten thousand Chinese talking and talking. And when the Chinese talk, "Ching, ching, chang, ching..."

The Americans were very puzzled. They said, "What is going on? How did you manage to get here? We didn't think you had the technology yet."

And the Chinese said, "What technology are you talking about? There is no need for any technology. We simply went on standing upon each other and we reached! What technology? Our population is enough that we can reach any planet we decide to – and we have only come for a holiday, a picnic!"

People are more interested in reaching Everest, the moon, Mars, than in reaching their own innermost self, because that is no challenge to the ego.

God is so obvious; that's why he is missed. Truth is so easily available; that's why nobody is interested in it. Nirvana is now, and the mind is not interested in now at all, it is always somewhere else.

A longtime ago in China, a mandarin had three beautiful daughters. He wished to marry them off to nobles of wealth and status. In those days a man's position in society was indicated by the number of dragons embroidered on the front of his robe.

The mandarin called his daughters, announced his intentions and asked the eldest what kind of man she wished to marry.

"Oh, Daddy," she said, "I'd like to marry a man with three dragons on his chest!"

"Very good," replied the father, "I will arrange it." Then turning to the second daughter he asked, "What kind of man would *you* like?"

"Oh, Daddy, get me a man with two dragons on his chest!"

The father was very pleased, and turning to the youngest daughter said, "I suppose you want to marry a man with one dragon on his chest?"

In a voice charged with emotion she replied, "Oh no, Daddy, I want a man with one draggin' on the floor!"

All desires are insane! The only sanity is to be desireless. The only sanity is to be herenow. This moment is more than enough.

And the last question

I am a Catholic nun. Can I also become a sannyasin?

Certainly! I am here just to destroy monks and nuns; that's my very purpose for hanging around. It is to sabotage the old idea of monks and nuns, it is to bring a new kind of sannyasin into the world. The monks and nuns of all the religions— Catholic, Protestant, Hindu, Mohammedan, Jaina, Buddhist—have all been escapists. They are people who are basically afraid of life.

I teach you fearlessness.

Live as totally and passionately as possible, because it is through intense living that you will find God. God is nothing but life lived at the optimum, with total abandon, a dance danced so totally that the dancer disappears; only the dance remains. Then you have found and you have come home.

If you are a Catholic nun, then be quick! There is no time to waste, because it will take time for me to uncondition you. The Catholics condition people in a very scientific way, in a far more scientific way than Hindus and Mohammedans and Buddhists can do, because the West knows the latest methods, techniques, strategies to condition people. Buddhist strategies are twenty-five centuries old; Jaina strategies are even older, perhaps fifty centuries old. Christianity has been learning continuously whatsoever becomes available through psychological research, and has been trying to use all the modern methods of conditioning which have been developed by Pavlov, Skinner, Delgado and others.

So it will take a little longer for me to help you get rid of your nunhood. But I am also aware of the latest – not only the latest, I am also aware of many other techniques which have not yet been developed. I have come a little ahead of my time, at least one hundred years before, so all those things can be sabotaged. I can dynamite...

You are welcome. Don't hesitate at all.

The saints were really bored, so they sent Mary, The Holy Virgin, to Pune to see what was going on and make a daily telephone report back to them.

The first call was answered by Peter. "Hello, Peter, this is Mary, The

Holy Virgin. Today I dyed all my clothes orange. What do you think about it?"

"That's okay," said Peter, "if everybody does it."

The next call came: "Hello, Peter, this is Mary, The Holy Virgin. Today I did Dynamic Meditation, what do you think about that?"

"Well," responded Peter, "if everybody does it, it's all right."

On the third day the call came: "Hey, Peetsey Weetsey, this is Veet Mary, the Holy...um...er... Ciao, bello!"

Don't waste time!

Malcolm and Eddie were out joyriding when they smashed into a brick wall. When they arrived at the gates of Heaven, Saint Peter said to Malcolm, "Since you were a good boy and didn't sin very much we're going to give you this new Buick to get around in up here."

Peter turned to Eddie and said, "You were not so good, my son, so you drive this Volkswagen."

Just as the boys were about to get into their new cars, a big Lincoln Continental pulled up. Inside, a fat guy smoking a big cigar sat behind the wheel. He smiled and drove on.

"Who was that?" Malcolm asked.

"Oh," said St. Peter, "that was the last pope John!"

Malcolm and Eddie drove off in their new cars, out to tour Heaven. Later that day Malcolm saw Eddie's Volkswagen parked along the side of the road. Eddie was a little way away, rolling on the grass, laughing hysterically.

"What's so funny, Eddie?"

"You won't believe this!" Eddie roared. "I just saw Jesus coming down the road on roller skates!"

Enough for today.

CHAPTER 6

A Thousand and One Ways to Laugh

The first question

The other day in discourse you mentioned that when a woman wears red lipstick it is ugly, because it is not natural. I am from New York where it is required that women shave their legs, underarms, dress stylishly, have their hair neatly combed, wear makeup, and act in a ladylike manner. Yes, it is all very admirable how your sannyasins are so natural, but the girls at the ashram do not excite me. You see, natural is not always the best or the most beautiful. My feeling is that you are so against makeup because you have never seen good makeup. I am a freelance makeup artist and would like to do a makeover on an ashramite so that you can see how makeup can be used to spiritually enhance a woman's natural beauty. Anything to say?

There are many things to say. First, makeup is the invention of the ugly people. It is not that makeup is ugly, but makeup itself is the invention of the ugly. The ugly feels inferior compared to the naturally beautiful – jealous, competitive. The ugly tries to compensate for it with artificial methods. The natural has no need to compensate. But naturally beautiful people are very few; hence makeup has become almost a routine thing.

For thousands of years, man has been trying to hide in every possible way all that is ugly in him—in the body, in the mind, in the soul. Even people who were naturally beautiful started imitating the ugly and the artificial, for the simple reason that the artificial can deceive. For example, breasts naturally are not as good looking as they can be made to look. Even if a woman has naturally beautiful breasts, she will start feeling that the women who have no natural beauty in their breasts can at least pretend and show that they are far more beautiful. So the naturally beautiful also start imitating.

Makeup, and the whole idea of makeup, is basically hypocrisy. One should love and accept one's nature—and not only on the physical level, because that is where the journey starts. If you are false there, then why not pretend the same falseness as far as mind is concerned? Then what is wrong in pretending to be a saint, a sage, when you are not? The logic will be the same. And sometimes it happens that the pretender can defeat the real, because the pretender can practice, can rehearse, can manage and manipulate in many ways.

It happened in the life of Charlie Chaplin...

On one of his birthdays his friends arranged a competition for who could act most like Charlie Chaplin. There were going to be three prizes, and from all over the world many people participated in the competition. And the final competition was going to be held in London. Charlie Chaplin, just to have fun, entered the competition from a faraway place. And because there were so many pretenders, nobody could even see that Charlie Chaplin was part of the competition. He was certainly hoping—in fact, he was absolutely certain—that he would win the first prize and that he would have the last laugh. But it turned out otherwise. He got the second prize. Somebody else was more authentically Charlie Chaplin than Charlie Chaplin himself.

It is possible that a woman with makeup can, as you say, look very beautiful. But she has to be ugly in the first place; otherwise why should she bother? And it is not that I have not seen good makeup; I have seen it. For thousands of lives what have I been doing here? Although I have not seen *you*, I have seen so many people like you that I can say many things even about you.

The first thing is that you must be fat. If you are not you can stand up and everybody can judge. Only fat people become interested in makeup. Secondly, you must be a 'homo', because only 'homos' become interested in the artificial. And if so many beautiful women here are not turning you on, that simply means one thing: that a woman as such cannot turn you on; you need men to turn you on. In that way, homosexuality is a very great spiritual development, because heterosexuality is just natural, it is biological; homosexuality is an invention of man. The bisexual person, who is both, of course, is far more rich. He can be turned on by both men and women; he has a far richer sexuality.

And from your name it is clear that you are a Jew. Now, a Jew, homo and fat...what else is needed to become a freelance makeup artist? You have all the qualifications for it.

You say, "The other day in discourse you mentioned that when a woman wears red lipstick it is ugly because it is not natural." In the first place, that woman is ugly—that's why she wears lipstick. If she had beautiful lips, who would bother to paint those beautiful lips with something tasteless, ugly?—ugly in the sense that your lips are no longer part of your face. They stand out, they become separate; they are no longer an organic unity.

I would like women to have red lips, but those red lips should come through the inner health—through blood circulating within your body, through exercise, through breathing; through long walks, through sunbaths, lips should become red. It is beautiful to have red lips, but to pretend...! And for whom are you trying to pretend? Everybody can see the lipstick is there. The lipstick does not hide your lips, it simply reveals that something ugly is hidden behind it. And I am not saying that all that is not natural is bad. Nature *can* be improved upon. That's what intelligence is for, but it should not be against nature. For example, the lips can be red through better food, through better exercise, through better medicine. That too is improving upon nature, but improving upon nature in a natural way.

Putting on lipstick is cheap; it is not really improving. It is good for the stage. Makeup artists are needed for the stage, not for real life. On the stage it is good, because the people who are looking at you are far away from you; they don't have to kiss you. They can throw kisses from far away; that's perfectly okay. But they don't have to taste your lipstick. Layers and layers of lipstick! It is so rotten and old, and continuously your saliva is giving it all kinds of germs. In each single kiss at least one hundred thousand germs pass between the lovers. And that is when the lips are without lipstick. With lipstick nobody has yet counted what is being transferred. And when the lipstick is there you never come in contact with the lips.

You must have misunderstood me. I am not saying that improving upon nature is bad. I am not saying that. Women can shave their legs and underarms. It is good, it is hygienic; nothing is wrong in it. Unless you take every care to clean your body...

Sobel, your New York women must not be taking baths everyday it seems. If you take a bath everyday and clean your body, then the hairs under your arms are not bad. There is nothing wrong about it. There is no need to remove them, they have their place. But if you are not taking a bath and if you are not being hygienic and clean, then certainly they will collect dust and they will collect perspiration and they will stink. Then it is good to remove them. I am not against removing them. It is beautiful to shave the hairs on your legs and give your legs a beautiful shape.

Improve upon nature, rather than impose. Make people more aware of their beauty and how to take care of it. Help them in natural ways. Man is the only animal who can go beyond nature, but he should go through nature, not cover nature. So I am not saying that that which is not natural is necessarily ugly.

But you must have misunderstood me. You must have heard with your freelance makeup artist's mind.

One Negro from South Africa was sent by his family to study at the university. So he went to the director to ask for admission.

"Which branch would you like to take?" asked the director.

"Can't I have a desk like everybody else?"

Now the poor fellow is coming from Africa. His mind can understand only in his own way...!

Sex was a big problem on the American nuclear submarine which was at sea for months at a stretch. The captain, however, had solved the problem by buying a life-size rubber doll which he put to frequent use. In fact, he became so satisfied that his crew became suspicious of his good moods and soon discovered the reason.

When the captain was on the bridge, they began to sneak into his cabin to visit the doll.

A few months later, when the submarine returned to San Francisco, the captain went along to the shop where he had originally purchased the doll.

"Look," he said, "I want to congratulate you guys on the lifelike qualities of that doll I bought. You know, it is so good I even got syphilis."

Be natural. Try to improve upon it.

It is good in films, on the stage and in theater to have makeup, because people are simply looking at you—and from a distance. You can deceive them. But when you are living with a person, in love, as a wife, as a husband, as a son, as a father, as a mother—how can you go on deceiving? The truth will be known— your false breasts will be discovered!

You can deceive others, but how can you deceive people who are close to you? And is it right to deceive them? And if they love you because of your breasts, the moment they discover that the breasts are false—plastic or rubber— will their love remain? It will disappear. The whole of humanity has become false. The idea seems to be to deceive, to pretend.

I am not against your art, but it has its own place. Life is not its place; life should be lived naturally. Yes, if some woman is so ugly, or some man is so ugly that he is disgusting, help him. Then your art can be helpful, because to be disgusting is immoral. When a woman passes by and you feel like vomiting, then certainly the questioner is needed, just to protect people from falling sick!

He has written a letter to me in which he says that he is not turned on by any sannyasin, although they are so beautiful. But he was turned on by an Indian woman in the Blue Diamond Hotel who was wearing lipstick and everything that he would like everyone else to wear.

My own understanding is that people become attracted only to persons who are unavailable. Now that Indian woman is almost an impossibility for him. She will not be available—that creates attraction. Whatsoever is impossible is attractive.

My sannyasins are very natural people; they are not pretenders. They are open, vulnerable, available. If love knocks on their doors, they will not reject it. But there are many people who are attracted only to the impossible, for the simple reason that they cannot get it. Getting it creates troubles, so it is better to be infatuated with something you can never get.

Indian women can be very attractive to Westerners, because they are closed, completely closed, and they are absolutely unavailable. And that very thing makes them so far away, like stars, that you can become interested. In fact it is one of the oldest strategies of women to make themselves as unavailable as possible. That creates infatuation in people, that creates sexuality in people. That keeps people tethered to the lowest kind of sexuality. Hence, people are interested in Indian women, they are interested in film actresses, because they will not be available to them. They will not be able to pay, they will not be able to afford them. They are always attracted to something which is beyond their reach. It gives them a challenge.

My effort here is to make this commune sexually free. And when I say sexually free, it has two meanings. In the beginning, people will be easily available to each other, and in the end the very availability will make their minds transcend sex. And that is happening everyday.

Hundreds of sannyasins write to me, "What has happened? When we came, we were so full of sex, and now all that has disappeared. There seems to be no desire for it. Even if we are interested in somebody, it is more like friendship than any sexual relationship. We love to be together, but there is no need to jump into bed immediately."

In fact, there are many sannyasins writing to me that sex has so completely disappeared, that for months or for years they have been celibate. Go and ask a Catholic monk or a Hindu sannyasin: they are trying to be celibate, and their minds are full of sex. We are not trying to be celibate here, but celibacy is happening.

Whatsoever is easily available, automatically becomes uninteresting.

In the West many people are turning towards homosexuality, lesbianism, for the simple reason that a man seems for another man to be a faraway goal because he is so unnatural; a woman, for a woman, seems to be a faraway goal, it seems so unnatural. A man and woman relationship is natural. So people are turning into homosexuals, lesbians. The reason is that when you make anything difficult, condemn it, repress it, it will become more and more attractive.

In my commune nothing is repressed, hence everything, by and by, loses its attraction. One becomes more and more calm and quiet and settled.

You say that in New York the women act in a ladylike manner. They have been forced for centuries to act in a ladylike manner. They have been changed from women into ladies. To be a woman is beautiful; to be a lady is ugly— ugly for the simple reason that acting like a lady is phony, it is snobbish. Acting like a woman is a natural phenomenon. And of course, when you want to act like a lady then you will have to have many kinds of makeup on many planes: physical, psychological, spiritual. You will go on hiding yourself behind curtains. You will never show your real face, your authenticity. You will become just a phony phenomenon.

The word "phony" is beautiful. It came into current use when telephones were invented, because when you speak on a telephone you do not sound real. It does not sound exactly like you; it becomes *phoney*. The word "phony" is beautiful—you are not in direct contact.

When I am talking to you, it is a direct contact. When it is a long-distance call, you sound phony, I sound phony. But that's how people are living. They are not allowing closeness; they are creating all kinds of barriers to create distance. Lipstick is a distance, so that lips should not come in direct contact. It gives a phoniness. All makeup is phony.

But let me remind you, I am not saying that anything that is natural is good. It is not inevitably good. It can be improved upon— it has to be improved upon. But it should be improved according to nature, not against nature. Nature should be helped to go beyond itself, it should not be repressed.

If nature is repressed, you start becoming schizophrenic. You start having double individualities: one that you are; one that you show to others. And you can get very messed up within yourself. Who are you?— this or that? It is not only a question of having two personalities, you will have to have many personalities. The mother will have one personality towards the child—she has to pretend to be a mother—and to the husband she has to pretend to be a wife. And to the lover she has to pretend to be a lover, and so on, so forth. So she will have many personalities around herself, and in the jungle of all these personalities her own individuality will be lost. She will find it very difficult to discover her original face.

You say to me, "Makeup can be used to spiritually enhance a woman's natural beauty..."

That is sheer nonsense. Spirituality cannot be enhanced by any makeup. Spiritual beauty has nothing to do with anything that can be done from the outside. Spirituality is your original face; it is the discovery of your intrinsic nature. It has not to be tampered with, it has not to be painted, it has not to be arranged. It has no hairs on the legs because there are no legs, no armpits, no lips. Your innermost being is pure consciousness. It needs no makeup.

But I understand his standpoint. People are even pretending there. That's what your so-called saints are doing. They are trying to cultivate spirituality. They are trying to condition themselves in a certain pattern of being holier-than-thou. But the really spiritual person is very simple, simple in the sense that he is in a natural flow; he is in a let-go with existence.

I will not allow you to work on any one of my sannyasins – not at all. It is hard work for me somehow to remove their lipstick, and somehow to make them drop their phoniness, and somehow to help them to discover their original face. I don't want you to do some makeup, and I don't see that you can make any of my sannyasins more beautiful in any way by makeup. The makeup will simply make her somebody else; she will not be herself. She may look like an actress, she may look like a model, but she will not be herself.

My whole effort here is to help you to be yourself, to be totally free from personalities. Personality is the false thing that surrounds you, and individuality is the gift of God. It is already there inside you. If you drop your personalities, you will discover it. The moment personalities are removed, it wells up.

Rather than doing that, I can help you to be natural. If you are fat, your fatness can disappear. Become a little more loving, become a little more natural. Your fatness will disappear. Fat people are people who are in some way repressing their sexuality. Whenever you repress your sexuality, you will start eating more. That's a substitute. You will go on stuffing yourself. Hence, I suspect your Hindu monks —because they are all so fat.

Have you seen Muktananda's guru's picture? If you have not seen it, it is worth seeing. It is a rare treat. I think he is unique— Nityananda *is* unique. You may have seen people with big bellies: Nityananda is a belly with a head! The belly is so big, you cannot say that he has a big belly. You can only say that the belly has a small man. And this is bound to happen to sexually repressed people.

But rationalizations.... Muktananda writes in his memoirs that when he was practicing his great *siddha yoga*, his *kundalini* started rising. And what really happened he describes in detail. Not knowing anything about Freud, Jung, Adler, Wilhelm Reich...these Indian so-called gurus are absolutely noncontemporary. They don't know anything that has happened in these last one thousand years. They are at least one thousand years behind. So when he talks about kundalini, he says that his genital organs became so strong, so erect, that they started hurting; that his prick was so erect it started touching his belly button. Kundalini rising...!

These fools go on teaching the West that this is the kundalini rising. This is simply repressed sex and nothing else. It is such a simple fact.

When the kundalini rises, something just the opposite happens.

An African native was bathing in the river by his village when a group of tourists arrived on the scene. They stared in awe at the enormity of his prick. The native looked back at them, embarrassed, and said, "Why is it so amusing? Don't yours shrink in cold water?"

When the kundalini rises it is taking a bath in cold water, in ice-cold water...! But Nityananda's disciple cannot be anything else. Whenever you repress your sex, you will start eating more, you will become fat. You will become ugly, you will lose all proportion.

Rather than trying makeup out on any of my sannyasins, allow some of my sannyasins to remove some fat from you. That will be far more enhancing for your spiritual beauty. And if you are not turned on by the beautiful sannyasins here, that simply shows that you have become fixed, fixated on homosexuality. Jews have suffered the longest from homosexuality0151—from the days of the Old Testament. Three thousand years of homosexuality— it has become almost natural to them by now.

Let my people help you to become a little bit natural. It is beautiful to be attracted to a woman. It is a little bit berserk to be attracted to a man; something is wrong. It never happens to the wild animals when they are in a natural state. It always happens when you put them in a zoo. In a zoo, animals start behaving homosexually.

The reason is that each animal needs a certain space and freedom. There is a categorical imperative: each animal needs a certain space for his territory. When that space is disturbed, he goes crazy. Then he cannot see any difference, who is who – who is man, who is woman; who is male, who is female. He forgets all that, and he becomes so tense that he wants to release his sexual energy on anybody.

Mankind has become too overcrowded; that is creating homosexuality. The earth has become like a zoo. Nobody has space, which is an absolute necessity for growth, for natural growth. So everybody is becoming a little crazy. Homosexuality is not a good sign. It simply shows something has remained retarded in you.

When a child is born, he passes through many stages. The first stage is masturbatory, because he loves himself. So every child wants to play with his genital organ; that's a natural development. Then he moves to a second phase, and that is homosexuality. The boys become interested in boys, and the girls become interested in girls. That's how friendships arise, and that's how later on you will always feel that those friendships of your childhood were something superb. Nothing like that happens again. It cannot happen; it was confined to a particular phase of your life. And if things don't go wrong, then homosexuality turns into heterosexuality. This is natural growth.

The child first loves himself. He is the center of his world, he does not relate with anybody else. That is dangerous, because if he remains stuck there he will never be able to get on with people. He will remain very egoistic, selfish; he will never be able to share.

The second step is: he moves towards the boys if he is a boy, or towards girls if she is a girl, because moving from oneself to the same sex is easier. And then from that point he can move to the opposite sex. The boy starts becoming interested in girls, the girls become interested in the boys—that's natural growth.

These are the three natural phenomena. And the fourth, celibacy, is going beyond nature. That is the most beautiful phenomenon.

So I am not saying all that is natural is beautiful, but that the transcendental should come through the natural. The natural should be transformed into the transcendental.

Celibacy comes at the fourth stage, when you have lived with the woman or with the man, and you have gone through all the pleasures and all the pains. You have suffered, you have enjoyed, and you have become ripe enough, mature enough, to see that that too is a game—a beautiful game, very engaging, but a game is a game. Then you start moving beyond it. Then sexuality disappears; then silence descends in you. You relate with people without any sexual idea behind it. Your relating with people then has a pure fragrance of love, and it comes more and more close to prayer.

I am all for transcendence, and transcendence is not natural. But I am not for artificiality. Your art can be used by my theater group, by my fashion people, by my other artists; you can be of immense help to them. But remember, it is only for the stage. It is showmanship; it has nothing to do with the real life.

The real life has to be natural, and the real life has to go one day beyond nature. But nature has to become its foundation – not against nature, not hiding it, but discovering the innermost core of nature. Then is the transcendence, and that is the most beautiful experience. It beautifies you, your body, your mind, your soul. It not only beautifies you, it beautifies even people who come in contact with you. This beauty belongs to the beyond; it is called grace. Something descends from the above and floods you.

The second question

Why is it so difficult for me to laugh?

It must be that you have come here conditioned by wrong people. And the wrong people constitute the majority, almost ninety-nine point nine percent. The religious, the moralists, the puritans—they are all serious people. They destroy the very possibility of laughter in you. They destroy the very sense of humor in you. To them, humor is something earthly, mundane.

That's why Christians say Jesus never laughed. That is absolutely wrong. I know Jesus. It is impossible that Jesus never laughed. It cannot happen. But the Christians go on believing in this—that Jesus never laughed. Two thousand years of seriousness has made it incomprehensible that a man like Jesus can have a sense of humor.

Look at the statues of Jesus that Christians have made. He looks so serious, as if he has been on the cross for thirty-three years. And the cross became very significant to Christianity for the simple reason that the very idea of the cross will destroy all sense of humor in you. The cross has become the symbol of their religion.

Krishna is far closer to life. The flute is the symbol of life, not the cross. And have you seen the pictures of Krishna? Dressed beautifully, standing in a dancing posture, the flute in his hands on his lips, it looks like he is going to sing a song at any moment. He looks so alive, and he is wearing a beautiful crown of flowers with peacock feathers. This is far truer to life. That's how life is. It is tremendous joy.

But Buddhists say that Buddha does not even smile. And Jainas say that Mahavira has no sense of humor, cannot have. All these people are trying to create a certain idea of religiousness which is devoid of laughter. It is as if man's misery is not enough for them, and they want man to become even more miserable. They tell you, "Carry your cross on your shoulders"—as if your life is not already a cross.

Your conditioning of a wrong approach towards life is why you cannot laugh. But you will have to learn laughter here, because to me laughter is one of the most essential qualities of a religious man. If you cannot laugh you can never be a sage. If you cannot laugh totally, then something is missing in you. Then you have not understood the beauty of existence, you have not understood the mystery of existence.

Bodhidharma laughed for seven days when he became enlightened—nonstop. His friends became very worried; they thought he had gone insane. They asked him, "What is the matter? Why are you laughing?"

He said, "I am laughing because now I see the whole ridiculousness of my search. I have been searching for lives together for the truth, and it has always been within me. What I was searching for was in the seeker himself. I was looking everywhere and it was within me. I was running hither and thither and there was no need to run anywhere. I could have just calmed myself down, and it was mine. It has always been mine. From the very beginning it was within me. It is my innermost being, my very being.

"The seeker is the sought—that's why I am laughing. I cannot believe how I could remain in such a deception for so long, how I managed to be such a fool. And I am also laughing because I see all around millions of people searching in the same way—searching for bliss, for God, for truth, for nirvana—and all that they are searching and seeking and looking for can be found within themselves. There is no need to go anywhere. There is no need to do anything. Just close your eyes and look within, and the kingdom of God is yours. Hence, I cannot stop laughing."

The sense of humor is very significant, particularly for my sannyasins, because I am introducing a new kind of religiousness to the world: a non-escapist religiousness, a religiousness which is not against life. I would like you to be Zorba the Greek and Gautam the Buddha together, simultaneously. Less than that won't do. Zorba represents the earth with all its flowers and greenery and mountains and rivers and oceans. Buddha represents the sky with all its stars and clouds, and the rainbows.

The sky without the earth will be empty. The sky cannot laugh without the earth. The earth without the sky will be dead. Both together—and a dance comes into existence. The earth and the sky dancing together—and there is laughter, there is joy, there is celebration.

Look around, watch life. Don't be too bothered with religious scriptures. Ninety-nine percent of those religious scriptures are written by people who know nothing of religion. They are written by scholars, theologians. They are written by ascetics, anti-life people. The person who is anti-life is bound to be anti-laughter, anti-love— he will be anti-everything. His whole life is nothing but a denial, a constant denial. He is suicidal, he goes on cutting himself chunk by chunk. He is destructive, he destroys himself— how can he laugh?

I teach you life, I teach you love, I teach you how to sing, how to dance. I teach you how to transform your life into a festival, into a carnival of delight. Hence, laughter has to be one of the most essential qualities. Even if you cry and weep, your tears should have the quality of laughter in them. They should come dancing and singing; they should not be tears of sadness and misery. They should be tears of overflowing cheerfulness, of bliss. This is possible not through scriptures, but only if you look at life. All that is needed is a clarity.

You are an Indian— that creates difficulty. When you look at life, inside you are reciting the Bhagavadgita, Ramayana...Vedas are going on and on. You are chanting *Vishnu Sahasranam*— the one thousand names of God. How can you see life? Stop all this nonsense. Be silent and look at life, and you will find surprises everywhere—each moment, on each step. During the Second World War, a house in a London suburb is nearly totally destroyed by a direct hit of a rocket. All the inhabitants survive; only one man is missing. Suddenly, they hear a tremendous ughter coming out of the toilet which stands undestroyed amongst the ruins.

The man climbs out of it still laughing loudly, and they ask him, "What the hell are you laughing about?"

"Well," he says, "isn't it funny? I pull the chain and the whole house collapses!"

Just look around and you will find a thousand and one ways to laugh...

Little Siddhartha, our great sannyasin, walks up to a little girl, another sannyasin, and asks her to dance.
She replies, "No, thank you."
He replies, "Don't thank me. Thank God someone asked."

A few sannyasins were talking. One asked the others, "What is long, hard, and when put into something warm and wet, gets soft and drippy?"
And little Siddhartha answered, "Spaghetti."

The big boss and his wife had accepted the junior executive's dinner invitation. And as dinner was being served, the little son and daughter of the host left their beds and walked through the dining room absolutely naked. The polite guests ignored them.

At the first opportunity, the furious father went upstairs to scold them. But before he could say anything, the little boy cried, "Ah, Daddy, it is wonderful. We rubbed ourselves all over with Mummy's vanishing cream, and when we went downstairs to the dining room nobody saw us!"

In a small German town a Catholic priest caught red-handed a young boy picking out all of the raisins from a big loaf of bread which the priest had just brought from a nearby bakery shop.

"Are you not ashamed, my son, picking out all the raisins from this bread?" inquired the priest.

The boy looked straight at him and said, "Firstly, I am not your son. Secondly, my mother ordered a loaf without raisins. And thirdly, I am Protestant anyway."

While visiting Pierino's parents, a woman keeps telling them how much she would like to have a child like him, but that the stork has unfortunately not brought her anything.
Pierino says, "Why don't you change to a cock?"

Just look around and you will find a thousand and one things to laugh about.

Life is full of laughter, full of ridiculousness, full of absurdities. But if you are serious you will miss all that. If you are nonserious you will be available. If you are nonserious you will be capable of seeing it.

Paddy had died from dysentery. While they prepared the body for burial, it was still excreting. The undertaker thought carefully for a moment, then went away to get a cork.

Two hours later, O'Reilly and Muldoon came to carry the prepared corpse downstairs for the wake. As soft music played, the two friends solemnly carried the body down the stairs. Suddenly there was a loud pop, and a fountain of shit poured over O'Reilly's head. He promptly dropped the body, which slid down the stairs into the crowd of waiting guests.

The undertaker rushed up to O'Reilly saying, "What did you do, you clumsy bastard?"

O'Reilly looked at him coolly and said, "Look man, if he can shit, he can fucking walk!"

Sartini stalked into a police station and told the desk sergeant he wanted to swear out a complaint against a truck driver for assault and battery.

"What happened?" asked the bored cop.

"I was in a phone booth, and this creep came along and wanted to use the phone," explained Sartini. "I told him to wait a while, but he could not. Finally, he slammed open the door and yanked me out of there."

"No wonder you got mad," agreed the sergeant.

"Damned right, I got mad," said the Italian. "The son-of-a-bitch did not even give my girlfriend time to put her panties on."

Lady Maria's business is doing badly. As a whore in downtown Rome she tries hard, but for some reason or other it does not work out well.

One night she gets a great idea: "I will buy me a few small firecrackers, and when I am making love to a guy I will set one on fire and start screaming that something inside me has been torn and he should pay extra for it."

That night she happens to meet a man and takes him to her room, where they start making love on the bed. She slips one hand under the bed and lights a firecracker. Unfortunately she lights the whole box full of fireworks, and an enormous explosion follows.

"Oh, oh!" she screams, "you hurt me inside. Ten dollars extra."

The man looks at her and groans, "How about a hundred dollars if you can find my balls?"

Enough for today.

CHAPTER 7

Aes Dhammo Sanantano

The first question

> Is it possible that you are not enlightened? If it is the case, would that make any difference for me?

It is not only possible, it is absolutely certain that I am not enlightened! Enlightenment happens only when one is not, hence *one* cannot be enlightened. Either one is, or enlightenment is; both cannot be together—that is an impossibility, that is not in the very nature of things. Buddha will say: *Aes dhammo sanantano*, "This is the ultimate law of life."

One cannot be enlightened. To be is the barrier, not the bridge. It hinders; in fact, it is the only hindrance. To dissolve, not to be, that becomes the bridge.

Hence, the word Buddha uses for enlightenment is tremendously significant and beautiful. It contains the most profound truth ever uttered, but it is untranslatable; "enlightenment" is a very faraway echo of it. The very word "enlightenment" gives you a totally different sense. Buddha's word is nirvana; nirvana means cessation, disappearance. Literally it means when you blow a candle out, when the light of the candle is blown out, when the light disappears... One cannot ask where it has gone, one cannot say where it is now; it is simply no more. This is nirvana: the disappearance of the light.

"Enlightenment" gives you just the opposite meaning. It makes you feel that *you* become enlightened, that *you* become full of light, that darkness disappears, not you. You remain; in fact you are far more than you were before. Before, you were hidden in darkness; now, all the darkness is gone and your being is revealed.

Buddha says there is no being in you; you are a non-being— *anatta* is his word. Anatta means no-self, no-soul, no-being. He not only denies the ego, he denies every possibility of the ego; otherwise, the ego is so cunning it will go on coming back again and again. It will find subtle ways to catch hold of you. It will come in the name of the self; in fact it will come very loudly in the name of the self.

Ordinarily people write "self" with a lower case "s," and the people who philosophize about the ultimate reality start writing "Self" with a capital "S." It is ego magnified, it is ego decorated, it is ego pretending to be holy, it is ego pretending to be eternal.

Buddha uses the words "no-self," "no-soul," "no-being." He leaves no possibility for the ego to sprout again; he simply cuts it from the very roots. Never before Gautam the Buddha had it been done so efficiently.

My understanding, my experience, is exactly the same: nirvana cannot be claimed by anyone; to claim it is to falsify it. The *Upanishads* say: "Those who know cannot claim, and those who claim cannot know." The knower cannot say "I know," because in the knowing the "I" melts— there is nobody to claim, there is nobody to brag. Hence, I can only say one thing: it is absolutely certain that *I* am not enlightened. What is enlightened is not *me*; it is beyond the idea of *I*. It is transcendental to the ego, and in that sense you are also enlightened. You may not know it, that's another matter. Knowing or not knowing makes no difference to your nature; your nature remains the same, exactly the same. When you become enlightened you don't become a new person. In fact you don't gain anything, you only lose something: you lose your chains, you lose your bondage, you lose your misery, you go on losing.

Enlightenment is a process of losing; you don't gain anything. When there is nothing left to lose, that state is nirvana; that state of utter silence can be called enlightenment. *I* don't claim anything...

And you ask me, "If it is the case, would that make any difference for me?" It will make a difference, because you are not *here* with me. You are not here in a love relationship, you are here out of your greed. If it were not so, the question would not have arisen at all. Your questions show much about you. Your questions as questions may be meaningless, absurd, but they show much about you; they are indicators.

If you become absolutely certain that I am not enlightened, then your relationship with me is finished. Then you will start searching for somebody else who is enlightened; then you have to move to some other master. You will be caught by someone who brags, by someone who has a very subtle spiritual ego, who claims, who tries to prove his enlightenment through the scriptures or through miracles or through some other things. You need to be convinced that you are with the right person. The greedy person asks for proofs; love never asks for any proofs.

The people who were with Jesus were very greedy. They were all Jews— obviously they could not have been otherwise. They were continuously asking him, "Are you really the son of God— *really?*" In their question there is suspicion, doubt. They want Jesus to do miracles— walk on water, raise the dead, cure the blind. And even then they are not convinced— maybe there is some trick in it. Walking on water or curing the blind man or raising the dead— who knows, there may be some trick; there is every possibility.

The whole story of Lazarus may just have been a managed act. Lazarus was one of the friends of Jesus. Jesus could have told him, "Lie down; pretend to be dead." He may have taught him a few yoga tricks— how not to breathe. Yogis know the tricks, and Jesus had been to India. He may have learned a few tricks, how not to breathe, how to stop breathing. Now it is a proven fact that there are yoga exercises which can do it.

One yogi from south India, Brahma Yogi, demonstrated it in many universities—in Oxford, in Cambridge, in Calcutta, in Tokyo, in many universities—in front of very learned scientific gatherings. He used to stop his breathing for ten minutes; for all practical purposes he was not breathing. Only very sophisticated instruments showed that there was some slight breathing still going on, but that was not visible to the eyes; the pulse had stopped.

The pulse can be stopped very easily, you can learn the trick— the trick is so easy. You do only one thing: count your pulse. Then, every day early in the morning when you get up, fresh—don't do anything else—sit on your bed and count your pulse. For five minutes focus your mind on the pulse and go on repeating inside, "It is slowing down, slowing down, slowing down..." and you will be surprised: within a week you will have learned the art of slowing it down. You can bring it lower and lower as your practice grows. Within three months you will be able to stop it for a few moments, and if you practice for years you can stop it for a few minutes. The same is true about the heartbeat and about breathing.

In front of scientists Brahma Yogi proved that he was capable of stopping the breath. Now, Lazarus may have been just pretending that he was dead. Suspicions can never be put aside; if you doubt, you will doubt everything. And I don't say that there is something wrong in doubting – the only thing is that you have not fallen in love with Jesus; the master-disciple relationship has not happened. Hence the questions, hence the desire for proofs. But your doubting mind will create new questions, will ask for new proofs. And it is an infinite regression.

I know of a Bengali saint, Bengali Baba, who once stopped a train at Calcutta station. He created much news all over Bengal and became famous because of that; otherwise nobody had heard about him. He entered a first-class compartment. The ticket collector came, he asked for the ticket, and Bengali Baba said, "I am a fakir, a saint, and saints don't need any tickets. You get lost!"

Of course the conductor became very angry. He said, "You have to produce the ticket; otherwise I will throw you out!"

Bengali Baba said, "You can throw me out, but remember, without me this train cannot move even a single inch!"

Now it was a great challenge! He was thrown out; the police were called and he was taken out. He stood there on the platform, closed his eyes, went into deep *samadhi*, and the miracle happened! The driver tried hard, the guard was waving his flag—but nothing happened. And the guard was puzzled because there was nothing wrong with the engine. Everything was working perfectly, but the train would not move a single inch.

A great crowd gathered, all the passengers gathered. Even the station master came and touched the feet of Bengali Baba and said, "Please, let the train go!"

Bengali Baba said, "It cannot happen this way. Bring that man who threw me out. He has to touch my feet, apologize, and promise never to ask a fakir for a ticket!"

The conductor was very unwilling, but the whole crowd pressed him, forced him, virtually dragged him: "We have other work to do and the train is getting late—somebody has to attend the courts, somebody has to go somewhere else—and just because of your foolish ego! What is wrong with asking forgiveness? And you have seen the power of the man!"

Finally, he touched his feet, asked the Baba to enter the train, and promised never to ask any fakir for a ticket. And the moment the Baba entered the train, the train moved.

He became famous all over Bengal, and the secret was very simple. He was a very good man; before he died he revealed his secret. He said, "The secret was this: I had bribed two persons, one was the ticket collector and the other was the driver. Just two persons were bribed, and the whole show was so perfect!"

So who knows whether Lazarus was pretending to be dead. It is possible. If you doubt, you can doubt anything. After all these miracles, still the apostles were asking Jesus again and again, "Give us proof!" Even at the last moment, when he was crucified, they were hiding in the crowd and waiting for the ultimate miracle to happen. And when it did not happen they were really very disappointed. So their whole life was wasted by this man! He had been doing all kinds of tricks, and now on the cross everything failed. So there was no God behind him; otherwise this was the time to prove it! They were all greedy people.

Your question is full of greed. So when you ask me, "If it is the case, would that make any difference for me?" even in asking, you know it will make a difference, because you are not here for any love affair— not out of trust but out of greed. You want to gain something— and if the man is not enlightened, then why waste your time here? Move somewhere else, find the right person who can help you. If I am not enlightened, how can I help you to be enlightened? So what is the point of being here? And I say to you it is better that you move, because I have said clearly it is not only possible, it is absolutely certain that I am not enlightened.

So those who are here out of greed, spiritual greed, should not be here; this is not the place for them. This is not a business place! It is only for those who are gamblers, who can risk. It is only for those who are a little bit mad, drunkards.

I don't promise you anything. I don't promise you the kingdom of God, I don't promise you enlightenment – I don't promise at all. My whole approach is of living moment to moment; enlightened or unenlightened, what does it matter? Living moment to moment joyously, ecstatically, living moment to moment totally, intensely, passionately...

If one lives passionately, the ego dissolves. If one is total in one's acts, the ego is *bound* to dissolve. It is like when a dancer goes on and on dancing: a moment comes when only the dance remains and the dancer disappears. That is the moment of enlightenment.

Whenever the doer is not there, the manipulator is not there; whenever there is nobody inside you and there is only emptiness, nothingness, that is enlightenment. And out of that beautiful space whatsoever is born has grace, has glory.

Paradise is not something geographical, it is not somewhere else; it is a way of living. It belongs to those who can live totally and intensely. Then immediately, herenow, paradise descends— or, even better, wells up within their own sources, within their own beings. Just the space is needed for it to well up.

And I don't tell you to drop the ego, because if *you* drop the ego then the dropper will become the ego. I don't say become humble, because if *you* become humble then behind the facade of humbleness there will be a very subtle ego hiding.

So my devices are different. I say dance to abandon, sing, play music! Do whatsoever you like doing and move into it so totally that nothing is left behind. When nothing is left behind, the ego dissolves of its own accord.

That's the meaning of nirvana: you have blown the candle out, suddenly it is not there. Then whatsoever is, is divine.

The ego is human; egolessness is divine.

The ego is hell; egolessness is paradise.

The second question

Can I ever be happy with my wife?

It is almost impossible. Nothing is wrong with your wife, but the very institution of marriage is ugly, the very institution is anti-love. It is based on denying love a chance to flower within you. Marriage is an invention of those who don't want the earth to be full of flowers of love.

Love is dangerous to the establishment, the most dangerous thing, because if people are loving then this society is doomed. This society depends on hatred, not on love. Our whole politics and our whole so-called religions are based on hatred. Nations are divided – for what? The earth is one, what is the need for nations? India and Pakistan and Afghanistan...what is the need for nations? Can't humanity live together? Why all these boundaries? These boundaries are needed by the politicians.

Without the boundaries the politicians will disappear; without the boundaries there will be no politics. These boundaries create the whole game, and these boundaries are just big prisons. You don't feel as if you are imprisoned because the prison is so big you cannot see it. But try to cross over the boundary from India to Pakistan, or from Pakistan to India, and then you will see that it was all nonsense to think of yourself as free. You cannot go beyond the boundary: you need a passport, a visa, a permit, a this and that. Then suddenly you become aware that the prison was so big that you were not aware of its walls—but there are walls all around you.

Man has not yet become civilized enough to be allowed to move around the earth in freedom. When you pass from one prison to another, you have to fulfill many conditions. And these nations go on fighting, continuously fighting. Seventy percent of human energy is wasted on war—and the people are starving and the people are dying. The same energy can transform the whole earth into such a rich planet that nobody will bother about heaven at all. We can create a far better heaven here; we are more scientifically equipped. I have read the descriptions of your heavens in all the scriptures of the world. They are all living in the world of the bullock cart; they don't even know anything about bicycles. I have never come across any description of angels on bicycles! —what to say about anything else.

Your conceptions of heaven were developed at least three thousand years ago. Man has come of age. We now have a far better technology, far greater efficiency in creating, in producing, but for stupid reasons the whole thing goes into the war effort.

Now, what is the point of Iraq and Iran fighting? Utterly foolish—but they are destroying each other. And in destroying each other they will be destroying everybody else too, because the whole world depends on these two countries for all kinds of things: diesel, petrol and other petroleum products. These are two giant countries, and they are destroying each other's capacities. Once they are successful in destroying each other, they will have destroyed the whole world in a way; the whole world will be dragged back. And there seems to be no point: the whole question is of boundaries, where the boundaries should be. On the earth there are no boundaries, only on the maps!

Mulla Nasruddin was going on an airplane trip – it was his first trip. When he was passing the boundary of India and Pakistan, he was looking out of the window with his big binoculars trying to see the boundary, and he could not see anything.

And the pilot was saying, "Just two miles ahead is the boundary of India and Pakistan, and within seconds we will be crossing it." So he was looking very intently...but no boundary!

He asked the passenger sitting by his side, "Where is the boundary? I cannot see it!"

The very idea that the boundary existed on the earth was so foolish that his neighbor played a joke on him. He said, "You look carefully, concentrate on it. It is a very delicate thing and we are miles away, but if you look minutely you will see it."

He put one of the hairs from Mulla Nasruddin's beard on the lens of the binoculars, and Mulla said, "Yes, now I can see! Yes, there is the boundary! And at the end of the boundary line I can see there is a camel also, but such a very strange-looking camel I have never seen!"

The neighbor said, "This is a Pakistani camel—how can you have seen it before?"

He was looking at his own beard!

On the earth there are no boundaries, but politicians need boundaries. Religiousness has no boundaries, but priests need them. Religiousness is neither Christian nor Hindu nor Mohammedan, but then what will the priests do? They will be out of a job, completely out of a job, and millions of people depend on these boundaries. Their whole business is to go on insisting: "Only Christianity is the right religion; only Hinduism is the right religion. Unless you are a Christian there is no hope for you." And the same is the claim of all the other religions. Everybody is trying to pull you into his fold because numbers create power.

Society, up to now, has existed in deep hatred – hatred for other countries, hatred for other religions, hatred for other-colored people, hatred in every possible way. So the love quality has to be destroyed, and we start destroying the qualities of love from the very childhood. We start teaching the child: "You are a Hindu, Mohammedan, Christian – hate others." But we don't say it directly, it is a very indirect maneuver. We start making every child ambitious, and ambition means you cannot love; ambition is anti-love. Ambition needs fight, ambition needs struggle, ambition needs you to use others as a means.

Love is a totally different perspective. Love says respect the other as an end unto himself or herself; never use the other as a means. Nobody is a means for you, everybody is an end. But then ambition will flop, and our whole educational system depends on ambitiousness, our politics depends on ambition, our religions depend on ambition. Politics is the religion of this world and religion is the politics of the other world; that's the only difference between the two. And the politician and the priest have been in a deep conspiracy for centuries. They have divided everything up amongst themselves: "You will rule here, we will rule there; you will rule before death, we will rule after death – fifty-fifty!" But both have to do one thing: destroy any potential for love.

For thousands of years only child marriages were allowed. It was a subtle strategy. The questioner himself may have got married when he was a child, not knowing what was going to happen. Once you become older it becomes difficult for you to accept any woman or any man as your wife or husband: you will start asking your parents embarrassing questions: "I don't love this man, I don't love this woman...?" Love is something that cannot be enforced—if it happens, it happens; if it does not happen it does not happen. So the cunning people decide that before you start asking about love it is better to arrange a marriage.

All other relationships are given by birth. There was only one freedom for you: to choose your wife or your husband. Even that has been destroyed. You cannot choose your mother, you cannot choose your father, you cannot choose your brothers and your sisters— that is all accidental. You cannot choose your uncles, your aunts; that is beyond your choice. The only freedom was that you could choose your beloved—but that too was denied.

People were married when they were so small, six years old, seven years old. In India marriages used to be arranged even while the child was inside the womb. People used to arrange that "if your child turns out to be a boy, and my child turns out to be a girl, or vice versa, we will marry them." The marriage was already decided before the birth! This was a strategy to poison love. So the child would grow with the wife or the husband just as one grows with one's brothers and sisters: he would become accustomed, love would never happen.

The society is very much afraid of love. It condemns love, it calls love blind. The fact is, love is the only phenomenon which is not blind; everything else is blind. Logic is blind, not love, but you have been told that love is blind, you have been told that love is mad. In all the languages of the world this type of expression exists: "falling in love"—as if one falls! I would like to change it. Whenever you are in love never say, "I have fallen in love," say, "I have *risen* in love." It is reaching higher than you have ever been before. It is not a fall, it is growth.

You ask me, "Can I ever be happy with my wife?" It is not a personal question at all, remember, and I am not answering you in a personal way either; it is a general question. You cannot be happy with your wife unless you respect her as a person and not as a wife. Unless you accept her as independent, free to be herself, you cannot be happy. And the man has been told that he is the possessor, the wife is only a possession.

In China, for centuries the husband was allowed to kill his wife if he wanted, because the wife was just a thing. In India, the wife is thought to be the property of the husband. Certainly, if the wife is your property, how can you be happy with her? You are insulting her, you are humiliating her, you are destroying her individuality. She will take revenge. Of course her ways will be feminine ways of taking revenge, but she will take revenge. She will create a situation in which you will be in constant hell.

Society has been dominated by the man for too long, and he has reduced the woman to a commodity. Now it cannot be done anymore. The woman has equal rights with any man; and she has to be respected—

she is a human being and nobody's property! At the most, the husband and the wife are friends – not more than that. And don't take her for granted, because nobody can take anybody for granted. One cannot be certain about the tomorrow. Tomorrow she may be yours, she may not be yours. This risk has to be accepted; only then can there be joy in relationship. When relationship is free, when there is freedom in it, there is joy, because freedom is the ultimate value; nothing is higher than that.

If your love leads you towards freedom, then your love will be a blessing; if it leads towards slavery it is not a blessing, it is a curse.

On his golden wedding anniversary a man was asked if his marriage had turned out better or worse than he had anticipated.

"Well," he said, "originally I thought our marriage would be a fifty-fifty proposition. It has turned out that way, but not as I expected. My wife has had her way the first fifty years, and I'll have my way the second fifty!"

Something like this arrangement happens between husbands and wives. It is an arranged phenomenon, it is not out of love. Both are trying to get as much out of it as possible and to give as little as possible.

"We got a divorce because we were incompatible," explained one bar fly to another. "My wife hated me when I was drunk, and I couldn't stand her when I was sober."

These are arrangements!

The newly-enlisted rookie was being examined by the army psychiatrist. "What do you do for social life?" he was asked.

"I just hang around the house."

"Do you ever go out with girls?"

"No."

"Don't you ever want to?"

"Yes."

"Then why don't you?"

"My wife won't let me!"

Husbands and wives are protecting each other, guarding, detecting. They are not friends but enemies, trying to prove in every possible way who the master is.

How can you be happy with your wife? If you are a husband you cannot be happy. The very word "husband" is ugly; it comes from husbandry. The wife is thought to be like a field and you are the farmer; you have to sow the seeds— the wife is just like a field. You are the owner, the sower of the seeds, the reaper of the crops, and she is just the earth. We should change our language. Very ugly words still go on being used. "Husband" is an ugly word; it should be dropped from all languages.

The wife and the husband should come to a better understanding. They are together to make life a joy; they are together not to quarrel, not to nag, not to destroy each other but to enhance each other in every possible way—physical, psychological, spiritual. Love should be a journey, a pilgrimage towards the ultimate.

An elderly couple are lying in bed. "Joseph," she says, "you remember the days you used to kiss my ear?"

Joseph turns over and kisses her ear.

"And Joseph," she says, "you remember the days you used to fondle my hair?"

Joseph gently strokes her hair.

"And Joseph," she continues, "you remember the days you used to bite my neck?"

Joseph gets up and walks through the room, "Hey, Marge," he says, "do you remember where I put my false teeth?"

Love is not a demand, love is a deep understanding. One cannot ask for it; one should give for the sheer joy of giving. Certainly it comes, a thousandfold it comes, but it has not to be asked for.

There is no future for the institution of marriage. We will have to discover new forms of relating, new forms of loving, new dimensions in which people can join together. Marriage is out of date, but old habits die hard—we go on clinging. Even young people...

Just the other day a girl who is only twenty-two- and not even Indian, she comes from Germany— told me, "I want to get married." For what? Can't you see the insanity all around? Her father has divorced her mother; her mother has gone with some other man. Her father is living with some other woman, and still, she wants to get married! Everybody thinks that his life is going to be an exception. That foolish idea destroys people's whole lives.

The first thing is love: love deeply. If you have been with a person for a few years, in deep love, and you have experienced all the joys and all the miseries, and still you decide to be with the person, then marriage is okay. Because marriage is only a legal arrangement, it cannot make anything more beautiful than it is. It can only make it ugly, it cannot beautify it. Once it is settled legally, once you start taking each other for granted, things will start going down rather than rising high.

So before one settles with anybody, one should learn to live with as many people as possible. My own understanding is that there are no two persons alike; hence, unless you have experienced many love affairs you will not know the multidimensionality of love. Only after knowing the multidimensionality of love will you feel enriched. Only when you know that now you have known the world enough and you have experienced and observed many kinds of relationships with many types of people...only then can you choose. No astrologer can decide it for you, and no parents can decide it for you. Even *you*, just by your instinct, cannot decide it.

Love affairs have been failing, and parents feel very happy. People come to me and they say, "Look, in the West love affairs have been failing. Then why are you against marriage?" they ask me. Love affairs are failing because first the marriage was arranged by the astrologer, then it was arranged by the parents, and now it is being arranged by biology, by instinct. You suddenly feel that you like a woman, but you don't know how long this is going to last and you are not even aware why you like her. You are not even alert to what it is in you that likes her. Maybe it is just her hairstyle. Now, are you going to get married to a hairstyle? You can get married, but tomorrow morning when you see her hair disheveled you will be at a loss: "Is this the same woman I fell in love with?" How long can you be interested in the hairstyle? Soon you will get fed up. The same hairstyle again and again—the whole day, twenty-four hours a day...!

People are falling in love because a certain man has a certain type of nose. People are falling in love with fragments! Nobody is bothered about the totality of the person—and it is a vast thing. The nose does not count for much— after two days you won't look at it at all. Or the color, or the shape, or the proportion of the body— all these things are very minor. The real thing is the total functioning of the person, and that can be experienced only when you live together. Before one decides to get married, one should live with many people so one can choose in awareness, and one should live with the person one is choosing for a few months, for a few years.

My own observation is that nobody should get married before the age of thirty-five. If you are going to live seventy years, then thirty-five is the right time; if you are going to live more than that, then you can prolong it. If you are going to die at eighty, then forty. If you have decided to live a hundred years, then fifty. The longer you wait the better, because if you wait long enough you may decide not to get into it at all! That's the most beautiful thing: if you wait long enough.

Just the other day Amrit Chinmayo asked me...Now, she is nearabout fifty; she is a beautiful woman and I like her because she is outrageous! She asked me, "I don't see many sannyasins of my age here. There are beautiful people, stunning people, but they are nearabout thirty or at the most thirty-five, and I am fifty. There are very few people who are fifty or beyond fifty. Am I transcending sex or is it just because I cannot find people of my own age?"

My feeling about you, Chinmayo, is that you have lived an outrageous life and it is time to transcend. Only outrageous people can transcend quickly. The orthodox, the conventional, the people who live in a lukewarm way go on and on repeating the same stupidity to the very end. Even when they are dying they will be thinking of sex, women— and you can always find a copy of Playboy under their pillow! Maybe a very old copy from when they were young, or just a hangover they are still carrying, or something like a memoir of their youth, their young days...

Chinmayo is a woman who has really lived, and if you live totally and really authentically, you will get beyond all this nonsense sooner. Fifty is the right time to go beyond, but don't force it because forcing will not help. Transcendence has to happen in a silent, whisperlike manner. One becomes aware of it only when it has happened.

But it is going to happen sooner or later, Chinmayo; it will not take long for you. Those who live intensely can live more in ten years than ordinary people can live in fifty years.

Once a man asked Emerson, "What is your age?"
Emerson said, "Three hundred and sixty years."
The man could not believe it—he looked no more than sixty. And he could not believe that Emerson would lie because he was well-known for his authenticity. He thought, "I must have heard wrongly." He said, "Pardon me, I could not hear. What did you say? What is your age?" years then they will come close to me, although I have lived only sixty years. But I have lived intensely and totally. Each moment I have squeezed the juice of life; I have not left a single drop behind. So in sixty years I have lived six times more than people ordinarily live."

And that's my feeling about Chinmayo: she has lived more in fifty years than people will live in a hundred years. And it is time to transcend, it is time to go beyond.

Sex is animal, love is human.
And to go beyond love is divine.
Then arises prayer.
Sex, love, prayer: these are the three stages of life.
If you die without knowing prayer, you have lived in vain.

The last question

Why are you not serious? Why are you always joking?

God is not serious—what can I do? God is always joking. Look at your own life— it is a joke! Look at other people's lives, and you will find jokes and jokes and jokes.

Seriousness is illness; seriousness has nothing spiritual about it. Spirituality is laughter, spirituality is joy, spirituality is fun.

Two hunters were in a forest looking for game, when they came across a huge black bear. The first hunter took aim, but missed. The second hunter took careful aim as the bear drew closer to them, but his gun jammed. The two hunters fled in terror with the bear in hot pursuit. They came to a small cabin at the edge of the forest, ran inside and bolted the door just before the bear reached them.

The enormous bear circled the cabin, found an open window and climbed in after them. Loud crashing and terror-stricken screams ensued, then silence...

Finally, after three days, the door burst open and the first hunter staggered out, walked ten paces then fell face first onto the ground.

Not long after, the second hunter staggered out, walked about twenty paces then fell to the ground. Hours later the bear appeared, staggered up the track about half a mile, then collapsed.

Shortly after, a beautiful young lady appeared at the door of the cabin. She walked up to the first hunter and said, "Him, he owes me ten dollars!"

Walking up to the second hunter, she said, "Him, he owes me twenty dollars." Then she looked up and began scanning the horizon. "Now, I wonder what happened to that big guy in the fur coat? He had another free one comin'!"

Enough for today.

CHAPTER 8

Silence and Song Meet

The first question

When I am among people, after a while I want to be alone. When I am alone, after a while I want to be among people. So I cannot enjoy one or the other fully. Should I live on the inside or on the outside?

This is one of the most fundamental questions every human being has to encounter; it is part of the challenge that life presents to us. The mind functions in duality; it is like a pendulum. When the pendulum moves towards the right, you see it moving towards the right, but at the very same time it is gathering momentum to go to the left. When it is moving towards the left it is gathering momentum to go to the right.

This inner duality in the pendulum represents your mind. The mind is a pendulum; hence, when you are alone you cannot enjoy aloneness, you start gathering momentum to be with people, and as you start thinking of people, aloneness turns into loneliness. Aloneness is tremendously beautiful; it is like a sunlit peak, something beyond the clouds. But loneliness is ugly; it is a dark hole. If you cannot enjoy aloneness everything goes upside down: the peak becomes the valley, the light becomes darkness. You are bored, you don't know what to do with yourself; you feel empty, and you want to stuff yourself with something—either with people or with food or with a movie. These are all different ways not to feel lonely. And when you are with people, the same will happen again from the other end. When you are with people you feel interfered with, trespassed upon, because others start encroaching on your space, they destroy your freedom. So being with others is no longer love; it becomes a bondage. And one hates bondage — one wants to get rid of it as quickly as possible. It is a prison; you start feeling suffocated. Even with the person you think you love, you start feeling fed up. You cannot enjoy love because suddenly you realize that to be alone is beautiful, because now you can see that aloneness is freedom. But when you are alone you see love as joy!

This is the dichotomy of the mind. It exists in every dimension. If you are poor you hanker to be rich; this is a well-known fact. But the other side has not been recognized: everybody knows the beggar wants to be the emperor, but have you not watched Mahavira renouncing his kingdom, Buddha escaping from his marble palaces? What is that? It is the same phenomenon! The poor man wants to be rich, and the rich man wants to be poor. And when Buddha started initiating disciples he called them *bhikkhus*. The word "bhikkhu" means beggar.

Alexander the Great, at the last moment of his life, realized that he had wasted his life in accumulating unnecessary, nonessential things, and now death would take everything away. Suddenly he remembered the great Greek mystic Diogenes whom he had met just a year before. Diogenes was naked and lived without any possessions, and Alexander had felt tremendously infatuated with him. He had told Diogenes exactly this, that "If I am to come back to the world I will ask God to make me Diogenes next time, and not Alexander."

This is the same dichotomy; there is no difference. When you are a child you want to be older, and when you are older you start thinking how beautiful were the days when you were a child. Everybody as he grows older starts fantasizing about his childhood; he starts decorating it in every possible way. And when he was a child he was in a hurry to grow up.

When you are alive you think of the life that is after death. People come to me and say, "Tell us something about what happens after death." And I am always intrigued with their question. Rather than answering them, I ask them, "First tell me what happens before death!" Nobody seems to be interested in that — what happens before death; everybody is interested in what happens after death. And if you meet a ghost, it is absolutely certain he will tell you, "I am suffering very badly. I missed my life, now I am hankering for it. I would like to have the body again, the mind again, to have all the senses again."

Silence and Song Meet

Different aspects, but the problem is the same: you hanker for the opposite because the grass looks greener— not your own grass but the grass beyond the fence in the neighbor's garden. It always looks greener. It is a simple phenomenon: whatsoever you have loses meaning—the moment you have it, it loses meaning—whatsoever you have not becomes immensely significant. The mind hankers for that which it has not got, and the mind gets bored with whatsoever it has got.

It is said about the great English poet Byron that he must have loved at least sixty women. He did not live so long; he died young— and this number, sixty, is a very conservative estimate. This is from the known stories; there may have been other relationships which are not known. When he would go mad about a woman, he would risk everything. He risked his whole respectability. He was expelled from England for the simple reason that he was creating chaos. He was a beautiful man— very beautiful, extraordinarily beautiful—and a great poet. He had all those qualities which women are attracted to. He was a legend in his own time.

It had become a routine phenomenon that if he entered a restaurant the men would clutch the hands of their wives and run away! He was not allowed into clubs, he was not allowed into good society. Everybody was afraid of the man; he had some charm, some magnetism, some charisma. And for months he would go mad and chase a woman. And the moment he got the woman he would lose all interest, all interest would absolutely disappear. He represents mind in its purity, in its essential quality.

One woman forced him to marry her because she insisted that she would not allow him even to kiss her, or even to hug her, or even to hold her hand unless he married her. And he was so mad about her that he agreed to marriage. When they were coming out of the church, just married, and the guests were taking leave of them, standing on the steps, holding the hand of his wife, he saw another woman walking down the road and he forgot his wife. His wife immediately recognized it; she could see that he had forgotten all about her, and she told him so.

But he was a sincere man too. He said, "It is true, I have lost all interest in you. For six months I was mad—day in, day out, I dreamed about you, fantasized about you, wrote poems about you. I was dying! I was thinking that without you I could not live a single moment longer.

And now that you are mine and your hand is in my hand, I only feel perspiration! That woman for a moment caught my whole being. I simply forgot you." He apologized—but apology is not love.

This is the way the mind functions: its whole interest is in that which you have not got. Hence your question is significant and it has tortured humanity since the very beginning. And people have been choosing, just as you are asking: "Should I live on the inside or on the outside?"

Wherever you live you will be in trouble. If you live on the outside, the inside will function like a magnet. If you live on the inside, the outside will go on sending invitations to you: "Come out! It is a beautiful morning. The flowers are blossoming and the air is fragrant," or, "It is a tremendously ecstatic sunset. Look, the starry night..." And if you are outside you will continuously worry, "What is inside me? Who am I? What is this consciousness?"

Science has become focused on the outside; religion has become focused on the inside. Both are lopsided, because the inside and the outside are not two separate things, they are inseparably one. To separate them is arbitrary, artificial.

In the past the monks decided to be alone because they saw the misery of love, they saw that to be with someone is to suffer. What Jean-Paul Sartre said in this century, the monks all over the world—Christian, Hindu, Jaina, Buddhist, Mohammedan – have known all along; it is one of the most ancient experiences. Jean-Paul Sartre is not original at all; he looks original because nobody has said it in exactly that way. Jean-Paul Sartre says, "The other is hell"— and this is the experience of all the monks, of all the mahatmas, of all the saints. Whatsoever denomination they belong to does not matter; on one point they all agree: "The other is hell— escape from the other!"

They escaped to the Himalayan caves, they escaped to the monasteries, they escaped from the world—they were really escaping from the other. But were they happy in their monasteries, in their caves? That question has not been raised. It has to be raised. Were they blissful? Maybe they were more silent than you are—but silence is not bliss, silence is not a song. Silence has no warmth; it can be cold and dead. And it *was* cold and dead.

Your so-called monks have lived in such a suicidal way that they have become living corpses. They chose half of life, and whenever you chose half you will be in trouble, because what are you going to do with the other half? You will remain only fragmentary, and the other half will take its revenge.

The remainder of humanity has chosen to live in the world, and it is very rare to find a person in the world who does not feel once in a while the desire to escape from all this. The world is too much; it is anxiety, anguish; it is nothing but suffering.

Psychologists say that the average person thinks at least four times in his life of committing suicide—at least! Why do people think of committing suicide? And not only do people think of it, many commit suicide. That's also a way of escaping from the world, escaping totally, because if you go to a monastery you can come back. You know it yourself: if you go to the Himalayas, who can prevent you? —you can come back again.

Suicide seems to be irreversible. Suicide is a total renunciation of life, and what you have called the renunciation of life is nothing but slow suicide, suicide in installments—the American way, part by part!

My own observation is that both extremes have been wrong, and both have created a very ugly situation. There is no need to choose; we have to live both. Of course it is easier to be silent in a cave, but that silence will not give you a dance, and without a dance you will remain dead. If you are in the world it will give you a song, but the song will not have any depth; it will be superficial, formal.

One needs silence in the heart, and yet a silence which is not cold but warm, a silence which can sing and dance.

When silence and song meet, the man is whole.

When you are capable of moving between the inner and the outer easily, just as you move in and out of your house...in the same way as when it is too cold in the morning you simply move out of the house into the sun. You enjoy the warmth of the sun, and when it becomes too hot you move inside. There is no problem in it—it is *your* house! The inner is as much yours as the outer, and to be capable of moving from the inner to the outer and vice versa, in a flexible way, creates the whole man. And I call the *whole* man the holy man.

My sannyasins have to be whole.

You are not yet a sannyasin. If you are really interested in solving this problem, my sannyas is the only way to solve it, because I teach flexibility. All the old ideas are rigid: "Either be extrovert or be introvert"— but both are pathological. The introvert becomes moribund, the introvert becomes a little bit insane because he loses contact with objective reality; he starts hallucinating. That's why it is easy to experience God if you go to the Himalayan caves. There is no objective reality to hinder you from deceiving yourself. There is no objective reality to remind you that this is a dream, that what you are seeing is not there, it is a hallucination.

It is a well-known psychological fact that if you live in deep isolation for just three weeks you will start hallucinating. And you can hallucinate whatsoever you want: if you are a Christian you will see Christ, if you are a Hindu you will see Krishna, if you are a Buddhist you will see Buddha. This is very strange! No Christian ever sees Buddha, no Buddhist ever sees Christ! Whatsoever you have been conditioned for, your hallucination will be colored by it. You will start visiting heaven, but your heavens will be different.

The Tibetan heaven is very warm; it has to be—Tibet suffers so much from cold. The Tibetan hell is cold, ice-cold, but the Indian hell is just fire. The very idea of ice to the Indian will give him great joy! The Indian idea of heaven is that it is very cool— it is air-conditioned! The Indian will dream about his heaven, and the Tibetan will dream about his heaven.

In the Mohammedan heaven there are rivers and streams flowing with wine, because the *Koran* is very much against wine. It is repression. When you repress you are bound to erupt in hallucination. The Mohammedan idea of heaven is that you will have beautiful women there, and not only beautiful women but beautiful boys too, because in the Arabic nations homosexuality has been one of the longest traditions— repressed, very much repressed. But whatsoever is repressed is bound to assert itself somewhere. In heaven even homosexuality is allowed, available. Here it is condemned; there it is allowed.

Hindus go on saying that all desires are wrong, but in heaven you have wish-fulfilling trees. You just sit underneath the tree— *kalptarus*, wish-fulfilling trees— you desire anything, and immediately, instantly it is fulfilled. Instant coffee is a very new thing – Hindus have known instant fulfillment for all desires! Just sit under the *kalpavrisksha*. Here they go on talking against desires, and there the same desires are going to be fulfilled. Here they go on talking against women...

The Hindu saint goes on saying that the woman is the door to hell, and in their heaven there are beautiful *apsaras*, beautiful women— Uruvasi, Menaka...thousands... They have golden bodies; they are always young. In fact, they have been stuck at the age of sixteen for millions of years; they have never grown beyond it. It seems they were born at exactly sixteen and they have remained sixteen. Here, the woman is the door to hell, and the saints are hoping that sooner or later all this austerity, asceticism will be finished and they will enjoy heaven forever and forever. And what are you going to enjoy there? – the same women who are the doors to hell here!

The same money, the same gold which you go on calling dust...in heaven even the flowers are made of gold. I would not like such a heaven! Flowers made of gold cannot have any perfume. A roseflower made of gold will be ugly, it will be dead. Gold cannot be alive.

The extrovert is half: he is continuously running after things and continuously feeling guilty that he is missing the inner —maybe the real bliss is there. Perhaps the Buddha and the Jina and the Christ are right, that the kingdom of God is within. And the person who is sitting silently, looking inside, is continuously wondering, "Am I wasting my time? People are enjoying and I am foolishly sitting here, waiting for the spring to come and the grass to grow by itself! And who knows whether it grows by itself or not? And even if it does grow, so what? It will still grow whether I am sitting silently or not! The spring will come and the grass will grow, so let it grow! And there is some juicy party going on, and there are so many beautiful hotels and restaurants and clubs and nightclubs..."

Even a man like Morarji Desai...can you imagine Morarji Desai visiting a nightclub? Now he has confessed that when he was the prime minister—he must have been eighty-three at that time—he went to visit a nightclub in Canada, of course without declaring it. He has kept it a secret up to now. Why did he suddenly talk about it? He was bragging; he did not think that he was saying something wrong— he was bragging. He was telling the Gujarat Vidyapeeth students in Ahmedabad, "I have attained to the ultimate celibacy. For example, I visited a nightclub in Canada just to see what was going on there." But why should a man who has attained to ultimate celibacy even be interested to know what is going on there? Some rationalization, some strategy of the mind entering from the backdoor. He was not even being honest enough to say, "I wanted to see the naked women." No, he says, "I wanted to see what was going on there." But why should he be worried about it?"

And he says, "When I went there, knowing that I was the prime minister, the four most beautiful girls were sent to me and they started dancing around me, making all kinds of gestures—very inviting, very appealing—but I remained controlled! I was not affected at all." He emphasized it so much that it simply shows he must have been affected.

And those girls seem to have been far more intelligent than this poor guy. After a while they said, "We thought you were a man, but you are just a Morarji Desai!" Now do you know what Morarji Desai means? The girls said, "We thought you were a man, but you are nothing—just a Morarji Desai!"

But he even brags about that—stupidity is such! He thought they recognized that he was no ordinary person, he was Morarji Desai—that he was not a man in the ordinary sense, he had transcended all human weaknesses.

The people who are living extrovertly will remain interested in the inner world, and the people who are living introvertly will remain interested in the extrovert world, and they will both be torn apart. That creates anguish, strain.

My own suggestion is to live a relaxed life. It is beautiful to be alone, it is also beautiful to be in love, to be with people. And both are complementary, not contradictory. When you are enjoying others, enjoy, and enjoy to the full; there is no need to bother about aloneness. And when you are fed up with others, then move into aloneness and enjoy it to the full.

Don't try to choose—if you try to choose you will be in difficulty. Every choice is going to create a division in you, a kind of split in you. Why choose? When you can have both, why have one? And it is a very natural process. It is just like when you are hungry you eat, and when you are full you stop eating. You don't start saying, "What should I choose? Should I always remain hungry or should I eat continuously?" When you are hungry, eat, and when you are full, stop eating and forget all about it; there are a thousand and one other things to do. There is no need to go on a fast, and there is no need to go on stuffing yourself continuously; both are pathological states.

The same is true about love and aloneness. Enjoy people because they are manifestations of God, but remember the other side is also there. So when you start feeling fed up there is no need to remain with people just out of politeness. Don't try to be British— be authentic! It is very difficult not to be British, because we have always been told to be polite, to have certain manners, to follow a certain etiquette. Even if you are bored you go on smiling. Even if you don't feel good with somebody you say, "It is a blessing to meet you," and you are cursing them.

Why do you go on creating such strange splits in yourself? It is time— man has come of age— it is time to be authentic. When you are feeling good with somebody, say so and say it totally, and when you are not feeling good, then you can just say, "Excuse me..." I am not saying to be rude, but there is no need to suffer the presence of the other. Just say, "I would like to be alone, I would like my own space."

Up to now this has not been possible. If you love somebody you cannot say, "I would like to have my own space." This is sheer nonsense, inhuman! If you love somebody you should be sincere— that is the indication of love— you should be able to say, "Now I would like to have my own space." And you should allow the other also the same freedom to be with you or not to be with you.

It is good if two persons agree to be together for a time; it is beautiful. But it is also good to be alone. Aloneness will give you peace, silence, equanimity, meditativeness, awareness, a sense of integrity, centering, rootedness, groundedness—all these are great values. And love will help you to learn compassion, prayer, service—they are also great values, and they will enhance each other.

That's what I am doing here with my sannyasins—letting them enhance each other, letting them become backgrounds to each other.

Let your love help your aloneness.

It is like...when you look at the sky in the day you will not see any stars. It is not that they have all died or disappeared or evaporated; they are still there, but the background of darkness is missing, that's why you cannot see them. The sky is always full of stars; day or night makes no difference, but in the night you can see the stars clearly. The darker the night, the brighter the stars look. They are not against each other; they are complementary, not contradictory.

So are the inner and the outer world: the outer is part of the inner, just as the inner is part of the outer. They are like two wings — you cannot fly with one wing. Enjoy both, and don't create any rift, don't create any fight between them. Learn the art of being together *and* of being alone.

Hence, my whole teaching consists of two words, "meditation" and "love." Meditate so that you can feel immense silence, and love so that your life can become a song, a dance, a celebration. You will have to move between the two, and if you can move easily, if you can move without any effort, you have learned the greatest thing in life.

God is both the creator and the creation—this infinite universe outside and this infinite consciousness inside. And he has to be tasted and known in both aspects.

The second question

Chogyam Trungpa writes in one of his books:

"Nor is it helpful to choose someone for your master simply because he is famous – someone who is renowned for having published stacks of books and converted thousands or millions of people. Instead, the guideline is whether or not you are able to actually communicate with the person directly and thoroughly." The key words are "directly" and "thoroughly." How does this work from the sannyasin's end, in view of your virtually complete physical inaccessibility?

It is true that one should not choose someone as a master *just* because he is famous. Jesus was not famous when he was alive nor was Lao Tzu famous when he was alive. To be famous is one thing; to know the truth is totally another. In fact, there is a greater possibility that the master, the real master, will be notorious rather than famous.

Jesus must have been very notorious; otherwise why should he be crucified? And he was crucified with two thieves, one on either side, just to show the world that the people who were crucifying him did not consider him in any way more significant than two ordinary thieves. In fact they thought he was worse. It was a tradition in the Jerusalem of those days that each year one person could be forgiven. The day Jesus was crucified there were four persons to be crucified, and there was a possibility of one person being forgiven. Pontius Pilate asked the Jews, "Whom would you like to forgive?" He was thinking they would ask for Jesus to be forgiven, because in fact he had not done any harm to anybody—he was not a murderer, he was not a thief, he was not a criminal. But the people asked for a thief to be forgiven and insisted that Jesus could not be forgiven: "You can forgive any of the thieves, but not Jesus." He must have been very notorious—people were so angry with him.

They killed Socrates, they killed al-Hillaj Mansoor, they made many attempts on the life of Gautam Buddha. It simply shows these people were not famous, not respected by the crowd; the crowd was utterly against them. Hence, it is true that you should not choose your master simply because he is famous. He can easily be famous if he fulfills your expectations. And everybody has certain expectations, everybody has in mind certain qualities that a master has to fulfill — and anybody who fulfills your expectations is not a master at all. No master can fulfill your expectations; in fact he will sabotage all your expectations, he will destroy all your expectations. To fulfill your expectations is to strengthen your ego, and no master can do that.

And how can you decide what the qualifications of a master are? The Hindu will decide in one way, the Jaina will decide in another way; in fact, their decisions will be diametrically opposite to each other. The Hindu thinks Krishna is the perfect master, and the Jainas have thrown Krishna into the seventh hell. Hindus think Krishna is the perfect master because he lived a multidimensional life. Jainas think that he is one of the greatest criminals because he was the cause of the great war that destroyed India forever. Since that war five thousand years have passed and India has not been able to stand on her own feet again.

Millions of people were killed, and Krishna rationalized this killing with beautiful logic. He said to Arjuna, "Don't be worried about killing people, because the soul is immortal and the body is already dead, so you are not killing. There is no murder, there is no violence at all. The body is already dead, so dust will fall unto dust; and the soul is immortal, so you are only disconnecting them, that's all. You are not killing anybody; nothing is ever killed. *Na hanyate hanyamane sharire* — "By killing the body, nothing is killed."

A beautiful argument for violence! Now, the Jainas cannot forgive it. Their criterion for a perfect master is that he should be absolutely nonviolent—Mahavira is their ideal. Mahavira used to sleep in one position the whole night, for the simple reason that if he changed his posture, turned over on his other side, some ants or some insects might be killed. It was better to remain in one position the whole night. It is unnatural; the body needs the change. It helps the digestion to change your position — it is a little bit of exercise. But Mahavira remained like a statue the whole night. This is their ideal.

Krishna cannot fulfill it, Rama cannot fulfill it. Rama carries a bow and arrow, and they symbolize violence. Even Jesus cannot fulfill their criterion, because according to the Jainas you suffer only because of your past karmas. Jesus suffered on the cross, and that simply shows one thing and very definitively—that in his past lives he must have committed a great crime; otherwise why should he be crucified?

Who is going to decide? How are you going to know who the master is? Fame cannot decide, thousands of followers cannot decide. Then what is the way to decide? In fact, logic cannot decide. This is logic: looking at the fame of the man, looking at how many disciples he has. This is all logic, calculation, mathematics; these cannot be decisive. Only one thing can decide: if in your heart some bells start ringing for no reason at all, illogically. Even if you want to stop them they don't stop, they go on ringing. It is a heart-to-heart phenomenon.

So it is true: one should not choose a master just because he is famous, but the second part is not right either.

Trungpa says: "Instead, the guideline is whether or not you are able to actually communicate with the person..." The master has no personality, he is not a person—he has dropped personality. In fact, in the ultimate sense he is just a nothing, what Buddha calls *shunyata*; he is pure nothingness. How can you communicate with nothingness? Yes, communion is possible, but communication is not possible. And communion needs no direct personal contact; you can commune with the master from thousands of miles away. The physical presence is not needed. The physical presence is needed only for the beginners, for the people who are in the kindergarten class.

As the master starts working deeper and deeper, as he starts finding

Silence and Song Meet

his people, he will become more and more inaccessible physically, because once he has found the right people, who are ready to commune, there is no need for communication.

So that part is sheer bullshit, that the guideline is whether or not "you are able to actually communicate with the person directly and thoroughly." The whole thing depends on the disciple. If he can surrender his ego, then wherever he is there is communion.

Communion is a totally different phenomenon from communication. Communication is from intellect to intellect— and for that the physical presence is helpful – but communion is a totally different phenomenon. It is a love affair. The hearts can beat in the same rhythm thousands of miles apart. Even if you are on another planet, it doesn't matter; the hearts can dance in the same rhythm with the master, and then there is communion. You can be here physically with me, but if your heart is not beating with me, if you are not attuned to me, then communication is happening—I am talking to you, you are listening to me—but communion is not happening. The relationship between a disciple and a master is that of communion; it is a love affair.

Trungpa knows nothing about it. He is not a master, just a teacher. And remember the difference between a master and a teacher: the teacher is one who can inform you, the master is one who can transform you. The teacher teaches you, the master gives you a new birth. The master is like a midwife: he helps you come out of the cocoon of your mind; he makes you twice born.

There is no question of physical communication, so "directly and thoroughly" does not mean physically; "directly and thoroughly" means something different. According to me, if your ego is completely put aside, if the disciple is ready to trust, then there is a direct communication —direct, immediate. Even words are not needed; nothing is needed. And it is thorough communion too – total; it is an immersion.

It is like two lovers getting into a deep orgasmic state; that is a physical orgasm. The same thing happens on a higher plane with the master; it is a spiritual orgasm. Your soul and the soul of the master meet and merge, melt, lose their boundaries. There is tremendous joy; a great bliss surrounds you, a great grace descends in you.

Buddha had forty thousand disciples. Do you think it was possible for him to physically communicate "directly and thoroughly" with each one? Mahavira also had forty thousand disciples; it would have been impossible. But Buddha helped many more people to become enlightened than anybody else on the whole earth and in the whole history of man. And how did he help? Yes, there was a direct and thorough communion, but it was a silent phenomenon.

When Maulingaputta, a great philosopher, came to Buddha to ask questions, Buddha said, "If you really want your questions to be answered, for two years sit silently by my side, don't ask anything, and after two years I will answer you."

While Buddha was saying this, Mahakashyapa, one of Buddha's great disciples, started laughing. Maulingaputta felt a little embarrassed and he asked, "Why is this man laughing? He looks a little crazy!"

Buddha said, "You ask him!"

And Maulingaputta asked Mahakashyapa, "Why are you laughing?"

Mahakashyapa said, "I am laughing because this man deceived me too! And I warn you, if you want to ask your questions, ask right now! After two years you will not be able to ask. He played the same trick on me! For two years I was sitting silently by his side, and then slowly, slowly all questions disappeared."

Buddha said to Maulingaputta, "I will stick to my promise. If your questions disappear, then what can I do? But after two years I will remind you."

And after two years Buddha actually reminded him. Mahakashyapa was also present. Maulingaputta was sitting somewhere behind, afraid that Buddha would ask. Two years had passed, and Buddha asked Mahakashyapa, "Where is Maulingaputta? Find him! Two years have passed, exactly two years since the day he came. Now he can ask."

Maulingaputta stood and he said, "Forgive me, I have no questions. Now I know why you insisted that I should be silent."

When the mind becomes completely silent, there happens a direct and thorough communion. Answers are not given but received. Nothing is said but everything is heard. So it is not a question of how many sannyasins I have. I will tell you a beautiful story.

Two sannyasins meet in London and get into conversation. The first says, "Yeah, I just came back from Pune. Osho asked me to come back

Silence and Song Meet   131

to the West and start up a few small buddhafields here and there to help his work."

The second swami says, "Oh, if there were only a hundred sannyasins like you!"

The first continues, "Well, I'm really close to Osho, I suppose. I think he's starting to send future *bodhisattvas* out into the world. You know—to be in the world and yet not of it."

The second swami says, "Oh! If there were only a hundred sannyasins like you!"

The first swami goes on speaking, "I'm going to try to raise enough money to buy an island in the Pacific for the new ashram. I know he wants to leave India, and so I'm going to find the perfect place for him. I expect I will get to live in his house there."

The second swami sighs, "Oh! If there were only a hundred sannyasins like you!"

"Well," the first swami says, "I probably shouldn't tell you this, but when he told me to go back to the West, I knew he was preparing me for something special. I have a feeling that I'm going to be the first male medium when I go back there. He said a few of us were ready and I could swear he was looking straight at me."

"Oh! If there were only a hundred sannyasins like you!" said his listener.

"Look," laughed the first swami, "I'm just an ordinary guy like you. Why do you go on saying if only there were a hundred like me?"

"That's why!" said the other. "If only there were only a hundred sannyasins like you instead of two hundred thousand!"

But it does not matter—communion is possible. Two hundred thousand or twenty hundred thousand makes no difference. As far as I am concerned, to commune with one person or to commune with one hundred million people is the same, because communion from my side is a simple phenomenon. I am just a zero. All that is needed is a preparation on your part: if you are also a zero, then two zeros become one zero. And thousands of zeros can go on meeting and disappearing into one zero.

Neither fame should be decisive nor your expectations, but only your heart. If your heart says take the jump, then take the jump, then risk, then be adventurous.

And I will become more and more inaccessible. As the new commune arrives I will become more and more inaccessible to you physically so that I can become more accessible spiritually. I am going to be silent sooner or later, I am not going to speak at all. So be quick— get out of your kindergarten classes. Be fast! Don't waste time and don't postpone.

The last question

Do you want to attract or prevent Polacks with your jokes?

I never thought that you were also a Polack! There are many Polacks here—through my jokes I have discovered them; otherwise they hide themselves so perfectly! It is my way of discovering who are the Polacks among my sannyasins.

In Poland all are not Polacks, and outside Poland all are not non-Polacks either. So don't be worried—I am not saying anything against Polacks as such. They are beautiful people, innocent people; they are simple people. And sometimes simple people are also simpletons, but I love them. Those who can understand me will be attracted, and those who cannot understand me, whether I tell the jokes or not will not make any difference to them.

A Polack traveling on a train goes to the toilet for a piss. As soon as he opens the door to the toilet he sees himself in the mirror opposite and thinks that he is someone else. He apologizes for the intrusion and closes the door.

Ten minutes later he returns. "Oh, sorry!" he says, closing the door.

He comes back a third time and the same thing happens. He can't hold on any longer. With his hands thrust tightly in his pockets, he goes to the conductor to complain.

The conductor, another Polack, is outraged and goes to the toilet with the passenger to see what the problem is. He opens the door and shuts it again immediately, saying, "Oh, the conductor is in there. Use another toilet!"

Prisoner Pozinski, serving a twenty-year sentence in a Michigan jail, was reminiscing with a fellow inmate about his wife. "We used to have such fun at the seaside burying each other in the soft white sand!"

"Must have been nice!" said his cell mate.

"Yeah!" said the Polack. "When I get out I think I'll go back and dig her up!"

How many Polacks are needed for an electrical repair job?

Seven: one to be the negative pole, one to be the positive pole, and five to keep them apart!

Do you know why we have a Polish pope?

During the conference of cardinals, when they were trying to choose a successor to John Paul the First, the conference was deadlocked at three candidates.

Then one of the Italian cardinals who had been to America suggested, "Look, in the United States when they have elections, they always have a poll!" And that decided the matter.

Finkelbaum and Protski worked as chefs in a fine hotel.

In time they quit and Finkelbaum opened up a Jewish restaurant. Protski opened up an eatery directly across the street.

Within six months Finkelbaum's was thriving, and Protski's was practically out of business. He decided to ask his old friend for advice.

"It's easy," said Finkelbaum. "You gotta excite the customers. One day I have my waitresses go topless, the next day I have them go bottomless."

Protski, exhilarated by the idea, rushed back to his restaurant and called his waitresses together.

"From now on," announced the Polack, "one day you are all gonna go topless, the next day bottomless. So, tomorrow no babushkas! The next day, no boots!"

A Polack went to the dentist. The diagnosis was grim. "All the teeth need to be removed, my friend," said the dentist.

"My God!" said the Polack.

"But no need to worry, it won't hurt a bit. We'll fix you up with an immediate denture—it will be fitted straight into the sockets, it will look great, and it won't hurt at all."

"My God!" said the Polack.

"If you have any doubts you can phone Goldstein, the town's famous Jew. He had the same thing six months ago," the dentist told the worried Polack.

"My God! My God!" said the Polack. "I'll phone Goldstein—I know him—and let you know."

He phoned Mr. Goldstein and asked if there had been any pain with his new teeth.

Goldstein replied, "Pain! In the last six months I've taken up rowing on Sundays with my grandchildren. Last Sunday, in the middle of the lake I lost one oar. As I reached over to get the oar, it floated away. The boat rocked, and I caught my balls in the rowlock— that was the first time in six months I have forgotten the pain of my new teeth!"

Enough for today.

CHAPTER 9

The Very Alphabet of Love

The first question

I love you, and I have been in love before and been hurt. I am afraid. Will you help me?

Love never hurts anybody. It is something else pretending to be love which feels hurt. Unless you see this you will go on moving in the same circle again and again. Love can hide many unloving things in you. Man has been very clever, cunning, in deceiving others and in deceiving himself too. He puts beautiful labels on ugly things, he covers wounds with flowers. This is the first thing you have to go into.

Love ordinarily is not love, it is lust. And lust is bound to feel hurt, because to desire somebody as an object is to offend. It is an insult, it is violent. When you move with lust towards somebody, how long can you pretend it is love? Something which is superficial will look like love, but scratch a little bit and hidden behind it is sheer lust. Lust is animalistic. To look at anybody with lust is to insult, humiliate, is to reduce the other person to a thing, to a commodity. No person ever likes to be used; that's the most ugly thing you can do to anybody. No person is a commodity, no person is a means towards any end.

This is the difference between lust and love. Lust uses the other person to fulfill some of your desires. The other is only used, and when the use is complete you can throw the other person away. It has no more use to you; its function is fulfilled. This is the greatest immoral act in existence: using the other as a means.

Love is just the opposite of it: respecting the other as an end unto himself or herself. Had you loved anybody, Mimi, as an end unto himself, then there would have been no feeling of hurt; you would have become more enriched through it. Love makes everybody rich.

Secondly, love can only be true if there is no ego hiding behind it; otherwise love becomes only an ego trip. It is a subtle way to dominate. And one has to be very conscious because this desire to dominate is very deep rooted. It never comes naked; it always comes hidden behind beautiful garments, ornaments.

Parents never say that their children are their possessions, they never say that they want to dominate the children, but that's actually what they do. They say they want to help, they say they want them to be intelligent, to be healthy, to be blissful, but—and that "but" is a great but— it has to be according to their ideas. Even their happiness has to be decided by their ideas; they have to be happy according to their expectations. They have to be intelligent, but at the same time obedient too. This is asking for the impossible.

The intelligent person cannot be obedient; the obedient person has to lose some of his intelligence. Intelligence can say yes only when it feels deep agreement with you. It cannot say yes just because you are bigger, more powerful, authoritative—a father, a mother, a priest, a politician. It cannot say yes just because of the authority that you carry with you. Intelligence is rebellious, and no parents would like their children to be rebellious. Rebellion will be against their hidden desire to dominate.

Husbands say they love their wives, but it is just domination. They are so jealous, so possessive, how can they be loving? Wives go on saying they love their husbands, but twenty-four hours they are creating hell; in every possible way they are reducing the husband to something ugly.

The henpecked husband is an ugly phenomenon. And the problem is that first the wife reduces the husband to a henpecked husband and then she loses interest in him, because who can remain interested in a henpecked husband? He seems to be worthless; he does not seem to be man enough.

First the husband tries to make the wife just his possession, and once she is a possession he loses interest. There is some hidden logic in it: his whole interest was to possess; now that is finished, and he would like to try some other women so he can again go on another trip of possession.

Beware of these ego numbers. Then you will feel hurt, because the person you are trying to possess is bound to revolt in some way or other, is bound to sabotage your tricks, strategies, because nobody loves anything more than freedom. Even love is secondary to freedom; freedom is the highest value. Love can be sacrificed for freedom, but freedom cannot be sacrificed for love. And that's what we have been doing for centuries: sacrificing freedom for love. Then there is antagonism, conflict, and every opportunity is used to hurt each other.

Mimi, you say to me, "I love you, and I have been in love before and been hurt...." If you love me in the same way as you have loved before, you will be very hurt. In fact, all your past hurts will be nothing compared to this hurt; this will be the greatest wound in your life. Then you will never think of love again, because with me there can be no relationship of lust, no relationship of ego, no relationship of any subtle kind of domination. With me the only possibility is of the purest love, of a love that is almost a prayer. And then there is no question of your being hurt.

Love in its purest form is a sharing of joy. It asks nothing in return, it expects nothing; hence how can you feel hurt? When you don't expect, there is no possibility of being hurt. Then whatsoever comes is good; if nothing comes, that too is good. Your joy was to give, not to get. Then one can love from thousands of miles away; there is no need to be physically present even.

Love is a spiritual phenomenon; lust is physical.

Ego is psychological; love is spiritual.

Mimi, you don't know what love is. You will have to learn the very alphabet of love. You will have to start from the very beginning, from scratch; otherwise you will be hurt again and again. And remember, except you nobody else is responsible. Now even in this question you are trying to lay your trip on me! You are asking: "I am afraid. Will you help me?"

Only you can help yourself. How can I help you? I cannot destroy your ego. If you cling to it, nobody can destroy it; if you have invested in it, nobody can destroy it. I can only share my understanding with you. The buddhas can only show the way; then *you* have to go, then you have to follow the way. I cannot lead you holding your hand in my hand.

That's what you would like: you would like to play the game of being dependent on me. And remember, the person who plays the game of being dependent will take revenge. Soon he would like in some way for the other to be dependent on him or on her.

If the wife is dependent on the husband for money, then the wife makes the husband dependent on her for other things. It is a mutual arrangement. They both become crippled, they both become paralyzed; they cannot exist without each other. Even the idea that the husband was happy without the wife hurts the wife, that he was laughing with the boys in the club hurts her. She is not interested in his happiness; in fact she cannot believe: "How did he dare to be happy without me? He has to depend on me!"

The husband does not feel good that the wife was laughing with somebody, was enjoying, was cheerful. He wants all her cheerfulness to be totally possessed; it is *his* property. The dependent person will make you dependent also.

My sannyasins are not dependent on me; I am not dependent on them. This is a relationship of total freedom. They are here because of themselves; I am here because of myself. It is beautiful that somehow we have coincided to be here in this place— but nobody is dependent on anybody else.

There are a few sannyasins who think that they are dependent on me. And how do I know they think that? I have come to know from their questions and their letters. They write angry letters to me, angry questions to me. Then I know that in some way they must be feeling dependent on me— this is their revenge. Otherwise there is no need to be angry with me. I do not possess you— you can leave at any moment. Not even for a single moment will you be prevented from leaving. It is absolutely up to you to be here or not to be here, to be a sannyasin or not to be a sannyasin. I am not obliging you to be a sannyasin, I am not obliging you by initiating you into sannyas. It is my joy.

Remember, it is my joy to share my vision with you and it is your joy to commune with me. Otherwise there is no dependence at all.

Even in your question, Mimi, you are repeating your old pattern: "I am afraid..."

Fear is never love, and love is never afraid. There is nothing to lose for love. Why should love be afraid? Love only gives. It is not business, so there is no question of loss or profit. Love enjoys giving, just as flowers enjoy releasing their fragrance. Why should they be afraid? Why should you be afraid? Remember, fear and love never exist together; they cannot. No coexistence is possible. Fear is just the opposite of love.

People ordinarily think hate is the opposite of love. That is wrong, absolutely wrong. Fear is the exact opposite of love. Hate is love standing on its head; it is a *shirshasan*, a headstand, but it is not opposite to love. The person who hates simply shows he still loves. Love has gone sour, but love is still there. Fear is the real opposite. Fear means that now the whole love energy has disappeared.

Love is outgoing, fearlessly reaching to the other, tremendously trusting itself that it will be received— and it is always received. Fear is shrinking within yourself, closing yourself, closing all the doors, all the windows so no sun, no wind, no rain can reach you—you are so afraid. You are entering into your grave alive.

Fear is a grave, love is a temple.
In love life comes to its ultimate peak.
In fear life falls to the level of death.
Fear stinks, love is fragrant.

Why should you be afraid? Be afraid of your ego, be afraid of your lust, be afraid of your greed, be afraid of your possessiveness; be afraid of your jealousy—but there is no question of being afraid of love.

Love is divine!
Love is like light.
When there is light, darkness cannot exist.
When there is love, fear cannot exist.

Hence, I am against all words like "God-fearing," because the person who is God-fearing is not religious at all, although in all the languages of the world such words exist or such phrases exist; the religious person is known as God-fearing. That is the most stupid idea one can imagine. The religious person is God-*loving*, not God-fearing. The God-fearing person will be angry at God.

Friedrich Nietzsche is God-*fearing*, that's why in his outburst of anger he says, "God is dead." You have heard this statement, but it is only half of the statement. The full statement is worth consideration, because unless you know the full statement you will not understand the meaning of the first half. The full statement is: God is dead, and now man is free. The second part shows reality: he is so afraid of God that even his presence seems to be anti-freedom.

And not only Nietzsche is convinced of this fact, that God's presence means fear; there have been other thinkers who have simply denied God. The Charvakas in India, the Epicureans in Greece—they all denied God for the simple reason that if God exists, man cannot be free. If God has made you, he can destroy you at any moment. You are just a puppet, and what right has the puppet? The strings are in God's hands: you are dancing his dance, it is nothing to do with you. He pulls this way and that way, and you start dancing. You are just manipulated. This will create fear, and unless God is dead, man cannot be free of this fear. Nietzsche seems to be the really religious person according to the traditional idea of God-fearing.

God-loving is a totally different phenomenon. Jesus says, "God is love." If God is love, how can you be afraid of God?

Omar Khayyam, one of the Sufi mystics, says in his *Rubaiyat*: "Don't be worried about your small sins. They are so small that God, out of his love, cannot even count them. And God is compassionate, he will forgive you." Omar Khayyam says, "I guarantee that you will be forgiven, don't be worried. What you are doing are just small things, and God cannot take note of these small things. He cannot be so nasty, so small minded, so pigheaded!"

Omar Khayyam is right. God means love, God means forgiveness; there is no question of fear. But people are afraid of God also for the simple reason that their God is again a projection of ambition.

The day Jesus was going to be crucified, he gave a farewell party for his disciples—The Last Supper. He was going to die the next day, and do you know what the disciples were asking? They were asking, "Lord, tell us one thing, because now this is the last time we will be able to ask you. You will be raised to divine glory, you will sit by the side of God on the golden throne, on the right hand of course. What will our positions be?"

These twelve apostles, these twelve who had been so long with Jesus, remained utterly deaf, blind; they did not understood a single word. They may have heard him, but they had not listened. They were asking, "What will our positions be? Who will be next to you?" Jealousy, politics,

The Very Alphabet of Love

ambition, ego! Now they were worried about who was going to be next to him—who would be chosen as the most beloved disciple of Jesus.

It is the same politics! It does not matter that it will be in paradise; the mind is the same. Then there will be the fear—who is Jesus going to choose? All twelve cannot sit next to him; one person will be next to him. Who is this person?

Jesus must have wept—the question was so stupid! And these are the apostles who created Christianity. These are the people who are the pillars of Christianity.

And this is so in every religion, everywhere; small people gather around the enlightened masters. The enlightened master talks about his peak, the sunlit peak, and the disciples listen from their dark holes, and everything becomes distorted.

Mimi, you ask me, "I am afraid. Will you help me?" That is a strategy. I never help anybody—you have to help yourself. I am available like a river is available, but if you are thirsty you have to help yourself. You have to come down to the river, you have to make a cup out of your hands, you have to take the water up to your mouth, you have to drink it.

The river is available—I am available.

You can drink out of me as much as you want—there will be no condition from my side—but I cannot help you. In that very desire you are creating your old gestalt, your old pattern: "Will you help me?" And then immediately you will start complaining that help has not arrived, or it is not according to your needs, your expectations, or it is not enough, as much as is needed. You will start complaining, you will become grumpy. That's how you must have destroyed all your love experiences before. Please don't destroy it again.

Here, be loving. I am available. Drink as much as you can, take as much as you can. Remove all the hindrances—and that is all your responsibility. I am doing my work; about my own work I am absolutely open and available, but that's all I can do. I am like a light: I can show you the path, but you have to walk.

My feeling is, Mimi, that you have not yet taken any mature step in your life; you have remained immature, *un*grown up, you are still behaving like a child. You would like a father figure – I am not. Then you can go to the Polack pope! The word "pope" means father; in

Italian it sounds even better, *papa*. It is exactly the same as "papa" in English; it means father. These are all childish desires: calling God, "the Father"; then calling his representative in the Vatican, "Father"; then calling his representative in your local church, "Father." These are just substitutes. You want some father figure to take care of you; **you don't** want to take responsibility.

This is my first requirement: the people who are around me have to be absolutely responsible for themselves. Nobody else is responsible. There is no church here, no father figure here, no creed, no dogma. Everybody is here out of his own **personal love**, out of his own individual understanding.

To be totally responsible is the beginning of freedom, and freedom is the highest phenomenon. Out of the peaks of freedom flows the Ganges of love. Attain to freedom, and love will surround you naturally, spontaneously. And then love has never hurt anybody—how can it hurt you?

Something else is masquerading—uncover it. At least be naked in front of yourself, and then by and by be naked, totally naked, to your friends, to your lovers. And you will be surprised: to be true is such a joy, to be authentic is such a blessing; there is nothing compared to it.

Love can make a great celebration out of your life – but only love, not lust, not ego, not possessiveness, not jealousy, not dependence.

The second question

I am convinced that the rich exploit the masses. Now you are telling me that capitalism is the best system for freedom. I have never supported Russian totalitarianism, but I thought that Mao Zedong improved life for the majority in China. Your statement about anti-capitalists being jealous rings true, but don't some rich capitalists use their power to exploit others through such means as monopolies, selling at a loss for short periods of time in order to ruin smaller businessmen, acquiring more land than they need, and thus denying poor people the ability to own and use land, et cetera? Although the Soviet-bloc countries restrict freedom, are not the socialist and communist parties in the West dedicated to more personal freedom—that is, freedom from the powerful, manipulative, rich capitalist?

It is true that the rich exploit the masses, but the powerful in Russia exploit the masses in the same way, and the powerful in China also exploit the masses. Only the name has changed. Now the capitalist is not called a capitalist in Russia or China; now the Communist Party functions instead. The people who belong to the Communist Party, the power elite, they exploit.

So the question is not who exploits, the question is: unless we produce so much that the need for exploitation disappears, exploitation will continue. Names will change; structures will be different.

Before capitalism arrived on the scene there was feudalism, and then the kings and the queens and their prime ministers were exploiting. Capitalism started a different pattern of exploitation. Feudalism disappeared, but the exploitation continued. Communism has changed the structure again, but the exploitation continues.

It is time to understand that two things are needed, and the most important is that the earth should be provided with more richness than it needs. Only then will exploitation disappear; otherwise not. The educated will exploit the uneducated; how can you prevent it? In India the exploitation is there. The educated will exploit the uneducated; the brahmin will exploit the sudra, the untouchable; the politician will destroy and exploit the non-political masses.

If water is available nobody accumulates water, but if water is scarce then people will start accumulating. And of course those who are powerful—and there will be some who will always be more powerful than others—they will accumulate water for the times when water will become so scarce that people will be dying without water.

Right now, in poor countries the air is not polluted – nobody bothers about it. But sooner or later in cities like New York, Los Angeles, the rich people will start finding ways to have more oxygen for themselves. The poor will suffer from the pollution, not the rich. And by "rich" I don't mean only the rich who have more wealth, I mean the rich in any way—the educated who have more education, the politician who has more power. In any way, whosoever is powerful will have the first right.

In the feudal days the king would have the first right about everything. If a beautiful girl was born she would first go to the king's palace; if he rejected her, then somebody else could have her. The first fruits would go to the king, the first flowers would go to the king.

Everything is bound to go to the hands of the powerful. For example, if the earth becomes too polluted then the rich and the powerful will be the first who will start moving to the moon or to Mars. Of course everybody cannot go there; it will be too costly to live there. Only the few will be able to afford it, and they will dominate the earth from there.

The question is two-sided. One is the extrovert side, that the earth has to be provided with more facilities than are available. And it can be done by science today; there is no problem about it. Science can produce as much wealth as we need or even more, so that is not a big problem. It is not really a political problem; it is changing more towards being a scientific problem: more technology, more industry, more science, and in tune with ecology. Then the earth need not in any way suffer through exploitation.

This is the outside of the problem, and the inside of the problem is to change the greed to have more than others, because even if the earth has enough there will be mad people—the braggarts, the egoists—who would like to say that they have more than you have.

Krishna is said to have had sixteen thousand wives. That was the time when a person's wealth and power was measured by wives, how many wives he had. The more wives you could afford, the richer you were. And obviously, how could a poor man afford sixteen thousand wives? Even to afford one is very difficult!

And I don't think that this is just a story; it must have been true—because even in the beginning of this century, the twentieth century, the Nizam of Hyderabad had five hundred wives. So if in the twentieth century a person can have five hundred wives, what is wrong in having thirty-two times more? And that was five thousand years ago, so it doesn't seem to be improbable or impossible. It was traditional in the Nizam's family to have at least five hundred wives so that you could say that you were not an ordinary man.

So from the inside, the greed has to disappear. On the outside, more science is needed. On the inside, more meditativeness is needed— or you can call it science *and* religion, it is the same. Science will help to produce more, and religion will help to make you less greedy. This is the solution that is going to help, not communism, not socialism.

And to me, capitalism is the only state where we can experiment with all these things; in a communist society it is impossible. There are nearabout fifty sannyasins in Russia, but they cannot wear orange, they cannot wear the mala—they cannot show that they are sannyasins. They meditate but they have to meditate underground in some friend's basement; they cannot make it public. They cannot publish a book of mine—and they want to publish books there. They have translated at least five books into Russian—handwritten, typed, cyclostyled. They are mixing with thousands of people, but underground. If even a single copy is seized they will be in trouble.

Now, in such a society, how can you think of tackling the problems to change them? There is no freedom to think at all. And the same is true about Mao Zedong's China. Just as Russians insulted Joseph Stalin after his death...when he was alive they could not say anything because he was too powerful. To say anything against him only meant one thing: death. You would disappear the next day and you would never be heard of again.

Now the same is happening to Mao Zedong. Now his portraits are being removed, his statues are being removed, his name is being brought down. Soon you will see that Mao Zedong has become an ugly name in China, just as Stalin has become an ugly name in Russia. In China Mao Zedong's name is going to become just the same. Why? Why this revenge? If Mao Zedong has done such great work and helped the masses, why should the masses behave with such enmity? It was not really a help, it was just an imposition. Forcing people violently to do something is not going to help. Any society that creates slavery is not going to help humanity.

And you say to me: "Your statement about anti-capitalists being jealous rings true, but don't some rich capitalists use their power to exploit others through such means as monopolies...?" Yes, they do, but somebody else will be doing the same—the communists will do it.

And you ask, "Are not the socialist and communist parties in the West dedicated to more personal freedom...?" Until they achieve power, everybody is dedicated to more freedom. The Russian Communist Party was also dedicated to absolute freedom, and what came to exist was absolute slavery. The Russian Communist Party was dedicated to absolute freedom, but the moment you get the power you are the same type of people. Your communists and your socialists are not meditators, they are not buddhas.

Only a buddha will not change; whether he gets the power or not he will remain the same. But your so-called socialists and communists, once they get the power will behave in the same way; it is absolutely predictable. When you don't have power then it is different.

It happened in India...

The followers of Mahatma Gandhi were great servants of the people. They lived in poverty, praised poverty, and even started calling the poor, *dharidra narayan*—the real people of God, God's people. And when they came to power, all that changed. Immediately all that changed; all their service disappeared. They became masters and rulers, and they started exploiting more than anybody else. Even the Britishers have not exploited this country so much as the Gandhians have done. This country has never been in such a dark space as it is today. The whole responsibility goes to Gandhian followers, and they were all good people when they were not in power.

Power corrupts, and absolute power corrupts absolutely.

The people who are communists and socialists—who are they? They are by-products of the same society, with the same ambitions, with the same desires.

Once Diogenes saw a man being led to the gallows by the magistrates and officers of justice. The criminal had stolen a silver cup from the public treasury. A bystander asked him what was going on.

"Nothing unusual," the philosopher replied. "It is merely the big thieves bringing the little thief to justice."

Whosoever is in power becomes the big thief and starts torturing the small thieves.

We have to change the outer world by more science, and the inner world by more religion. Then only can there be a real revolution, not otherwise.

Enough for today.

CHAPTER 10

Everybody Can Laugh

The first question

You say fear is the opposite of love. Have you any practical or impractical suggestions how one can drop fear?

Love is existential; fear is only the absence of love. And the problem with any absence is that you cannot do anything directly about it.

Fear is like darkness. What can you do about darkness directly? You cannot drop it, you cannot throw it out, you cannot bring it in. There is no way to relate with darkness without bringing light in. The way to darkness goes via light. If you want darkness, put the light off; if you don't want darkness, put the light on. But you will have to do something with light, not with darkness at all.

The same is true about love and fear: love is light, fear is darkness. The person who becomes obsessed with fear will never be able to resolve the problem. It is like wrestling with darkness—you are bound to be exhausted sooner or later, tired and defeated. And the miracle is, defeated by something which is not there at all! And when one is defeated, one certainly feels how powerful the darkness is, how powerful the fear is, how powerful the ignorance is, how powerful the unconscious is. They are not powerful at all—they don't exist in the first place.

Never fight with the nonexistential. That's where all the ancient religions got lost. Once you start fighting with the nonexistential you are doomed. Your small river of consciousness will be lost in the nonexistential desert—and it is infinite.

Hence, the first thing to remember is: don't make a problem out of fear. Love is the question. Something can be done about love immediately; there is no need to wait or postpone. Start loving! And it is a natural gift from God to you, or from the whole, whichever term you like. If you are brought up in a religious way, then God; if you are not brought up in a religious way, then the whole, the universe, the existence.

Remember, love is born with you; it is your intrinsic quality. All that is needed is to give it a way—to make a passage for it, to let it flow, to allow it to happen. We are all blocking it, holding it back. We are so miserly about love, for the simple reason that we have been taught a certain economics. That economics is perfectly right about the outside world: if you have so much money and you go on giving that money to people, soon you will be a beggar, soon you will have to beg yourself. By giving money you will lose it. This economics, this arithmetic has entered into our blood, bones and marrow. It is true about the outside world—nothing is wrong in it—but it is not true about the inner journey. There, a totally different arithmetic functions: the more you give, the more you have; the less you give, the less you have. If you don't give at all you will lose your natural qualities. They will become stagnant, closed; they will go underground. Finding no expression they will shrink and die.

It is like a musician: if he goes on playing on his guitar or on his flute, more and more music will come. It is not that by playing on the flute he is losing music—he is gaining. It is like a dancer: the more you dance, the more efficient you become. It is like painting—the more you paint, the better the painting.

Once, while Picasso was painting, a critic and friend stopped him in the middle and said, "One question has been bothering me and I cannot wait anymore, I cannot contain it. I want to know: you have painted hundreds of paintings; which is your best painting?"

Picasso said, "This one that I am painting right now."

The critic said, "This one? And what about the others that you have painted before?"

Picasso said, "They are all contained in it. And the next one that I do will be even better than this—because the more you paint the greater is your skill, the greater is your art."

Such is love, such is joy! Share it. In the beginning it will come only like dewdrops, because the miserliness has been very long, very ancient. But once even dewdrops of love have been shared, you will soon become capable of sharing the whole oceanic flood of your being—and you contain infinities. Once you have known the higher mathematics of giving and gaining, you will find that just by giving you gain. Not that something is returned; in the very giving you are becoming richer. Then love starts spreading, radiating. And one day you will be surprised: where is the fear? Even if you want to find it you will not be able to find it at all.

So it is not a question of dropping the fear; nobody has ever been able to drop it. It is only a question of sharing your love, and the fear is dropped on its own accord.

You ask me: "Have you any practical or impractical suggestions...?" Practical suggestions, no—that is not my business at all. Impractical suggestions, yes—and many!

The second question

> There are so many religions in the world which cause so many divisions amongst people, although all religions have good things in them. Why can't there be a religion which has the good things of all religions, which is accepted universally and which breaks down all divisions, thus causing a world fraternity? Kindly show the way.

The first thing to be understood is: there are many types of people in the world, and they can't belong to one religion. It is inevitable that there will be many religions. To impose one religion on the whole of humanity will be ugly, it will destroy the immense richness that variety brings. Just think of a world where only *The Bible* exists— no *Vedas*, no *Upanishads*, no *Koran*, no *Dhammapada*, no *Bhagavadgita*, no *Tao Te Ching*. It will be a very poor world. The world certainly needs a brotherhood, a fraternity, a great love, a universality, but that cannot come by imposing a certain religion. Any religion that you choose will be applicable only to a few people, and the majority will feel imprisoned.

For example, just look around... Mahavira has a certain appeal, but only to a few people. I myself would not like the life that he lived. Still I say he lived beautifully, as far as he is concerned. He lived beautifully, authentically, but he is not the person that I would like to follow. He lived naked, fasting for days at a time. To me that seems to be a kind of self-torture.

Animals live naked—they can, because they have a totally different kind of skin, a thicker skin. And moreover, whenever winter comes their bodies start growing thicker hair. Man is no longer an animal, he has lost that hairy growth on his body. To leave him in the cold, standing naked, is an unnecessary masochistic attitude. It may suit a few people, because people are different in many ways. It must have suited Mahavira—nobody was imposing the idea on him to live naked. He may have had a certain different kind of body structure, different hormones, hotter blood, a thicker skin.

I am not saying that he should not have lived naked, and I am not saying that there is nothing beautiful in it. If somebody enjoys it, if somebody feels beautiful in it, it is good, but it cannot be made into any universal religion. The whole of humanity shivering in the cold, in great fraternity, chattering their teeth, will not be a very good scene. I cannot support it.

Buddha ate only one time every day. It may suit a few people's bodies; in fact, it cannot suit the majority—because man has come from the monkeys, that's what scientific research proves. And you can watch the monkeys on the trees: they are all Americans, munching the whole day! To force a monkey to stick to one meal a day will destroy his life. In fact, only lions eat one time a day, because their diet is nonvegetarian. Only nonvegetarians can live on one meal a day. The vegetarian cannot survive, or even if he survives, the survival will be only at the minimum level of his energies. The vegetarian has to eat many times, at least two times and at the most five times. One meal a day is not good for vegetarians, and if you are pure vegetarians, just living on vegetables and fruits, then you will have to eat many more times because larger quantities have to be taken and absorbed. Meat is digested food; the animal has already done the work, but eating vegetables you have to do the whole work of digesting.

Now, it is very strange that Mahavira and Buddha are both in favor of vegetarianism, and still they insist on one meal a day. I think the reason is that they both came from nonvegetarian families, they both belonged to the race of the warriors. They must have become accustomed to eating meat, and so it was easy for them. But if people who have lived for centuries on vegetables try to live on one meal a day, they will be living in a state of undernourishment, malnutrition. And it not only disturbs your body, it disturbs your mental faculties too. You can see it happening all over the world: only very rarely does a vegetarian win a Nobel Prize—it affects your intelligence. You become a vegetable! If you are uneducated, you are a cabbage, or at the most a cauliflower. A cauliflower is a cabbage with a college education!

People are different, their systems are different. For example, women and men cannot belong to the same system. The women can accumulate more fat, men cannot; that is a biological difference. The woman needs it because when she becomes pregnant and a child is growing in her womb she cannot eat well. She starts vomiting, eating becomes difficult, she feels sick and nauseous. For those emergencies the body accumulates layers of fat. Man has no need to be fat because he is not going to become pregnant; hence man's physiology is different. That's why women can fast very easily.

This is my observation: the Jaina nuns are far more true to their religion than the Jaina monks. The Jaina nuns can fast very easily; they accumulate fat. And what is fasting in fact? When you fast you are eating your own meat; that's why when you fast one kilo of weight disappears everyday. Where does it go? You have eaten it! Fasting, in fact, is a nonvegetarian activity—I don't believe in it! It is eating yourself! The woman can fast more easily; the man cannot— he does not accumulate so much fat.

Then in different climates, in different geographies, different kinds of things are bound to happen. You cannot have one religion around the earth. Yes, you can have one kind of religiousness, but not one religion.

You can see gathered around me here all kinds of people from all countries, all races—but we are not a new religion. I am not trying to create one religion; we are just creating a quality: religiousness, meditativeness, prayerfulness, trust, gratitude towards existence. Yes, on these things humanity can become a great brotherhood, but about details many things are bound to remain different—and they should remain different. There is no reason to destroy this variety. It will be like when you love roses, so you start growing only roses.

One of my friends is a lover of roses. He has a very big garden. Because he loves roses, in his garden there are only roses—no other flowers, no other plants. When I went to see his garden I told him, "This is not a garden, this looks like a field. Just as somebody grows wheat, you grow roses. But this is not a garden!"

He was a little bit shocked, but his manager understood it immediately. He said, "You are right; that's my feeling too. For years we have forgotten about the garden. We are selling roses; we are treating roses as a crop."

When you have only roses, the variety, the multidimensionality is lost. The world will be really very poor if you have only Mahaviras or only Christs, or only Buddhas or only Krishnas. Jesus is beautiful with his cross, but so many Jesuses all trying to hang themselves on their crosses won't make a beautiful scene. It will be like a nightmare! Krishna is beautiful playing on his flute, but how many Krishnas can you allow...? If the whole world is playing the flute you will go mad!

I accept multidimensionality in every field of life.

You say: "There are so many religions in the world which cause so many divisions amongst people..." The divisions are not needed; that is human stupidity. If you love the rose, good; there is no question of fighting with you. I love the lotus and you love the rose, but we both are lovers of flowers. That's the meeting point, that we both love flowers. You love Christ, that is one flower; I love Buddha, that is another flower; somebody else loves Lao Tzu, that is another flower. We are all friends because we love flowers. And I can appreciate your rose, you can appreciate my lotus. There is no need to create any divisions.

The divisions come from man's political mind; it has nothing to do with religions. It is man's politics that brings divisions, conflicts, quarrels, wars, bloodshed. The whole history of humanity is full of calamities created in the name of religion, but not created by religious people.

A Buddha, a Zarathustra, a Chuang Tzu—these are not the people who create trouble. It is the priests and the politicians. They are a totally different kind of person, a different species, but they hide behind masks. They hide behind religious doctrines, churches, and they start playing their games in a very subtle way. The manyness of religions is not bad, but divisions in the name of religion are ugly. That simply shows man is not religious yet.

You say that "Although all religions have good things in them..."

True, but they also have many bad things in them. Each religion has some good things and some bad things, and the problem is, those good things and those bad things are not separable; you cannot separate them. You *cannot* separate them. You cannot choose just the good and leave the bad; that's impossible. If you choose the good, the bad comes in through the backdoor.

....For example, if you choose the idea of fate.... Many religions believe in the idea of fate. It has something good in it because it helps you to relax, it helps you to trust existence, it helps you to be unworried. But then there is something bad in it too: it makes you lazy, lousy. It makes you Indian! It makes you slaves, it makes you accept any humiliation.

For twenty-two centuries India has been in slavery for the simple reason that it believes in fate. Now, how can you separate these two things? If everything happens according to God, it will give you a few good things. You will be able to tolerate, to accept many miseries, sufferings, with equanimity, with a certain tranquillity, calmness, quietness. That will give you strength, integrity, a grace, but then you will also become a slave. Anybody can dominate you, anybody can exploit you. And the same is true about every other idea.

For example, Jainas believe that life is dominated by the theory of karma, and not only Jainas but Hindus and Buddhists too. All the three great religions of India believe in the theory of karma—that whatsoever you are now, you are the by-product of your past karmas. You have something to fulfill. You have to suffer if you have done anything bad and you will be rewarded if you have done anything good.

Now there is the Jaina sect of Acharya Tulsi, Terapanth. It says that because of the theory of karma, one should not interfere in anybody's life. For example, somebody is dying of thirst in a desert, and a Jaina monk from the sect of Acharya Tulsi comes by. If the man begs for water, the follower of Acharya Tulsi has to remain utterly cool, indifferent, because the man is suffering his karma. You should not interfere; interference is bad. If you give him water, then he will have to suffer someday again. You cannot escape from the inevitability of your karma, so why postpone? Let him be finished with it! You go on your way. Let him die, let him suffer. This is a logical consequence of the idea. Moreover, they say, if you save him, if you give him water and he is saved and tomorrow he commits a murder, then you will also be responsible for that murder; without you the murder would not have happened at all. Then *you* will suffer in your next life for a murder that you have not done, but in a way you have been part of it. So it is better not to interfere for his sake and for your own sake. It is a beautiful theory but it has also a dark side to it. You have heard the saying that every dark cloud has a silver lining. I would like to remind you that every silver lining also has a dark cloud to it.

Yes, the religions have good things in them, that is true, but those good things also have bad sides. And a truly religious person will not bother about choosing; he will start living according to his consciousness. He will not follow Jesus, Buddha or Mahavira or Mohammed. To follow is to be political. Only the blind follow, the superstitious people follow, gullible people follow. The people who are intelligent try to understand Buddha, Mahavira, Krishna, but it is just an effort to understand the message, what these people were doing, what they were living. Finally, you have to discover your own inner light.

That's what I call meditation: the moment you have discovered your own inner insight, you follow it. Then you are religious – neither Hindu nor Mohammedan nor Christian. A religious quality, a fragrance will surround you. You will be more loving, more compassionate. And these will be the qualities: you will be more authentic, more sincere, and you will be able to understand different points, different angles and the different paths leading to the same goal.

Truth is like the sunlit top of Everest: thousands of paths can reach there; there is no need to make one asphalt road. Let people follow their own paths, let them discover. The joy of discovery is far greater than the joy of arrival. Let them discover their path, let them inquire, and let them follow their own insight. Of course they will fall many times, they will go astray; that is part of freedom. That is beautiful; nothing is wrong in it.

You say: "Why can't there be a religion which has the good things of all religions...?"

That is impossible; that will be just a hotchpotch. It will be the same as if you are suffering from an illness and you go to the druggist and tell him, "Make a medicine out of all the good medicines that you have got. All that is good in every medicine, put it into one combination." That combination will kill you! Certainly it will destroy your illness, because it will destroy you too. Your illness needs a certain medicine only; you don't need all the medicines and all that is good in all the medicines.

You ask why one religion cannot be accepted universally. People have so many different minds, different attitudes, different visions, different lifestyles—why should they live in one uniform way? They should be allowed freedom. Freedom is one of the greatest religious qualities. And if they are allowed freedom, then they are free to choose.

If somebody loves the Koran I don't think he will be able to love the *Tao Te Ching*; they are totally different visions. You can recite the *Koran*; there is no need even to understand the meaning of it. The very reciting is tremendously beautiful, ecstatic. The *Koran is* really meant to be recited, not understood; there is not much to understand in it.

Many Mohammedan friends, many of my Mohammedan sannyasins go on writing to me, "When are you going to speak on the *Koran?*" I cannot really speak on it—I have thought about it many times— because there is not much to say about the *Koran*. It is a song, it is a shout of joy. What can you say about it? You can dance and sing, you can recite, but nothing can be said about it.

But one can go on commenting for years on the *Tao Te Ching*; it is inexhaustible. But you cannot sing it; there is no song in it. For those people who have a musical ear, the *Koran* will be the right thing. For those people who have a philosophical bent, the *Tao Te Ching* will be of immense value. But to reduce the whole of humanity to one type is not a good idea.

Man can become a family without destroying the variety. There is no need to destroy the different angles of seeing; they all enhance existence. The birds sing differently, the flowers bloom differently, the trees have different colors, shades, different leaves. Every river has its own song, every mountain has its own poetry, and so is the case with every individual.

To me, each individual is far more valuable than society as a whole. Let me say it in this way: the individual is the goal, not the universal. The universal is only an abstract idea. Have you ever seen the universal? Have you ever met the universal? Have you ever said to the universal, "Hello! How are you?" You will always meet the individual. The individual is the real; the universal is only an abstraction, an idea.

Don't be too interested in ideas; they don't exist. Remain more concrete, more realistic. Each individual has uniqueness, and I respect that uniqueness, and it is his freedom, whatsoever he chooses. And it is nobody else's business to give you a religion. It is not even your parents' business, or the priests', or the society's, or the state's. It is nobody's business to give you your religion. Everybody should be allowed to find his own religion. That will be the real state of fraternity. We have to respect the other with all his uniqueness. And we have to say to the other, "If it is good for you, you follow it; it is not good for me so I am going on another route. And if by chance we meet somewhere, it will be beautiful. I will share my journey with you, and you will share your journey with me, and we both will be enriched in that way."

The third question

I love it when you call a spade a spade – or the pope a Polack. I realize the religion of my childhood haunts me still, when I feel relief in laughing at the pope and all he represents. Then soon my laughter changes to anger at how organized religion has exploited my friends, my family and myself. What to do with this feeling of outrage?

It is natural. Humanity has been dominated by the priests and the politicians for so long that the people who are able to understand are bound to feel enraged, angry. They would like to destroy this whole stupidity that has prevailed all through human history. But just by being enraged, you are not going to help. The past is no more; nothing can be done about it. The future is not yet; nothing can be done about it either. All that we have got is the present, this moment. This very moment is all that is there!

And my feeling is that when you laugh, your laughter is not total. Something remains locked up within you, something remains unexpressed, repressed. You are not going totally into the laughter; you are holding back something unknowingly, unconsciously. But now become conscious. You must be holding something; that which you are holding becomes anger. If you totally allow the laughter, the anger will disappear.

It is the same as I was saying a few moments ago: when there is love, fear disappears; when there is laughter, anger disappears. Anger is because you are not allowing the laughter totally. It may be just because of your conditionings. We have so much conditioning that whatsoever we do is only half-hearted, fragmentary, and the remaining part remains imprisoned and wants to come out. That creates anger.

It is not a question of your feeling angry against organized religions. They have been there, but now you are out of it. Why remain so related? Now you are a sannyasin, you are finished with your childhood religion that has been given to you. Now you have found your own kind of religiousness. You have found that which fits with you, that which is natural to you.

Allow your laughter to be total.

A total laughter is a rare phenomenon. When each cell of your body laughs, when each fiber of your being pulsates with joy, then it brings a great relaxation. There are a few activities which are immensely valuable; laughter is one of those activities. Singing and dancing, are also of the same quality, but laughter is the quickest. Dancing you will have to learn; it may take years. Singing is a talent; it may not be possible for you. Everybody can sing, but to sing a beautiful song, talent is needed. You can sing and drive your neighbors crazy!

Once, in the middle of the night, a neighbor knocked on Mulla Nasruddin's door. Mulla staggered out of his bed, opened the door and asked, "What is the matter?"

The man said, "Stop singing, otherwise I will go mad!"

Mulla said, "What are you talking about? I stopped one hour ago!"

That man had already gone mad. He could still hear that Mulla singing.

Everybody can sing in that way. That's why people sing and hum in their bathrooms—except me! I have never managed to hum or sing in the bathroom. I have tried, but utterly failed, for the simple reason that I am not repressing anything. If I want to sing I will sing anywhere, I will not care whether it is the bathroom or not. If I want to sing I will sing in the marketplace; whatsoever happens to others, that is their problem!

Dancing, singing, laughing—of these three, laughter is the most simple, the most natural and the most spontaneous phenomenon. You don't want to learn, you don't need to learn—it is a natural gift. Everybody can laugh.

And what happens when you laugh totally? What happens when you dance totally? The dancer disappears in a total dance. That's my definition of the total dance: the dancer disappears, dissolves; only the dancing remains. When there is only dancing and no dancer, this is the ultimate of meditation—the taste of nectar, bliss, God, truth, ecstasy, freedom, freedom from the ego, freedom from the doer.

And when there is no ego, no doer, and the dance is going on and there is no dancer, a great witnessing arises, a great awareness like a cloud of light surrounding you. You are watching it, you can see it happen. You are not the doer; it is happening on its own. God has taken possession of you. That's exactly the meaning of possession: when the ego is no longer there, God immediately enters and takes possession of you. You become a vehicle, a passage, a medium, a hollow bamboo, and on the lips of the whole the hollow bamboo becomes a flute.

In laughter it happens more easily because it needs no talent, no learning, no discipline—unless you are a born donkey, and that's another matter. Laughter is simple—but let it be total. It has been crippled. Society has stopped you from going totally into it. If you go into a total laughter people think it is hysterical. It is not, it is historical!

A few jokes for you—and let it be a total laughter!

A businessman was about to enter a hotel bar after a heavy day at the office when he was stopped by a nun who delivered him a lecture on the evils of alcohol, assuring him that drink was the most certain path to hell.

"Sister," he interrupted at last, "I am a most temperate man and only have one drink every few days to relax me. One drink never hurt anyone. Even Jesus had the odd glass of wine! Besides, how can you condemn something you have never experienced? You should try just one drink yourself, just so you know what you are talking about!"

The nun protested indignantly at this suggestion, but in the ensuing discussion found it more and more difficult to rebuke the logic of the executive. "Okay," she said in the end, "you have convinced me. I will try a small drink of whiskey— may God forgive me! But you better bring it out to me in a teacup in case anyone sees me."

The businessman agreed happily and entered the hotel. "A pint of beer, please," he called to the barman, "and one Scotch, in a teacup, if you don't mind."

The barman looked up with a frown. "Don't tell me that bloody nun is still out there!"

A man visiting a whorehouse was astonished at the quality of the girl he was assigned. He said, "You look so beautiful and have such fine manners. You actually look like you come from a very fine, wealthy family."

"Actually, I do!" she said, "My family is Catholic and they are aristocrats."

He then noted how intelligent she was and she told him she had graduated cum laude from Vassar. He noted then that she must have traveled worldwide because of her cultured ways. And she said that indeed she had traveled the world many times.

Thereupon he said, "Well how in the world did you ever come to work in a place like this?"

She replied, "Just lucky, I guess!"

There was once a young man whose mind was filled with many burning questions about life. He learned of a wise old Catholic sage who lived on a high mountain, and decided to undertake the arduous journey.

After many months of caravans, hiking and climbing, he came upon the hermit sitting outside a small cave as still and peaceful as any statue.

The seeker knelt in front of him, bowed his head respectfully, and humbly asked, "Why am I here?"

"Why indeed!" grumbled the old man. "I told them to send up a girl!"

Enough for today.

CHAPTER 11

The Suchness of Things

The first question

> Lao Tzu is said to have said:
> "Knowing the not-knowing—
> that is high.
> Not knowing the knowing—
> that is an illness.
> The one who suffers from this illness is not ill.
> The wise is not ill
> because he suffers from this illness—
> that's why he is not ill."

Lao Tzu is one of those few masters who have tried to say the truth as accurately as it is humanly possible. He has made tremendous effort to bring the inexpressible to the world of expression, to bring the wordless experience within the confinement of small words.

The words we know are mundane; they are meant for ordinary day-to-day use. And the experience that happens in absolute silence is absolutely beyond them. But still it has to be expressed— if not expressed, at least hinted at.

Lao Tzu's words are fingers pointing to the moon. Don't cling to the fingers. Forget the fingers and look at the moon, and great insight will descend upon you.

There is no other scripture like the *Tao Te Ching* for the simple reason that each single word in it is immensely pregnant, not only with the unknown but also with the unknowable. Words have been used only as indicators, milestones showing the way, telling you to go ahead, not to stop there.

These words are very significant, but at the first reading they will look very puzzling, confusing, paradoxical, contradictory—unless you have tasted something of meditation. That taste makes everything clear.

Meditation is like eyes. When you talk about light to a man who has eyes, he immediately understands what you mean. When you talk to the blind man about light, he *hears* the word but listens to nothing, understands nothing. His ears are perfect; the word reaches him but empty, with no content. The content has always to be put by your experience.

These words are not ordinary words. Unless you come to them with great meditation it is impossible to figure out what is what. If you come with meditation, then things cannot be more simple than Lao Tzu's words are. He says, "Knowing the not-knowing—that is high."

The highest point is that nothing can be known, that everything is unknowable—and not only unknown, but unknowable. A distinction has to be made between the unknown and the unknowable; these two words have to be pondered over. The first is the known. That which is known today was unknown yesterday. That which is unknown today may become known tomorrow or the day after tomorrow. Hence the difference between the known and the unknown. It is not a difference that makes any difference; it is only a question of time. There is no qualitative difference between the two.

But the unknowable is qualitatively different. The unknowable is that which has never been known and will never be known; unknowability is its intrinsic nature.

This is the most profound truth, that life in its totality, in its organic wholeness is absolutely a mystery. It is not a problem that can be solved, it is not a question that can be answered. No amount of knowledge is going to demystify it. It will remain mysterious. Mysteriousness is not something accidental to it. You cannot take it away from it; it is its very soul. And whatsoever we know is just superficial, very superficial. Whatsoever we know is only befooling ourselves.

D.H.Lawrence, one of the mystic poets of this age, and a man I love and respect very much, was walking in a garden with a small child. The child asked him—and only a child can ask such a tremendously significant question... The knowledgeable people always ask foolish questions because they ask out of their knowledge. In fact, they have already got

The Suchness of Things

the answer and they are asking just to see whether you have also got the answer or not. They are searching for an argument to prove their knowledge. Their question is not authentic, is not true. Any question arising out of your knowledge is pseudo.

But when small children ask something they mean it; it is not out of knowledge, it is out of innocence, out of a state of not knowing. Whenever there is a question out of not knowing it has immense beauty, splendor.

The child asked D.H. Lawrence, "Can you tell me one thing: why are the trees green? Why not red? Why not blue? Why not black? Why not this, why not that? Why are they green and always green?"

A man of knowledge would have answered very easily. He would have told the child the chemistry of the trees, the biology of the trees. He may have told the child about chlorophyll: "Why are the trees green?— it is because of the presence of chlorophyll."

But D.H. Lawrence remained silent; he closed his eyes.

The child was puzzled – such a great man, world famous, author of many books, who could not answer such a small question? The child nudged him and said, "Why have you closed your eyes? Either you know or you don't know! What are you doing with closed eyes? If you know, say it; if you don't know, say so."

D.H. Lawrence said, "The trees are green because they are green."

And the child said, "That's right!" He was absolutely satisfied, contented. He said, "That's right—trees are green because they are green!"

But only a child can ask such a question, and only a child can receive such an answer. What Lawrence is saying is exactly what Lao Tzu is saying. To say that trees are green because they are green, is to accept the ultimate mystery, that nothing can be said. It is so.

That was Buddha's way of answering. His word was *tathata*. Tathata can be translated approximately as suchness. He was asked a thousand and one times, "Why is there death?"

And he would say, "Tathata—such is the nature of things." It is not an answer, remember. What kind of answer is this? "Such is the nature of things—that the water flows downwards and the fire rises upwards." Such is the nature of things...?

In fact, the word *dhamma*, used by Buddha, which is ordinarily translated as religion, exactly means suchness, the suchness of things, the dhamma of things. "Aes dhammo sanantano" —such is the ultimate nature of things. Nothing more can be said about it.

That which is born will have to die. The young will become old, the child will become young, the beautiful will become ugly, the healthy will become ill. Such is the nature of things – but this is not an answer, remember. And Buddha insisted again and again, "I am not answering your questions, I am only making your questions clear to you."

This is the difference between a philosopher and a mystic: the philosopher tries to answer your questions, the mystic simply helps you to understand your questions.

Whenever Buddha used to go to a new place, his disciples would go ahead and declare to the people: "Please don't ask these eleven questions. It will be a sheer waste of time, because all that he is going to say is, 'Such is the nature of things.' So *we* can say it to you! This will be his answer to these eleven questions: 'Such is the nature of things.' So don't ask these questions."

Neither is Buddha a philosopher, nor Lao Tzu; in fact, no one who has *known* is a philosopher. Philosophers are blind people thinking about light.

You must have heard the ancient Panchtantra story...

Five blind men went to see an elephant. They were not five blind men, they were five philosophers, but all these philosophers were blind. That story has two meanings: one for small children—then it is five blind people— and one for those who are a little more mature, and then it means five philosophers.

Those five blind men touched the elephant from different sides. Somebody touched his feet and declared that the elephant was like a pillar – and so on, so forth. They all described the elephant according to their very limited, partial observation. And they started quarreling, arguing. A great argument arose, and the whole village gathered. They were very argumentative people. They quoted scriptures, they tried to prove that what they were saying was right. They were philosophers, theologians and scholars. Of course there could not have been any conclusion. Philosophers have never come to any conclusion—they cannot, because a conclusion is possible only through experience, and the experience has to be total, absolute, categorical.

The first experience of the mystic is that existence is not a problem but a mystery; it is unknowable—not only unknown. Science divides existence into two categories: the known and the unknown. Hence science assumes that a day is bound to come when the whole unknown will be transformed into the known. That will be the end of all inquiry.

But religion believes in three categories. The known and the unknown belong to the lower world of knowledge, and the unknowable belongs to the higher world of knowledge. That higher will always remain the same; it will be always there to inquire into, to go into; to merge with, to melt into, to become one with.

Lao Tzu says: *"Knowing the not-knowing"* —knowing that life is absolutely mysterious, that there is no way to know it— "that is high." That is the ultimate of experience. There is no beyond to it, nothing more transcendental than that; one has arrived home. The moment you enter the mysterious, you have found the home. No knowledge can satisfy you unless you are merged with the unknowable. "Not knowing the knowing— that is an illness." Lao Tzu calls even wisdom an illness, because you are falling from the ultimate health, ultimate well-being.

"Not knowing the knowing..."

Even by saying, "I don't know," you have asserted something, you have said something, you have claimed some knowledge. For example, if Socrates had met Lao Tzu, Lao Tzu would have said, "You are ill— ill with wisdom! A good illness, but you are just a step below," because Socrates' famous statement is: "I know only one thing, that I know nothing." But there is a claim: "I know." Although the claim is that "I know nothing," still it is a claim of knowing, a claim of knowledge. Even though it claims that life is mysterious, the claim has come in.

Even to say that God is indefinable is a kind of definition. To say that truth is inexpressible is in a certain sense giving it some expression. To say that the truth cannot be said means you have said something about it. Your very statement falsifies it; it is self-contradictory. Hence he calls it illness—it is self-contradictory.

Lao Tzu was one of the most consistent men; it is rare to find a buddha so consistent as Lao Tzu. His whole life he never wrote. All the teaching that he gave to his disciples was not a teaching at all; his whole method was *via negativa*. The disciple would come to him with all his knowledge, and Lao Tzu would start dismantling his knowledge, destroying his knowledge; that was his whole and sole purpose. He would go on taking away your knowledge brick by brick. A moment comes when the whole building of your knowledge collapses; then you are left in a vacuum. That is the moment Lao Tzu would say, "Now you can sit by my side—just sit in this vacuum." And of course in a vacuum you cannot ask any question, you cannot expect any answer. If you can ask, if you can expect, it is not a true vacuum yet. A true vacuum means no answer, no question; nothing is left, all has disappeared. The very earth beneath your feet has been taken away; you are falling into a bottomless abyss.

These were the people Lao Tzu had gathered around himself. They would sit with him, they would walk with him, they would move from one village to another village. But he was not like Buddha or Mahavira, who were teaching, who were trying to convey something of the unconveyable.

His whole life he was asked again and again by the kings, by the emperors, by the rich people, "Please write something about your experience for the coming generations. Don't take it away with you. We know you know, whether you say it or not. We know, because your very presence is so pregnant it is almost tangible. We can touch it, we feel it, we become flooded with it. We know you know! Please write something, just a few words for the future generations to know that a man like Lao Tzu has been in existence." But he was very reluctant. He would simply laugh, he would not even say no.

Once a disciple asked, "At least just to be polite you can say no!"

And Lao Tzu said, "To say no means you are on the way to saying yes! If they can get a no out of me, sooner or later they will get a yes too, because yes and no are two sides of the same coin."

And he is right, he is absolutely right. If somebody says no to you, that means there is hope—yes *is* possible. There is a possibility; however far away it may be, there is a possibility. The no can turn into yes because yes can turn into no; they go on changing into each other. And you know that your no in the morning becomes yes in the evening, your yes in the evening becomes no in the morning; they are interchangeable. They are not so contradictory as they appear. Somewhere deep down they are joined.

Lao Tzu would not even say no, he would only laugh. Now, what to make of this laugh? You cannot make anything out of it. He is neither saying yes nor saying no; he is not falling from his high state. But at the last moment he was forced to write—this is the only document in the whole history of humanity which has been written under compulsion, which has been coerced—because he wanted to go to the Himalayas. The Himalayas divide China and India; in one sense they divide, in another sense they join. You can see— yes and no are not very different!

He wanted to go to the Himalayas. His disciples asked, "Why?" He had become very old. He must have been very old for the simple reason that... The story is beautiful; true or not, that is not the point. I am a lover of beauty; I don't bother whether it is true or not!

Beauty is something higher than truth. Truth is logical, beauty is aesthetic. Truth is of the head, beauty is something deeper—of the heart.

I love the story...

Lao Tzu lived in his mother's womb for eighty-two years! It is almost impossible. When he was born he was already eighty-two years old, with a long beard, long hair, and all white. He was already an ancient man—and then he must have lived at least eighty years more. That has been the habit in the East of all the enlightened people. Buddha lived eighty-two years, Mahavira lived eighty-two years, Krishna lived eighty-two years, but Lao Tzu defeated all of them. He lived eighty-two years in the mother's womb first! Then to balance things he must have lived at least eighty-two years outside the womb. He was a man of balance!

So by the time he started thinking about finding a right place to die, he must have been nearabout one hundred and sixty years old. He asked his friends and disciples, "Now give me permission. I would like to go to a faraway virgin peak of the Himalayas to die so that no trace of me is left behind, not even footprints on the sands of time. I would simply like to disappear into the wildness of the Himalayas. Nobody will ever know where I died, where my bones are, where my body is, where my grave is. I just want to melt into existence."

They were sad, but they knew their master—that when he said something he meant it. Reluctantly, they gave him the farewell.

When he was leaving the country, the emperor of the country ordered all the guards at all the posts: "Lao Tzu is not to be allowed to leave the country unless he writes down his experience in short, to be preserved for future generations."

He was caught at the border, and the military guards wouldn't allow him leave until he wrote something. Under such compulsion, he sat in one of the guards' homes for three days. Day in, day out he wrote his small treatise, *Tao Te Ching*. These are words from that treatise. And when the treatise was complete, he left.

But he begins the treatise with a very strange statement: "*Tao* cannot be spoken. The moment it is spoken, it is no longer true. Now you can read whatsoever I am writing, it is no longer true; it has already fallen. It has come down from its profound silence into the noisy world of words."

That's what he calls illness. To say something about the ultimate is a fall—you have lost the wholeness. To be whole is to be healthy. That's exactly the meaning of healthy: to be whole. Nothing is missing; all parts are functioning in deep harmony, in accord, in tune with each other. It is an organic unity. To be ill means some parts are missing, nonfunctioning. The accord is lost, the harmony is no longer there; some trouble has arisen, the balance has been lost. That's the meaning of illness.

"Not knowing the knowing."

So even if you say, "I don't know anything except one thing—that I know nothing," you have already fallen; you have said already something.

There is a Sufi story...

Four disciples of a mystic were told by the master, "It is time for you to go to the mountains and sit in silence for at least seven days, and then come back."

They went with the vow to sit there for seven days, in absolute silence. After just a few minutes the first said, "I wonder whether I have locked my house or not."

Another said, "You fool! We have come here to be silent and you have spoken!"

The third said, "You are a greater fool! What has it to do with you? If he spoke, at least *you* could have kept silent!"

The fourth said, "Thank God, I am the only one who has not spoken yet!"

There is an irresistible urge to say when you experience. You want to share it— it is uncontainable. You can see other people searching for it, and you have got it. It is as if you are standing at a crossroads: you know the right way, and people are searching for it; how can you remain silent? It is irresistible! But the problem is, the moment you say, "This is the right road," it becomes wrong. Saying it is falsifying it. Truth is infinite and words are very finite.

Hence Lao Tzu says: "The best is not to say, the next best is to say. The best is to be whole, the next best is to be partially true." But remember: because truth is indivisible, you cannot be partially true. Hence his insistence that the moment you say it, it becomes false. To be partially true means to be false, because truth is indivisible. But still he could understand the need of the person who has experienced to convey it, and the need of others who are in search of it, so he allowed it. He says:

"The one who suffers from this illness is not ill."

I am not condemning him, I am not saying that he is pathological. All that I am saying is that he is no longer the total, he is now only a glimpse, a faraway glimpse. He is now only a picture of the sunset, not the sunset itself. He is now only an echo. If this can be remembered, then even the echo can be used to find the original source. Then even the picture of a sunset can be of immense help. But people are such fools: they worship the pictures of the sunset, they forget all about the sunset. In fact, if you tell them, "This is not the sunset that you are worshipping, this is only a picture," they will be angry.

Go and tell the Hindus, "The gods that you are worshipping in your temples are not real gods. These are only pictures, photographs, and that too not true to the original, just imaginary, metaphorical!" They will be angry, they will throw you out of their temple. Or to the Christians, or to the Mohammedans, or to the Jainas...go anywhere, they will not listen to you.

Go to a Jaina temple and you will find twenty-four statues of their masters. And you will be surprised—they all look alike, exactly alike. Even Jainas cannot make the distinction! To be able to make the distinction, who is who, they have made small symbols underneath the statues. So they can tell who is who—that this is Mahavira and this is

Parshvanath and this is Neminath—they just make small symbols; otherwise the statues are exactly the same. These statues cannot be authentic; they can only at the most be symbolic. Who has ever heard of twenty-four persons exactly alike?—the same noses, the same ears...

You will be puzzled: all their ears are touching their shoulders. The earlobe...sall! It may have been that one person's earlobes may have touched, but now it has become absolutely necessary for a Jaina *trthankara's* earlobes to touch the shoulders; otherwise he is not a tirthankara. And you can find some absolutely dumb, dull, stupid person whose earlobes are touching his shoulders—just a donkey! That does not mean that he has become a tirthankara, that he has become a great enlightened master; otherwise all donkeys will become great enlightened masters! This is simply symbolic.

What can the symbol be? The Jaina method of meditation is to listen, to listen so absolutely and so silently, as if you have become all ears—that is the symbol. So they have made big ears just to indicate their method of meditation. Their method of meditation is listening: listening to the sound of the wind passing through the pine trees, listening to the birds, just listening to anything. The dog barking or the call of a distant cuckoo...just listening, with no judgment, no evaluation. Jainas say that if a person can listen totally, without any interference of the mind, he can become enlightened—just by listening: nothing else is needed. To show this, to represent it in the statue, they have made big ears. But people are worshipping the statues. They are not trying to find out where the sunset is, they have forgotten all about the sunset. It is as if you have seen the sunset through the window. You have forgotten about the sunset, and you are worshipping the frame of the window. Hence, Lao Tzu says that the best is not to say anything about the truth, about your experience.

Then what is a master supposed to do? He can say how he achieved, he can say what the pitfalls to be avoided are, he can help you to refine your methods; again and again he can put you on the right path, he can stop you from going astray. He can tell you about all the means that lead to the end, but about the end he should remain absolutely silent.

That's what I am doing to you: about the end I am absolutely silent. What I am talking about is the method—the meditation, the prayer. These are the ways. When you have arrived, only then will you know what it is; it cannot be said. The moment you say it, something goes "ill"— something goes wrong, something goes sour.

But still, Lao Tzu feels that sometimes the masters have spoken out of compassion for those who are still lost in darkness. Hence he says: "The one who suffers from this illness is not ill." He himself is not ill, but what he says is ill. He himself is whole, but his statement cannot be whole.

> *"The wise is not ill"*
> *because he suffers from this illness—*
> *that's why he is not ill."*

A strange statement! *"The wise is not ill because he suffers from this illness—that's why he is not ill."* This illness is worth suffering, because it is the closest point to perfect health. It is a great blessing! Hence, don't be misguided by the word "ill." It is illness if you compare it to the highest, but if you look back at the journey, it is not illness. And if it comes out of compassion—and it does come out of compassion...

The story about Buddha is that when he became enlightened, for seven days he remained silent. He remained in that ultimate wholeness, health, and he was not willing to come down from there. It has happened to everybody who has become enlightened; hence the story of Buddha is very representative.

But, the story says, the gods in heaven became very much disturbed because somebody becoming enlightened is such a rare phenomenon. Buddha was hesitating to say anything about it. He was deciding, coming closer and closer to the decision that it is better to remain silent. But before he came to a decision, the gods rushed from heaven, fell at his feet, and said, "Wait! Don't decide, because once you have decided then nothing can be done. Just listen to us before you come to a decision. It is rare that a man becomes enlightened and there are millions who would like your advice, your help. Don't be so hard! And you yourself have suffered—don't you feel anything for the suffering humanity? Tell them how *you* arrived!"

Buddha said to them, "I have pondered over all pros and cons, I have thought about all these things. My own reasoning is that whatsoever I say will not be the same as I have experienced, and that is betraying the truth. Secondly, I am ready to betray it, because I am not going to lose anything by betraying it, but the moment I say something, people will understand something else which I have not said at all. The first loss happens when I say something, I come down from my silence. And the second loss—which is far greater—happens when people hear it, because they start coloring it according to their ideas, according to their mind.

"The third loss, the greatest, happens when they start telling it to other people. And then it goes on falling. Soon the flower of the sky falls into the mud of the earth and is lost, trampled over by people. So what is the point? I have also thought of their suffering, but then too my reasoning is: those who can understand me will be able to find it by themselves. If they are so capable of understanding me, it won't take them long to find it on their own, so why bother? Those who can understand me will find it sooner or later. It is only a question of time, and time does not matter as far as eternity is concerned. And telling those who cannot understand me is not right; they will misunderstand."

The gods were at a loss; they could not find how to persuade this man. They asked for some time so they could go in private to discuss the matter amongst themselves and find a way. They just wanted to be given one chance.

They went into seclusion, meditated, talked, discussed, and finally they came with a solution. They brought a really very beautiful solution. They said, "We agree with you that out of one hundred persons there may be one person who may attain it by himself sooner or later, just as you have attained. And we agree that out of one hundred, at least ninety-eight percent of people will misunderstand you, but they don't matter. They are already in misunderstanding—what more misunderstanding can there be? So you will not be harming them. So two things are certain: you will not be helping the one percent who is going to attain it by himself, and you will not be harming the ninety-eight percent who are anyway confused and will remain confused whether you speak or not.

"But what about the remaining one percent, the borderline case who is neither here nor there, who does not belong to the ninety-eight percent and does not belong to the one percent either—who is just in the middle of both? If you say something, he may be helped; if you don't say something, he may not be helped at all for centuries to come. Can't you feel any compassion for that one person?"

And Buddha had to agree with them that the one percent certainly had to be considered: "I will speak for that one person."

In fact, all the masters have been speaking for that one percent. They have been taking this risk of coming down from their sunlit peaks into the dark valleys of humanity for that one person. The message of the enlightened people can never be for the masses, has never been for the masses. The masses are always against it; it can only be for very few people. But even those very few people are enough to give life, beauty, grandeur, splendor. They are the salt of the earth.

The second question

Why is it so difficult to recognize you?

It is a simple phenomenon: you can recognize only that which comes within your experience. How can you recognize something which you have not experienced? What I am saying to you and what I am being to you is something utterly unknown to you—not only unknown, but much of it is unknowable too. Recognition needs some experience within you to coincide with my experience.

Those who are falling in tune with me, recognize me, and only they can recognize; it is not for all. It is only for the disciples to have a glimpse of recognition and it is only for the devotees to be absolutely certain of the recognition.

But many of you have come here only as students searching for more knowledge, and I am imparting being, not knowledge. You have come with greed in your heart. Many types of greed are there...

Just the other day I received a letter from a very rich Marwari from Orissa. He has never written to me before; this is the first time. He writes, "I recognize you as the greatest incarnation of God. This is the time for you to prove whether you are really a god or not, because we Marwaris"—Marwaris are the Jews of India—"are in very great difficulty in Orissa."

In Orissa, Marwaris are being thrown out. They have exploited the poor people for so long that it has come to a climax. Now, suddenly, he remembers me. I have never heard of the man; he has never written to me. Now he writes that this is the time for me to prove! "We will worship you forever if you can save us from the anger of the masses." They are being burned, killed, looted. Naturally he can recognize me. But this is not recognition; this is greed, it is fear.

Just one day before that, a young man from Delhi has written another letter: "I am rich enough, but I don't see any meaning in life. I am so afraid of committing suicide that I am staying in a hospital permanently. I am afraid that if I am not looked after continuously by doctors and nurses, I may kill myself any moment. If you promise to save me then I am ready to come to you. I am ready even to become a sannyasin!"

Now, such a conditional sannyas is not possible.

Many people come to me—they may not say exactly why they have come, but there are deep motives. Then it will be very difficult for you to recognize, because I am not here to fulfill any of your greed, to fulfill any of your desire, to fulfill any of your expectations.

I can share my bliss, I can share my truth, I can share my being, but very few people are longing for all those things; their longings are of a very ordinary nature, almost animalistic.

"While fishing one day," said the old angler, "I ran short of bait and did not know what to do. I looked around, and there at my feet I noticed a snake which held a frog in his mouth. I removed the frog and cut it up for bait, feeling very elated that I had seen the snake at that moment.

"I did, however, feel somewhat guilty at stealing the poor reptile's meal, so to repay him for my supply of bait I poured a few drops of whiskey into his mouth. My conscience was relieved when I saw the snake crawl away in a contented mood, and I went back to my fishing.

"Some time had passed when I felt something hitting against my leg. Imagine my surprise when, looking down, I saw the same snake, carrying three more frogs in his mouth!"

You ask: "Why is it so difficult to recognize you?" You come with a greedy heart—and then it is difficult to recognize me. You come to see something according to your own ideas—and I don't exist according to anybody's ideas.

I am simply just being myself!

Hindus come to look for a Krishna—I am not. Jainas come to look for a Mahavira—I am not. Christians come to look for a Christ—I am not. If you have come to look for somebody else in me, you will not be able to recognize me, because I am simply myself. I have no obligation to be a Christ or a Buddha or a Lao Tzu. If Christ is free to be himself, he need

The Suchness of Things

not be me, why should I be him? There is no need. Such expectations create a barrier.

An elephant is walking through a forest and spies a naked man. He looks at him bewildered and asks, "Tell me, how do you breathe through that short thing?"

Just expectations! The elephant has his own ideas...

A sannyasin was sitting by a cliff, sobbing uncontrollably. A passerby stopped and asked what the matter was.

"A busload of politicians just plunged over this cliff to certain death!" sobbed the swami.

"That certainly is a catastrophe," sympathized the stranger, "but I did not think you sannyasins had much love for politicians!"

"That's true!" said the swami as he doubled up with a fresh wave of grief. "The fact is, five of the seats were empty!"

You will have to drop your old ideas if you want to recognize me. My whole approach towards life is different from anybody who has preceded me. It has to be so. Krishna lived on this earth five thousand years ago; Buddha, twenty-five centuries ago; Jesus twenty centuries ago; Mohammed fourteen centuries ago; Kabir and Nanak five centuries ago. Since then, so much water has gone down the Ganges!

Man has changed, the whole life pattern has changed. I am living in the twentieth century; I cannot adjust myself to anybody five thousand years old – that is impossible. That would be crippling myself, paralyzing myself, poisoning myself. I have to be now, here!

But you are all conditioned. Although your conditioning has not given you any joy, it has not given you any ecstatic lifestyle, still people cling to the familiar.

At a bar, a disheartened drinker complained to the man next to him that he had gone to the tracks for a whole month without backing a winner.

"Why don't you quit betting?" advised the other.

"What!" snapped the gambler. "And give up twenty years' experience in horse betting?"

Twenty years' experience! How can anybody give up so easily? And your experience of religion is five thousand years old or even more. How can you give it up? But unless you give it up, you cannot see me; your eyes will remain covered. That's why you see very few old people around me. Even the people who are old and around me are in some way not old, they are very young and fresh.

Sephalie, one of my sannyasins who is near seventy, writes to me again and again, "I am very puzzled. I feel myself so young, and nobody believes me!" Just the other day she wrote, "Not even your sannyasins believe me! They try to help me, thinking that I am an old woman. They are very good, but it hurts me because I am young! I don't feel old age at all! The body has become old, but they don't see *me*, and I am not the body!" And she is right.

Back in Europe she was creating much confusion amongst people because she started playing with small children. Her family and her friends said, "What are you doing? A seventy-year-old woman playing with small children, laughing, giggling, dancing – it does not look right!"

But she said, "I feel so young! I feel just like a child!" And her experience is right. Her feeling is coming from within her being.

So even the people around me who are old are not old in the ordinary sense, they are all young. Actually, only young people have come to me. This has been always so. The twelve apostles of Jesus were all young people, younger than Jesus. The people who surrounded Gautam Buddha were all young people. The people who lived with Lao Tzu were very young people. It has always been so for the simple reason that the old mind has so many conditionings that unless those conditionings are fulfilled he cannot see. Only somebody who is a fraud is going to fulfill your conditions.

No original man is going to fulfill your conditions because no original man has any desire for all the respectability that you can give to him. He is so blissful; what does he need your respectability for? Respectability is a substitute. Only miserable people hanker for respectability; the blissful people have never cared a bit about your respectability.

I am perfectly happy. Famous, notorious, it doesn't matter. It makes no difference to me, so I am not going to fulfill any of your expectations. You must be carrying expectations somewhere.

A Jewish father and his son go together to a Turkish bath.
"Yuk! Your feet are so dirty!" says the father.
"But, father, your feet are much dirtier!"
"How can you compare?" says the angry father. "I am thirty years older than you!"

The old mind always goes on bragging, as if oldness is something very valuable. Oldness simply means you have been accumulating junk! A really alive person is always young; to the very moment of death he is young.

For example, I know Sephalie – when she dies she will die young and fresh, as fresh as the freshly opened rosebud. I have given her the name Sephalie because "sephali" is the name of a beautiful flower. She will die like fresh dewdrops in the early morning sun.

My people have to live freshly and die freshly. They have to remain continuously young. The only way to remain young is go on dying to the past, go on discarding the old, go on dropping all your accumulated knowledge so you are always in a state of not knowing. That is the highest according to Lao Tzu, and according to me also: remaining in a state of not knowing. "Not even knowing that I know nothing" – that's the highest, the most beautiful space one can ever be in. And only then can you recognize me; otherwise there is no way to recognize me.

Meditate, become silent, so that you can feel some meeting, some merging with me, so that you can taste something of the joy that I have brought to you. It is a pure gift! All that is needed on your part is a little receptivity.

The last question

What is the connection between laughter and sex?

There is certainly a connection; the connection is simple. Sexual orgasms and laughter happen in the same way; their process is similar. In sexual orgasm you go on reaching a climax of tension. You are coming closer and closer to burst forth, and then at the peak, suddenly, the orgasmic release happens. After such a mounting tension, everything suddenly relaxes. The contrast between the mounting tension and the relaxation is so vast that you feel as if you have fallen into a calm, quiet ocean—a deep relaxation, a deep let-go.

That's why nobody has ever been known to have died from a heart attack while making love. This is strange, because love-making is an arduous exercise! It is great yoga! But nobody has ever died for the simple reason that it brings such relaxation. In fact, cardiologists and heart specialists have now started recommending sex as medicinal to the people who are suffering from heart trouble. Sex can be of immense help to them; it relaxes tensions, and when the tensions are gone, your heart functions more naturally.

The same is the process of laughter: it also builds up a tension in you. A certain story, and you go on expecting that something is going to happen. Then when something really happens it is so unexpected that it releases the tension. The happening is not logical—that is the most important thing to understand about laughter. The happening has to be ridiculous, it has to be absurd. If you can logically conclude it, then there will be no laughter.

While you are listening to a joke, if you can logically conclude what is going to happen, and if it actually happens the way you concluded, then there will be no laughter because there will be no build up of tension in the first place; and secondly, there will be no sudden change. These two things are needed: a building up of tension so you become more and more narrowed, more and more tense, and then suddenly an unexpected turn—the punch line. It triggers a new process; the whole logic falls flat. All jokes are illogical, and because they are illogical they bring great laughter to you.

In one other sense also sex and laughter are joined together deep in the mind. Your sex organs are only the outermost part of your sexuality; the sex is not really there, the sex is somewhere in the brain center. So, sooner or later man is going to get rid of this old-style sexuality. It is really ridiculous! That's why people make love in the dark, at night, under the blankets. It is such an absurd activity that if you watch yourself making love, you will never think of it again! So people hide; they close their doors, they lock their doors. They are very much afraid of children in particular, because they will see the absurdity immediately— "What are you doing? Daddy, what are you doing? Have you gone crazy?" And it looks crazy— it is like an epileptic fit!

Sooner or later it is going to be changed, because now science has found that the real center is in the brain, not in the sex organs. So now a small electrode can be fitted in the head, and you need not know about it, because inside the skull there is no sensitivity at all; anything can be put there. Even if a small rock is put there you will not know. In fact, that's how many people are— they are carrying rocks inside, not knowing! So a small electrode can be put inside your brain, just inserted inside your brain close to the sex center, and you can use a remote control. You can keep the remote control in your pocket so that whenever you feel like having an orgasm, you just push it. Just a little push on the button will trigger the sex center in the brain, and you can have an orgasm anywhere!

Then you can discard this wife, this husband, this relationship, and all this nonsense. It will be a great freedom! In fact, it is the only way humanity will be liberated. All the buddhas have failed; they could not liberate you from sex. Now Delgado is the name of the latest person who is going to free you from all sexuality. He has freed many white rats! Sometimes I wonder why they never try black rats. Maybe they think that they are Indians and may not like the idea because they are religious people, spiritual. They always try white rats!

But you will be surprised to know – and it is good to remember— that whenever he tried with rats, a very strange thing happened. That's what prevented him from making it a device on the market available to anybody wanting to purchase it. The thing that stopped him was that when he fixed the electrode inside the head of the white rat and showed him the remote control button, the rat pushed the switch in front of him and went through a beautiful spasm, a total orgasmic joy. And then Delgado watched...

The rat looked all around, and seeing that nobody was looking, he pushed the button, and went through it again. You will be surprised: in one hour, he pushed the button six thousand times—till he died! He forgot all about food, forgot all about everything. Beautiful damsels were passing by, and he didn't even care about all those beautiful girls after whom he had been going crazy; there was no need now. No woman can give a man such a total orgasm, and no man can give a woman such a total orgasm, because the sexual organs are far away from the center. By the time the message reaches to the center, it is already very, very diluted. Hence, ninety-seven percent of women never achieve orgasmic joy. And those are Western statistics. Ninety-seven percent in America—what to say about India? I don't think I have ever come across a single woman who has said that she achieves orgasmic joy. She cannot—the culture does not allow it. She has to lie down almost dead. She simply suffers the whole foolishness of the man, and deep down she thinks that this man is a sinner dragging her into hell. She is not interested at all because she knows nothing about orgasmic joy. And her orgasmic joy is far more profound than man's. Her whole body is erotic; man's whole body is not erotic. He is only partially erotic, locally erotic.

These centers of sex and laughter are very close in the brain, so sometimes they can overlap. So when you are making love, if you really allow it, the woman will start giggling. It tickles, because the center is very close! She may not giggle just out of politeness, because the man may feel offended—but the centers are very close together, and sometimes when you are really in deep laughter you may have the same orgasmic joy as you have in sex.

It is not a coincidence that many beautiful jokes are sexual. The centers are so close...what can I do?

The wealthy woman woke up, looked around her bedroom, then rang for her Chinese houseboy, Fu Ling.

She asked him how she got home the night before, and he said, "I bring missy home."

Then she asked him how she got undressed. Fu Ling said, "I undress missy."

She asked then how she got into bed, and he said, "I put missy to bed."

Whereupon she said, "God, I must have been tight!"

Fu Ling replied, "First time, yes, missy! Second timeÖno!"

Makowski, the agent, called his friend Lyssky, the producer of striptease shows. "Lyssky," he shouted, "I've got a girl for you that is gonna make a fortune for both of us. She is incredible – gotta a pair of lungs that will knock your eyes out! Listen to these statistics: hips – forty; waist – twenty-seven; chest – ninety-nine!"

"Incredible!" said Lyssky. "What kind of act does she do?"

"Act? What act?! She just crawls out and tries to stand up!"

The newlyweds arrived at their honeymoon hotel. The excited groom, quite pleased with his reputation as a lover, and eager to thrill his bride with his expertise, quickly threw her upon the bed and performed with the skill of a champion sexual athlete.

When it was over he whispered to his bride, "Ah yes, my dear, I could tell how pleased you were – I noticed your toes curling up in ecstasy. I promise you I will always bring you such joy!"

She whispered in reply, "Perhaps next time, Romeo, you could remove my pantyhose first!"

Enough for today.

CHAPTER 12

From Italy to Nirvana

The first question

I felt so much love pouring from you when I could not get the microphone to work the other day. With my hands shaking, and my heart thumping, I knew I had to do something–yet with your big, brown eyes smiling at me, I just wanted to sit there and melt into you. It was an exquisite tension.

That's exactly what I was telling you to do. Sit silently and do nothing – and the microphone starts working by itself! But you wouldn't listen; you continued doing something or other—and that was creating the whole mess! But it is natural, it happens.

One day my Rolls didn't start, and I was telling Heeren again and again, "Wait a minute!" But he wouldn't wait, he went on turning the ignition. Just one minute I was telling him to wait, and the moment I left in the other car, exactly after one minute it started. Then he realized that there are some times when if you don't do anything, things settle on their own accord. But it is difficult... .

A man goes to a cocktail party. When the waiter brings round the salmon rolls, the lady standing next to him bends over to pick one up and loses her glass eye amongst the hors d'oeuvres. Before she can do anything, the man picks up a salmon roll containing the glass eye and eats it.

A week later he finds himself suffering from severe constipation. The doctors cannot seem to cure it so they decide to get him into the operating theater to stick a tube inside him and see what the problem is.

The doctor takes one look down the tube, looks up at the patient and says, "You really don't trust me, do you?"

And moreover, what was the hurry? We were all enjoying! It was such a beautiful joke that without a single punchline to it people were bursting in laughter. I have received many letters: "What happened that day? Even when you are telling a beautiful joke, the laughter never goes so deep and so total. But that day neither were you telling a joke, nor had we heard anything, but the laughter was happening!"

Recently some tapes other than Watergate have been discovered by archaeologists, and they shed light on Daniel in the lion's den.

You must know the old story of Saint Daniel who was thrown into a den of lions because he refused to betray his faith. He came out of the den unharmed. It was thought to be a great miracle. But this recent discovery by the archaeologists says something else. It says, the tapes reveal, that at the precise moment when the lion was going to eat Daniel, Daniel quickly grabbed one of the lion's ears and whispered into it, "Don't eat me! Remember, after dinner come the speeches!"

So there was no hurry—only a speech was going to come after. Even if the microphone was not going to work, there was no harm at all. We would have sat, enjoyed, laughed and said good-bye to each other!

Learn to do nothing....

"What are you doing here?" asks one mouse to his friend.
"Nothing really, just sitting in the sun."
"Ah!" says the first mouse. "I guess that's what I am doing too!"

And that's what all these orange people are here to do – nothing.

You missed one opportunity. But next time, remember, imitation won't do! Just because I am telling you, "Do nothing," it won't help—you have to be original. But once it is said and if you follow it, the microphone is not going to work at all. That opportunity is lost, at least for this life!

The second question

The world seems to be getting more and more crazy from day to day. Nobody knows what is going on and everything is upside down and confused. This is what is told in the newspapers. Is it real? And if so, is there any intrinsic balance in life that is keeping everything stable?

The world is the s
 three thousand years man has fought five thousand wars. Can you say this humanity is sane? One cannot remember a time in human history when people were not destroying each other either in the name of religion or in the name of God or even in the name of peace, humanity, universal brotherhood. Great words hiding ugly realities! Christians have been killing Mohammedans, Mohammedans have been killing Christians, Mohammedans have been killing Hindus, Hindus have been killing Mohammedans. Political ideologies, religious ideologies, philosophical ideologies are just facades for murder—to murder in a justified way.

And all these religions were promising the people, "If you die in a religious war, your heaven is absolutely certain. Killing in war is not sin; being killed in war is a great virtue." This is sheer stupidity! But ten thousand years of conditioning has seeped deep into the blood, into the bones, in the very marrow of humanity.

Each religion, each country, each race was claiming, "We are the chosen people of God. We are the highest; everyone is lower than us." This is insanity, and everybody has suffered because of it. Jews have suffered immensely for one single folly that they committed: the idea that "We are the chosen people of God." Once you have the idea that you are the chosen people of God, then you cannot be forgiven by others because they are also the chosen people of God, and how to decide it? No argument can be conclusive, and nobody knows where God is hiding so you cannot ask him either; he cannot be brought in the court to be a witness. Then only the sword is going to decide. Whosoever is mighty is going to be right. Might has been right.

Jews really suffered for centuries, but the suffering has not changed them. In fact it has strengthened the idea that they are the chosen people of God. The same people who tell them, "You are the chosen people," also tell them that the chosen people have to go through many tests, many fires to prove their mettle.

I have heard about an old rabbi — he must have been a very sane man – praying to God. He was praying for years and years and never asking for anything—and you know, prayer is a kind of nagging: you go on nagging God every day, morning, afternoon, evening, night, five times every day. God must be getting tired, utterly bored... .

And the rabbi was not asking for anything; otherwise there was a way out. If he had been asking for something it would have been given and the rabbi would have been told, "Get lost!" But he was not asking for anything, just praying.

Finally God asked him, "Why do you go on torturing me? What do you want?"

And the old rabbi said, "Just one thing. Is it not time for you to choose some other people? Please, make some other people your chosen people. We have suffered enough!"

But this is not only so with the Christians, Jews, Mohammedans and Hindus; it is exactly the same with all the people that have existed up to now. The racial ego, the religious ego, the spiritual ego is far more dangerous than the individual ego, because the individual ego is gross. You can see it—everybody can see it, it is so visible on the surface. But when the ego becomes racial— "Hinduism is great"— you don't think you are claiming anything for yourself. Indirectly you are claiming, "I am great because I am a Hindu, and Hinduism is great." This is an indirect way, a subtle, cunning way: "I am great because I am a Japanese, because Japanese are the direct descendants of the sun God"; or, "I am a Chinese and the Chinese are the most civilized people, the most cultured."

When the Westerners reached China for the first time, looking at the Chinese, they laughed. They looked more like caricatures; cartoons rather than men— just four or five hairs sticking out of your face and that's your whole beard! What kind of people are these? The first Europeans wrote in their diaries, "It seems we have discovered the missing link between the monkeys and man."

And what were the Chinese writing in their journals? Even the emperor of China was very much interested in seeing the Europeans because he had heard many stories about them. They were invited to his court, not because he respected the Europeans, but just to see what kind of people these were. Never before...! And he could not contain his laughter; he started laughing when he saw the Europeans.

The Europeans were very much embarrassed: "Why is he laughing?" They were told, "That is his way of appreciating. He always laughs, enjoys; that is his way of welcoming the guests." But the reality was that he could not believe that these are human beings! He asked his people, "Have you brought them from African jungles? They look like monkeys!"

That's how the ego functions: the other is always reduced to the lowest possible; and compared to the other, one raises oneself higher.

You say, "The world seems to be getting more and more crazy from day to day." That is not right; it has always been so. Only one thing new is happening, and that is a blessing, not a curse at all. For the first time in the whole history of humanity, a few people are becoming aware that the way we have existed up to now is somehow wrong; something basically is missing in our very foundation. There is something which does not allow us to grow into sane human beings. In our very conditioning are the seeds of insanity.

Every child is born sane, and then, slowly, slowly, we civilize him—we call it the process of civilization. We prepare him to become part of the great culture, the great church, the great state to which we belong. Our whole politics is stupid, and then *he* becomes stupid. Our whole education is ugly. Our politics means nothing but ambition, naked ambition—ambition for power. And only the lowest kind of people become interested in power. Only the people who are suffering from a deep inferiority complex become politicians. They want to prove that they are not inferior; they want to prove it to others, they want to prove to themselves that they are not inferior, they are superior.

But what is the need to prove it if you are superior? The superior man does not try to prove anything, he is so at ease with his superiority. That's what Lao Tzu says: The superior man is not even conscious of his superiority; there is no need at all. It is only the ill person who starts thinking of health; the healthy person never thinks about health. The healthy person is not self-conscious about his health; only the sick, only the ill. The beautiful person, the really beautiful person is not self-conscious about his or her beauty. It is only the ugly person who is constantly worried and making every effort to prove that it is not so.

In fact, in proving to others that "I am not inferior, I am not ugly," he is trying to prove it to himself. The others function as a mirror. If the others can say, "Yes, you are great... ." But they will say it only when you are powerful, when you are rich; otherwise they are not going to say anything. Who is interested in your ego? They are interested in *their* egos, but reluctantly, when you have power to destroy, they have to accept.

Adolf Hitler was mad, but nobody in Germany dared to say it. Many felt that he was mad, but the moment he was defeated and committed suicide, many people started writing that they had always felt it. Even his own physicians who had never dared to tell the person himself— at least *they* were supposed to say the truth, they were the physicians— they had not said that he was sick, badly sick, and not only physiologically but psychologically too.

He suffered from many nightmares, he was constantly afraid of being killed. He was obsessed with the idea that he was going to be killed, so much so that he never got married. He got married only when he had decided to commit suicide, just three hours before. To avoid having a woman in the same room, he never got married— because who knows, the woman may be a spy, an enemy, and while he is asleep she may kill him, poison him. He never trusted even the woman he pretended to love. He had no friends, because to be friendly with someone means to trust, and he was so doubtful.

The politicians are insane, but we teach our children to be politicians. We teach our children the same culture that has tortured us, the same values that have been heavy on us, that have only proved to be subtle chains, imprisonment. But we go on conditioning our children. The same education that has destroyed our grace, our innocence—we go on stuffing the same knowledge into our children's heads. And we go on lying to our children as our parents lied to us.

And this has been going on and on for centuries. How can humanity be healthy, wholesome, relaxed? It is bound to be crazy. Just look what lies you go on telling your children.

A little boy rushed into his mother's room and said, "Mommy, I had always wanted to ask one question, but today it is very urgent—I want the answer right now."

The mother was changing her clothes, getting ready to go out, and the son asked, "What are these two things on your chest?"

The mother felt a little embarrassed: How to explain to the child about the breasts?

Now, it is a simple thing to explain, and children are very understanding. It could easily have been explained that they are meant for small children to get their nourishment, and the thing would have been finished then and there. But we have become accustomed to such lies— and the mother immediately invented a lie.

She said, "These are balloons. When a woman dies, God puffs up these balloons. They become bigger and bigger and bigger, and then the woman's body starts rising towards heaven."

The child said, "Now I know what is happening."

The mother said, "What is happening?"

He said, "Our maid servant is dying, but poor daddy is trying hard to prevent her. He is lying on top of the servant, holding her down, sucking her balloons to pull the air out, and the maid servant is saying, 'God, I am coming!'"

Now, these stupid lies— and you think humanity is going to be sane? It has always been insane. It has always remained upside down and confused, because you have been brought up on lies.

But one thing good is happening today: at least a few intelligent young people are becoming aware that our whole past has been wrong and it needs a radical change. "We need a discontinuity from our past. We want to start afresh, we *need* to start afresh. The whole past has been an experiment in utter futility!"

Once we accept the truth as it is, man can become sane. Man is born sane; *we* drive him crazy. Once we accept that there are no nations and no races, man will become very calm and quiet. All this continuous violence and aggression will disappear. If we accept man's body, its sexuality, naturally, then all kinds of stupidities preached in the name of religion will evaporate. Ninety-nine percent of psychological diseases exist because of man's sexual repression.

We have to make man free of his past. That's my whole work here: to help you to get rid of the past. Whatsoever the society has done to you has to be undone. Your consciousness has to be cleaned, emptied so that you can become like a pure mirror reflecting reality. To be able to reflect reality is to know God. God is just another name for reality: that which is. And a man is really sane when he knows the truth.

Truth brings liberation, truth brings sanity.

Truth brings intelligence, truth brings innocence.
Truth brings bliss, truth brings celebration.

We have to change this whole earth into a tremendous festival, and it is possible because man brings all that is needed to transform this earth into a paradise.

The third question

Is it true that you are really an Italian?

Not now, but I must have been in some of my past lives. One has to pass through all kinds of things; one has to be an Italian too. Without being an Italian you cannot become enlightened—that much is absolutely certain. If somebody becomes enlightened without being an Italian he will have to come back; he will relapse from his enlightenment. Hence it is a must to pass through.

To be an Italian is just the opposite of being enlightened. Have you ever heard about any Italian becoming enlightened? But it helps—to touch the opposite pole is very necessary; only then the journey begins towards the source. You have gone as much astray as you could, then the prodigal sons return. You have to come back—there is nowhere else to go. Once you are an Italian, where else can you go? What else can you do? You have reached the dead end of the road. So it is good to be an Italian— the sooner it happens the better!

To be an Italian is to be really upside down, and not half-heartedly! I must have been an Italian; otherwise whatsoever I am now today would not have been possible. And I can say the same about Gautama the Buddha, Lao Tzu, Jesus, Bahauddin: all these people must have been Italian in some of their lives! You cannot bypass being an Italian. If you bypass, you are bypassing it at your own risk; you will have to come back. The Italian experience is something nobody can afford to miss.

Why is there such a low suicide rate among Italians?
It's pretty hard to kill yourself jumping out of a basement window!

A German, a Frenchman and an Italian were captured during the second world war and brought to a prison camp.

"How many pairs of underwear do you need?" asked the quartermaster sergeant.

"Seven," said the German; "a pair for each day of the week."

"Four," said the Frenchman; "one for each week in the month."

"And how about you, Luigi?" asked the sergeant. "How many pairs of underwear do *you* need?"

"Twelve," replied the Italian.

"What the hell do you need twelve for?"

"One-a for January, one-a for February, one-a... ."

Luigi met his best friend Giancarlo in the street one day. "Hello, Giancarlo, what-a you got-a inna your coat?"

"Well-a," said Giancarlo, "you know-a that fascist bastard Francesco? Well-a, every time I come-a to town, he says-a to me, 'Hey, Giancarlo, how you doing today-a?' Then he punches me in the chest-a with his fist-a and breaks-a all my cigars. So today I got-a four sticks-a of dynamite in my pocket. When he comes-a, I am-a gonna blow his goddamn hand-a off!"

Pierino comes home from school and asks his father, "Papa, what does 'simultaneously' mean?"

"It means at the same time," replies the father. But Pierino still does not understand, so the father explains it.

"Well," he says, "if you were born from a relationship between your mother and another man, not me, what would I be?"

"A cuckold!" replies the little boy.

"Right!" says the father. "And simultaneously you would be the son of a bitch!"

The Italian experience is very fundamental for spiritual growth. If you are not born an Italian, you can learn to be an Italian— it is easy. All that you need to do is exactly the same that you do in meditation, just a little bit different. In meditation you go beyond the mind; in being Italian you go below the mind. In both cases you go out of the mind! And it is better first to try to go below the mind; that will give you an out-of-the-mind experience— and then there is no possibility of relapsing.

Once you have tasted being an Italian, then you start praying to God, "No more of it! Enough is enough!" Then you start praying, "I don't want any more birth and death. I am fed up with time, I want to dissolve into eternity." But without being an Italian, this longing will not arise in you.

That's why I am so much in love with Italians— every moment they are coming closer to enlightenment. The deeper they become Italians, the closer they are coming to enlightenment; then the jump can happen at any moment.

There are people who are just in the middle—neither here nor there; they don't have much hope. For example, Indians—they don't have much hope. They are middle-of-the-road walkers—very careful, very cautious; they never go to the extremes. Keeping themselves in the middle they miss both the ultimate in misery and the ultimate in ecstasy.

To be an Italian is to be in ultimate misery. The only hope is spaghetti; otherwise all is misery! Once you have experienced the ultimate in misery, now the only possible way left for you is to search for the ultimate bliss, and nothing less than that will help you. The ultimate misery can be removed only by ultimate bliss.

It is not an accident that so many Italians are here. They have tasted the misery there, they have seen. If you have seen Italy you have seen the whole world. It is a miniature world, and once you are fed up with Italy you are fed up with the world too. Then nirvana is possible. In fact, from Italy to nirvana there is a direct route; that is the most simple, direct and the shortest route.

Italians live a very earthy life; they are earthy people. That's what is good about them—they are down to earth. They are not too interested in heaven and paradise; they don't care much about that. This earth is enough. But because it is not enough, sooner or later they start feeling an urge to seek for something else.

The Indians live on the earth, they are very mundane, but they go on talking about spirituality. That keeps them in a kind of illusion. Because of their talk they think they are spiritual. Because of their beautiful words which they have become very efficient in repeating...thousands of years of repeating and chanting mantras. They can do it very easily and befool others, but that is secondary— they can befool themselves. Hearing themselves using beautiful words, they can become infatuated with their own words. Words have then their own magnetism. If you use great words you will be influenced by those words— and your reality will be the same, it will not change. Words cannot change your reality, but they can hide, they can cover it up. They can give you a respectability.

The Indian lives in respectability. His whole effort is how to remain respectable, religious, spiritual; how to show others that he is a holy man. He is continuously making deliberate and not so deliberate efforts at pretending greatness, other-worldliness. You can see around him that stinking, ugly phenomenon of holier-than-thou.

Italians are beautiful in that way. They are simple people, down-to-earth, no-nonsense people. They don't bother about spiritual rubbish. And it is good to be earthly. My own experience is, if you have never been earthly, down-to-earth, if you have never been really materialistic, absolutely earthly, if you have never been really an atheist, you will not become spiritual, ever. Materialism has to become the base; your down-to-earthness has to become your foundation. Then the temple, the shrine of spirituality can rise on top of it.

First be a Charvaka, an Epicurean, a Zorba the Greek; only then can you be Gautama the Buddha, Jesus Christ, Bahauddin, Nanak, Kabir.... If your foundation is missing, then your spirituality is hocus-pocus; it is just verbal.

I love the Italian rootedness into the earth, because from there the work can start. The body has to be accepted first, not only accepted but respected too. If you have not explored your body you will not be able to explore the soul. The methodology of exploration is the same, but begin with the body because the body is the visible part of your soul. Start with the visible and then slowly move towards the invisible. Start with the known and then move towards the unknown. Start from the periphery and then go deeper towards the center.

There are millions of people in the world who live in words—repeating *The Bible*, the *Koran*, the *Gita*, the *Dhammapada*—but they are like parrots, mechanical; they are gramophone records. They can repeat the scriptures perfectly, but they know nothing. Knowledge needs roots in the earth, just as a tree needs roots in the earth. The branches will rise towards the sky, the branches will try to reach to the stars. But at the same time the roots have to go deeper and deeper into the earth. Remember, there is a balance: the higher the tree goes, the deeper its roots have to go; it is totally balanced. You cannot have a big tree with small roots. It will fall, it will not be able to stand.

That's how India has fallen....a big tree with very small roots. The most basic thing is to grow roots. But the roots cannot be grown into the sky, they have to grow into the earth, into the body, into matter. Then your branches can rise into the sky, into the world of the spiritual. They can reach to God.

Friedrich Nietzsche is right when he says, "When a tree wants to touch the feet of God, it has to reach to the very center of hell through its roots. The roots have to go to the very rock bottom; then only can the branches and the flowers be offered to the feet of God."

By Italian I simply mean a certain symbol, just as by Indian I mean a certain symbol. The Indian represents the hypocrite. Wherever he is born, that doesn't matter; he may be born even in Italy. But wherever you find a hypocrite you will find an Indian, and wherever you find a realistic, pragmatic, practical person he will be an Italian. To me these words don't represent geography, they represent something metaphorical.

My commune is going to be one of the richest communes that has ever happened on the earth. I have chosen Deeksha to take care of your bodies – an Italian, a perfect mamma! And she is taking care as beautifully as possible.

My commune consists of all kinds of people. They will all pool their different energies to make it the richest commune in the whole of existence that has ever existed. Around Buddha there were only Indians, around Jesus there were only Jews, around Mohammed there were only Mohammedans. Around me there are all kinds of people—theists, atheists, materialists, spiritualists, Catholics, Communists, Jainas, Jews, Italians, Indians, Germans...all kinds of people, and they have all developed different sides of humanity. No country has developed the whole human being, only partial human beings.

We can create the whole human being, multidimensional, immensely rich, rooted in the earth and yet longing for the stars.

The last question

I am leaving this wonderful buddhafield to venture forth into the big, wide world to get everything ready to become part of our new commune. Please tell me a joke that will accompany me on my adventures and that will remind me of your eternal laughter.

This is the joke for you:

A recently-married traveling salesman came home early from his business trip. He arrived at one o'clock in the morning and tiptoed up the stairs to his bedroom, not wishing to disturb his young wife. When he opened the door, to his horror he saw another man sleeping in his bed, next to his wife.

In a burst of rage he grabbed the man by the hair and pulled him out of bed. He kicked him and pushed him down the stairs and out of the back door. He forced the naked man into the garden shed, grabbed his prick and put it in a vice, which he then tightened and padlocked. He took a hacksaw from the shelf, very methodically removed the blade and fitted a new one in.

The terrified young man's eyes bulged at this prospect.

"You-you are no-no-not going to-to cut my prick off, are you?" he stammered.

"No," smiled the husband, handing the saw to the relieved young man. "*You* are! *I* am going to set fire to the shed!"

Enough for today.

CHAPTER 13

Of Course the Grass Grows by Itself

The first question

People of almost all the religions try to convince other people to follow their respective religions. But I have met many of your followers and they always discourage me from adopting the way you are preaching. Why so?

The first thing: what I am teaching is not a religion but a religiousness. A religion is a creed, a dogma, an ideology; it is intellectual. You can be convinced about it— arguments can be given, proofs can be supplied, you can be silenced. Argumentation is a kind of violence, a very subtle violence. It is an attempt to manipulate you, control you, enslave you. All the religions have been doing that for thousands of years; it is a subtle strategy to create mental slavery.

What I am doing here has nothing to do with religion at all. It is a kind of religiousness —no belief, no dogma, no church. It is a love affair; you cannot be convinced of it. Do you think Majnu can convince others about the beauty of Laila? It is impossible. No body can convince anybody else about his love affair. It is far deeper than the intellect, it is of the heart, and the heart knows no arguments, no proofs; it is simply so. One can dance, one can sing, but one cannot prove it. One can shout with joy, one can say "Alleluia!" but those are not arguments, they are not convincing.

The story about Majnu is very significant. It is a Sufi story. It is not an ordinary love story as people have been thinking, it is an allegory.

Majnu fell in love with a woman called Laila who was not beautiful according to others. According to the public opinion she was very ordinary, homely— not only that but ugly too. And Majnu was mad, so mad that the very name of Majnu has become synonymous with madness. He was continuously praying to God, continuously moving around the city asking people for help, because he was a poor man and the woman he had fallen in love with belonged to an aristocratic family. Even to see Laila from far away was not easy. It was a Mohammedan country, and in a Mohammedan country it is very difficult to see even the face of a woman.

Seeing his agony, his anguish, even the king became a little concerned. He called Majnu; he felt great compassion for him. He told him, "I know that woman; that family is well known to me, and if Laila had been a beautiful woman she would have been part of my harem. I have not chosen her—she is not worth choosing. I have got all the beautiful women from all over the country, and I feel so much for you that I will give you a chance. You can choose any woman from my harem and she will be yours!"— and he called the most beautiful women.

Majnu looked at each woman in minute detail and said, "This is not Laila!" Again and again...he passed over a dozen women, and the remark was always the same: "This is not Laila!"

The king said, "You must have gone utterly crazy! Laila is nothing compared to these beautiful women! You can choose anyone. I *know* your Laila, I have known the most beautiful women of the world, and my women are some of the greatest that have ever been on the earth."

Majnu said, "But you don't understand me. And I can understand that you cannot understand. It is not a question of choosing somebody else; the choice is not in my hands. It has happened already; the heart has chosen! I am nobody, I cannot interfere in it. The mind is only the circumference; the heart is the center. The center has chosen, how can the circumference interfere?

"And moreover— forgive me for saying so, because you have been so kind—I still insist that there has never been a woman like Laila and there will never be again. But to see the beauty of Laila you need the eyes of a Majnu, and you don't have those eyes so nothing can be done about it. You have to see her through *my* eyes; only then will you be able to see the grandeur, the splendor of her being."

Remember these words: To see the beauty of Laila you need the eyes of a Majnu.

This is not a religion. The people who have gathered around me are lovers—not intellectually convinced of what I am saying, but existentially convinced of what I am. It is a question not decided by the mind but something to be felt.

That's why my people never try to convince anybody. Knowing perfectly well that you don't have the eyes of a Majnu, what is the point of going into hairsplitting logic? It is futile! They know perfectly well that it is not their intellect that has made them part of my buddhafield, it is their hearts. Something has started ringing in their hearts—a bell has started ringing in their hearts.

Their hearts have felt a new release of energy, a new dance. A new melody has been heard, not a new argument but a new melody. Their hearts were asleep, now they are awake. Their hearts were like a desert. Now the spring has come, now roses are flowering, bees are humming. Their inner beings are transformed. It is religiousness.

Religiousness happens only when a Buddha or a Krishna or a Mahavira or a Christ is alive. When Christ dies there is religion. Religion is the corpse of religiousness; it only looks like a real person. When a person dies he looks exactly like he was when he was alive. Just something very small is missing—he is no longer breathing; otherwise everything is perfectly good! You can paint his face, you can put his hair in a beautiful style, you can give him beautiful garments, and he will look very young and very alive, with red cheeks—everything can be done. In the West it has become an art: how to paint the dead man, how to make him look alive. But it is only an appearance; the real is no longer there. It is only a cage—maybe a golden cage, but the bird has flown away.

When religiousness dies, religion is born. Religiousness breathes; religion is a corpse. But many people feel good with religion; in fact, the majority. Ninety-nine point nine percent of people feel good with religion, because it is not dangerous at all. What can the corpse do to you? You can do anything to the corpse, but the corpse cannot do anything to you; the corpse is in your hands.

But when religion is alive and breathing—that's what I mean by religiousness—then you are possessed by it, but you cannot possess it.

You cannot possess a Buddha or a Lao Tzu or a Zarathustra. You cannot possess Bahauddin, Jalaluddin, al-Hillaj Mansoor...no, that is not possible. These are people who have known the ultimate freedom—how can you possess them? They cannot fulfill your expectations, they cannot move according to you; they will have their own way. If it suits you, you have to be with them. You will not be able to force them to be with you; there is no way possible.

The truth cannot be with you—*you* have to be with the truth. But the lie is in your hands. You can manipulate it, you can make it look the way you want it to look, you can give it colors, you can cut it; you can give it form and shape, you can make it fit with your unconscious life. You can be a Hindu; it does not disturb your unconsciousness.

You can be a Mohammedan; it makes no transformation in you. You can be a Buddhist with no trouble at all, with no danger, with no insecurity. But to be with a buddha is to walk on fire! All that is nonessential in you will be burned and only the essential will survive— and the essential is very small in you. So much of you is false, and it is going to die.

To be with a buddha means a death.
Life comes afterwards, but death comes first.

Resurrection first is not possible; it can follow only if crucifixion has happened. It comes after the crucifixion. To be with a master is to be ready to die and ready to be born anew.

Religion is consolation, conformation.
Religiousness is revolution, rebellion.

Ajai Krishna Lakanpal has asked a long question about the Sufis who have died in the past— Muhinuddin Chisti, Nijamuddin Auliya, Baba Jan and others. He has asked about their majars, their graves—have they any power? He is a worshipper of these majars— a worshipper of graves! And he is asking me, "Are they not still vibrating with the energy of those great mystics?"

Being here with me he has no courage, no guts to be a sannyasin, but he goes to Ajmer to pay his respects to somebody who was alive a few hundred years ago. And I know perfectly well that if Muhinuddin Chisti was alive today, Ajai Krishna Lakanpal would not go there at all. And even if he did go there he would ask about the Kaaba, Bodhgaya, the graves of Buddha, Mahavira, Christ... Asking about the graves of other enlightened people is such a stupidity, but it looks as if you are asking a religious question.

Being here with me, if you cannot risk then of course you have to go and worship graves. And if you cannot feel the energy here, where else can you feel the energy? All that energy is your projection and nothing else. I am not saying that there is not any energy, but that energy can only be felt by those who have felt it with someone who is still alive. If you can feel the energy here, if you can get in harmony with this energy, you may be able to feel it at the *dargah* of Muhinuddin Chisti in Ajmer. But if you cannot feel it here, you cannot feel it there—that is impossible. If you cannot see God in man how can you see God in a rock? First you have to see God in man; only then will your insight deepen and will you be able to see God in the rock too.

First you have to be in contact with a living religiousness, then all religions become true in a new sense; otherwise they are just corpses. But they are comfortable—you can go and offer flowers and you can bow down, and the grave cannot do anything to you! You can come back with good feelings, that you have done something great, and you are the same old fool— nothing has happened to you. At the most you are a little more foolish than you were before, because now you are a religious fool. Before you were just an ordinary fool; now you have some pretensions of religion too. Now you will come home with that haughty feeling of holier-than-thou— just by going to a grave! And let me remind you, I am not saying that those graves have nothing; they have much, but only for those who have eyes. If you cannot see it in a living Sufi, in a living master, you are blind, you cannot see it in a grave at all.

But graves are good, because you are also dead and there is a certain adjustment. You are dead, the grave is dead; it feels very good – in the right company. You are a ghost and you would like very much to live with the ghosts.

You ask me: "People of almost all the religions try to convince other people to follow their respective religions. Why so?" That's a significant thing to ask. You may be surprised: they are not really trying to convince others; by convincing others they are trying to convince themselves that "We are not wrong." When they are able to convince somebody, again they feel at ease: "My religion is right, I am not wrong. Look, even somebody who never belonged to my religion is convinced." Christians go on converting people all over the world. The only reason is that *they* are not convinced of Christ yet.

The two most ancient religions in the world have been non-converting religions: the Jews and the Hindus. The Jews never converted anybody – they were so utterly convinced that there was no need to convince anybody else – the Hindus never tried to convince anybody. And these are the oldest religions in the world; in fact, all other religions are, in a sense, branches. Christianity and Islam are branches of Judaism; Jainism, Buddhism and Sikhism are branches of Hinduism. The most ancient traditions have been non-converting. Why? The reason was that they were convinced; they were so ancient and they were not in need of new converts. Their very ancientness gave them enough ground to be convinced that they were right. Not that they were right, but they had this illusion of being right because of their long heritage going back into prehistoric times. They had the ancientmost scriptures, and that was enough for them; that served their purpose.

But Christianity was a new religion; Christ had to start from *ABC*. Buddhism was new; Buddha had to start from *ABC*. Mohammedanism was new; Mohammed had to start from *ABC*—he had nothing behind him to fall back upon. The only way for the Mohammedans was to convert others. They were substituting tradition by converting people and creating a great mass of followers; that was their way of convincing themselves.

Hindus and Jews were convincing themselves in a different way, but Christians, Mohammedans and Buddhists could not do that; that was not possible for them. That avenue was closed; they had to open a new door. They became converting religions. The most unconvinced of all these were the Christians for the simple reason that the Jews had crucified Jesus. Now there was a great fear in the followers.

When Jesus left the world, the followers were in a deep darkness: their founder had been crucified with two criminals, two thieves...on both sides. He was treated like a criminal and he could not manage to do any miracle on the cross. There was a great shaking of the foundations. The Christians were very shaky, they were not grounded. They were very much afraid: "Who knows, we may have fallen into a trap. Jesus may not be the right messiah. The Jews could not recognize him – great scholars, rabbis, saints, could not recognize him at all. Who knows...?" That doubt persisted. The only way to destroy that doubt was to convert as many people to Christianity as possible—"If we can convert the whole earth, then it will be proof that we are right."

People think that a majority in numbers proves whether you are right or wrong. Now, you can take numbers in two ways: either you can count all the people who have gone before you in the past, or you can count the people who are still alive. If the door of tradition is closed, then you have to convert the contemporaries.

Christians became great converters, and they have converted almost half of humanity. Still some wound remains, still the doubt has not disappeared— and this is not the way to make it disappear. The heart has not yet become convinced, but the doubt still persists, the shadow lingers on.

Christians go on writing thousands of books proving that Jesus was the right messiah. What is the point? Who are you trying to convince? You cannot convince the Jews; you have tried for two thousand years and you have not been successful. Hindus are not at all interested whether Jesus was the right messiah; Jainas are not interested; Buddhists are not interested. Who are you trying to convince? You are trying to convince yourself.

You must have known this psychological phenomenon... When you are going alone into the forest on a dark night, you start whistling or singing a song, as if by singing a song the danger is averted, or that whistling is going to help. But in a psychological way it does something. When you start whistling you forget all about the fear—because the mind can do only one thing at a time, so when you are whistling you forget the fear. Moreover, when you start whistling you start hearing the whistle, and when you start hearing the whistle it gives you the fallacious idea that somebody else is there who is whistling, and that makes you feel a little at ease. It is the same phenomenon.

Christians are still whistling, still doubtful. And they have to be doubtful —they are responsible for their doubts. To prove to the Jews that Jesus is the right messiah, they have to brag and tell lies. For example, they say that he was born out of a virgin mother. That is sheer nonsense! Now, how can you ever be convinced of it? You may turn the whole earth towards Christianity, yet the doubt will persist. Any man who has even a little bit of intelligence can see the point, that this is stupid— Jesus cannot have been born out of a virgin mother. And then they have been saying that Jesus raised the dead, cured the blind...

But Jesus could not prove anything on the cross, where the real test was, when one hundred thousand people had gathered to see the miracle. And he had been doing all these small miracles, but only in front of his disciples, and they were not many. He had only twelve apostles and they were all villagers, uneducated—fishermen, woodcutters, carpenters, farmers, gardeners — simple people. He walked on water in front of these people; he raised the dead in front of these people; he cured the blind in front of these people. And when one hundred thousand people had gathered, the most educated and sophisticated of all the rabbis and all the scholars and all the professors in Jerusalem, he could not do anything.

Jesus was thirsty on the cross, and he could not even produce a cup of water for himself. And he had done miracles like transforming water into wine! He was thirsty and begging for water— he was dying. A great doubt had arisen even in his own mind whether he was really the messiah, whether he was really the son of God. He asked God, "Have you forsaken me? Why have you forsaken me? Is this the time to leave me alone, to betray me? I lived the whole of my life in trust—why are you not doing something to save me?"

And nothing happened. The sky remained silent— no miracle. The people must have gone home laughing. They must have all enjoyed the picnic and laughed. It must have been the gossip for a few days in the town, and people must have giggled about the whole affair—that this man was a fool, a pretender. Christians have not yet forgotten it; the wound has gone deep. But they are trying to cover it up.

Mohammed came later still; he came just fourteen hundred years ago. By that time humanity was almost divided; it was very difficult to find converts. Of course when he was alive he turned many people on, but the moment he was gone it was impossible for his followers to find converts. And, as far as argument was concerned, Mohammedans could not argue with the Buddhists. Buddhism had reached as far as central Asia. By that time there were temples of Buddha all over Asia, particularly in central Asia. And to argue with Buddhist logicians is the most difficult thing. The Buddhist logicians and philosophers have touched the highest possibility of intellectual grasp. It is impossible to argue with the Jaina philosophers. Even Pythagoras remembers them. He met them in Egypt. He calls them gymnosophists, and he describes them as naked people who argued with such intelligence that it was impossible to refute them. It is very difficult to refute Buddhists and Jainas; it is very difficult to prove that Mohammed was a greater miracle man than Jesus.

So Mohammedans were in a difficulty, and the only way was the sword. Intellect was not going to work, so they started cutting off people's heads. If you cannot cut their arguments, cut their heads – because might is right! They went on a rampage. They killed thousands, murdered, butchered, and converted people forcibly: "For *your* sake, of course, for your own good, because if you are not a Mohammedan you are not going to achieve paradise, you will fall into hell." They were trying hard to save people, but in fact they were trying to convince themselves that Mohammed was as good as Buddha or Jesus or Mahavira or Krishna.

My people are not interested in converting anybody, because they don't have any doubt. They are not here with me to be convinced, they are here with me because they are already convinced as far as their hearts are concerned. And if they are not convinced, they are free to leave; there is no need to be here at all.

I am not interested in the masses and the crowds; I am interested only in the chosen few, I am interested only in the spiritually aristocratic, the very few intelligent people. So if your heart is dancing with me, good. If it is not dancing with me, then this is not the right place for you— you are free to leave.

And my people will never try to convince anybody—at least not while I am alive! When I am gone, nothing can be done about it; then there is no guarantee. While I am alive they will not try to convince anybody.

But without any of my people convincing you, you have come here; that is far more important. Something of their joy has caught you, some glimpse in their eyes has touched you. Something special in their vibe has brought you here. This would not have been possible if they had argued. Argument is very gross and the work of real energy is very subtle.

I receive thousands of letters from all over the world: "There is certainly something strange in your orange people. They don't argue, they are not like Jehovah's Witnesses. They are not like Hare Krishna people, always carrying the *Bhagavadgita* and trying to force things into your head whether you are willing or not. They don't interfere in anybody's life."

But their non-interference is far more effective. That shows that they have found something, that shows that they have discovered something. Their very being is vibrant with their discovery. They are joyous, they are happy, they are cheerful. They are living their life as creatively as possible.

Now all kinds of creativity are happening here. There are dance groups, there are music groups, there is a theater group, there is an art group, and soon there will be many more—sculptors, architects, scientists, poets, novelists. Everybody is going to be here, and they will all share their joy through creativity. If their creativity can convince you, then that is a totally different matter. If their very life can become a light to you, that is a totally different thing. But they are not going to force anybody. I am not in favor of coercing people.

You say to me: "People of almost all the religions try to convince other people to follow their respective religions." They are religious and this is only a religiousness – at least right now it is only a religiousness. It is only a quality, vague, fluid, flowing, dynamic; it has not become stagnant yet. It can become stagnant only when I am gone. While I am alive I will go on stirring—I will never allow you to settle anywhere. I will go on and on calling you to new adventures, challenging you to new explorations.

You also say: "But I have met many of your followers and they always discourage me from adopting the way you are preaching." They are not my followers, just my friends. To be a follower is ugly. I am not a leader, so how can you be a follower? For you to be a follower, first I have to be a leader, and that very word is ugly.

I am nobody's leader; I am just living my life, doing my thing. And the people who enjoy being with me, they are welcome. It is a friendship. We are fellow travelers. Maybe there is a little difference: I am awake, they are asleep—so what? I was asleep, now I am awake.

Of Course the Grass Grows by Itself

They are asleep, tomorrow they will be awake. Their very sleep proves only one thing, that they have the capacity to be awake.

And I don't disturb anybody's sleep prematurely! When I see the person is going to wake up anyhow, then I just give him a little nudge. I don't nag people, I don't go on nagging them, "Wake up! Wake up!" because if you nag a sleepy person to wake up too much, he may start dreaming that he has awakened. That is a difficulty...because the mind can create all kinds of dreams. It can even create the dream that one is awakened, that one is enlightened. And even here it happens to a few people.

Now Siddhartha is here from Germany; it is happening to him. In his dream he has become enlightened—or approximately. And, be aware, when a German becomes enlightened, then he becomes perfectly enlightened!

Just a few days ago I was talking about Proper Sagar, the perfect Englishman. Somebody has asked me, "Do you know why he is perfect?" I know, but I cannot tell you because he will feel very offended, very offended. He is such a perfect Englishman that if I tell you the truth he will be very offended. If you promise me not to tell anybody, then I can share it: he is really a German pretending to be an Englishman. No Englishman can defeat him! There are hundreds of Englishmen here— has anybody the guts to defeat Proper Sagar? Impossible! When a German tries to be anybody he is always perfect. To be German means to be perfect—they are synonymous.

So it is happening in Germany: Siddhartha is dreaming that he has become enlightened. And I go on playing jokes: I have given him one of my chairs and one of my robes! So with my robe on he sits in the chair— and being a German he is very methodical: on one side sits a woman who is Mukta; on the other side are two women, one who is Vivek, the other Laxmi. And in front of Laxmi is a man who is Shiva. Germans do things perfectly!

Another German, Gunakar, is here. Siddhartha is very simple, a nice guy, but Gunakar is an advocate, a great legal expert, so he is going about it more methodically, more legally. Now he has closed himself in a room...just the way I live in a room he lives in a room; he does not come out, he does not write.... He has a secretary— a woman, of course. He does not allow anybody to touch his body.

The reason people are prevented from touching my feet has nothing to do with enlightenment—it is just that my toes are in difficulty. To touch my toes hurts them badly, so people have to be prevented. Gunakar must have seen that nobody is allowed to touch my feet anymore, so he is preventing people from touching him "because his energy gets disturbed"! And both of them are here!

So if you try to wake up people in their sleep, the great danger is that they may wake up, but not really, only in sleep; they may dream that they are awake and in their dreams they may start playing all kinds of games of enlightenment, spirituality, religiousness. One has to be very aware not to disturb anybody before the right time.

So I persuade you, I seduce you towards awakening. But I am not in a hurry – it cannot be done in a hurry. I have to wait, and when I see that you are just coming out of your sleep, only then a little shaking helps and you are fully awake. Even if you are not shaken up at the last moment, you may awaken. It may be a little later; it is just a question of time. The master has to be watchful not to be in a hurry, because sometimes it happens that you see people in misery and you would like to help them immediately, but to help them immediately may harm them more if they are not ready to wake up.

So my people are not my followers, they are just my friends, my lovers—they have fallen in love with me. And as you know, love is blind; it is not a logical thing, so how can they convince you? They have not connected themselves with me through logic; it has been an illogical jump. They can only share their joy with you, and if that brings you here it is good.

And certainly my sannyasins will tell you not to follow me, because that's exactly what my teaching is: not to follow me. Each individual is unique; nobody has to become an imitator. And they will discourage you from adopting the way I am preaching—they will discourage you so that you can find yourself. Otherwise, people are very willing to believe. Belief is so cheap; it costs nothing to believe.

My people will discourage you from believing, from following, from adopting the way I am teaching. If you become interested you have to come here and explore yourself. It is an exploration. It is an adventure into the unknown. It is going beyond the familiar, beyond that which can be comprehended, beyond that which the mind can cope with. It is a journey into the beyond. It is very delicate, far more delicate than the petals of a rose. You can destroy it very easily; any coercive effort and it is destroyed. So they bring you here without any coercion, without any logic. They only invite you, and that too not directly—very indirectly. And they will discourage you from following me, because it is not a question of following me; the real question is of following your own light.

All that I can do is to help you find the way that reaches to your own innermost light. I can show you the way. And when you have found your light you will have to live your own life. It will not be as a Christian, it will not be as a Hindu, it will not be Mohammedan; it will simply be your life, nobody else's.

The second question

> I have heard you know something about this guy Murphy and some of his golden rules. Please tell us some!

I don't know much about this guy Murphy, but I don't know much about anything else either!

I am not a man of knowledge; I function from a state of not knowing, and I have found that that is the most beautiful space to function from.

I have heard a few of the golden rules of this guy Murphy, so I will tell you a few.

George Bernard Shaw has written a beautiful book, *Maxims For A Revolutionary*. The first maxim is a beautiful one: The first golden rule is that there are no golden rules. But Murphy has improved upon it, and George Bernard Shaw would have appreciated it very much.

Murphy's first golden rule is: Whoever has the gold makes the rules.

Second: Never think of the future – it comes soon enough.

Third: For every credibility gap there is a gullibility fill.

Fourth: Youth looks ahead, old age looks back, middle age looks worried.

Fifth: Youth is when you blame all your troubles on your parents; maturity is when you learn that everything is the fault of the younger generation.

Sixth: The best thing about the golden old days is that they cannot come back.

Seventh: Being frustrated is disagreeable, but the real disasters in life begin when you get what you want.

Eighth: The solution to a problem changes the problems.

Ninth: Almost anything is easier to get into than to get out of.

Tenth: Beauty is only skin deep, ugly goes to the bone.

Eleventh: Celibacy is not hereditary.

Twelfth: Friends come and go, but enemies accumulate.

And thirteenth: If you think education is experience, try ignorance.

The last question

Yesterday in lecture you said that laughter was natural. I have also heard you say that what is natural is easy and right. Why do I find it so difficult to laugh—even at your jokes?

Laughter is natural, but you are not natural; hence the meeting cannot happen. You will have to be natural too. And, yes, I say what is natural is easy and right, but because you are not natural you are neither easy nor right. Your whole upbringing makes you artificial, arbitrary; it destroys your nature. It imposes something else that others want— it imposes the opinions of others upon you. There are vested interests that would like you to be a certain way. They don't want you to be natural—they are afraid of nature.

Somewhere deep down in man there is fear of nature. That fear of nature has created many problems. It has created an ugly civilization, a rotten culture, an anti-nature technology, a science against ecology, a religion which is not in tune with your innermost being. It is time for man to revolt against all this that has happened to humanity in the past!

But why is man afraid of nature? There are reasons. The first is: nature is bigger than your ego, and if nature is allowed, the ego cannot be in control. Then nature will control you. Then you will not feel that you are in control, and you would like to be in control. So rather than being natural, you repress your nature and you claim only a small spot of your being. Only one tenth of your being can be controlled by the ego. Then you feel the master, you are the master. With nature you are not the master; with nature you are nowhere, you don't exist at all. And the ego creates everything—the ego creates morality, and morality is against nature.

For example, what can you do if you fall in love with a woman who is not your wife? That falling in love is natural, but you have to look to other things— your marriage, your prestige, your respectability, your society, your religion, your future, your salary, your job, your business—and not only in this world but in the other world too. You will have to answer to God why you fell in love. It is better to prevent nature, to close nature completely, so you remain confined in the rules and regulations of your society, culture, religion.

You are taught ambitiousness, and nature is non-ambitious. Nature has no instinct in it to be the president of a country or to be the prime minister of a country. Nature would like to dance, sing, love, eat, sleep, to go swimming, take a sunbath... But nature will not bother to become the president of a country—nature is not that stupid. Who wants to become President Reagan? A third-rate film actor has become the president of America. Now all the third-rate people will be feeling great, will be feeling that now they can also make it. All kinds of stupid fools, mediocre people, become so prominent that if you want to be prominent you have to be mediocre.

Nature is very intelligent. It is not mediocre, it is not stupid; it is tremendously clear, clean, transparent. You have to destroy its transparency, and then naturally you become sad. Then you cannot laugh. Laughter becomes impossible...because laughter is a natural phenomenon. You can be sad, you can be miserable; that is not natural, that is cultivated.

Kevala, you cannot laugh because you are not natural. Relax and drop all that is unnatural in you—all pretensions, pseudo coverings, masks. Be just ordinary. To be ordinary is the greatest thing in the world. Let me say it in this way: to be ordinary is the most extraordinary thing in the world. And why is it extraordinary?—because the desire to be extraordinary is very ordinary. Hence, to be ordinary is really extraordinary. Only very few people have been able to manage it up to now.

Just be ordinary and laughter will come to you, unless it has gone very deep in you—unless, Kevala, you have been brought up by Catholics, Jainas, or in some other kind of unnatural way of life; unless you are an ex-nun! Then it will be difficult, but not impossible. I have destroyed many nuns here! Now even if you try to find them you will be surprised— you will not be able to find any monks and nuns.

If you want to know a really destroyed nun, meet Chintana. She has been a great nun. When she came it was impossible for her to laugh, and now I think she is the most laughing woman around here! Whenever she comes to see me I always tell her to go into gibberish. She is the most perfect at gibberish. She makes such beautiful sounds, meaningless; she starts speaking all kinds of languages which nobody understands. But she goes into it really passionately, deeply. One would never have thought that a nun could do this!

How do nuns and monks make love?
Out of habit.

Kevala, are you a nun? Then drop the habit! Or perhaps you are in more dangerous waters— you may be a Polack! To be a nun is only a question of a few years of conditioning, but to be a Polack needs many incarnations!

Have you heard the story of the Polack lesbian?
She loved men.

The Polack patient lying on the operating table whispers to the surgical-masked doctor, "You can take your mask off now, doctor, I have recognized you!"

In a school in Poland the teacher asks, "Has any of you ever saved somebody's life?"
A little boy raises his arm, "Yes, my little nephew's."
"How did it happen? Tell us!" asks the teacher.
The little Polack says, "I hid my sister's birth control pills!"

The unmarried Polack cleaning woman had a baby. When asked by a social worker about the father of the child, she replied curtly, "Dunno! You think I turn around every time I clean the stairs?"

The phone is ringing in the doctor's office. He picks it up and hears the desperate voice of a Polack woman: "Hello, Doc! Did I leave my underpants in your room after the medical examination?"

"No," replies the doctor, "they are not here."

Half an hour later she calls again. "Hello, Doc, it's me again. Don't worry anymore, I found them—they were at the dentist's!"

Come out of your unnaturalness! Come out of your Polackness! Laughter is one of the most important things in life. The person who misses laughter is going to miss God too.

I can tell you categorically that when you reach God he is not going to ask you what sins you have committed and what virtues you have accumulated. He will ask, "Have you brought some new jokes?" He always asks that! He must be getting tired—since eternity he has been sitting there doing nothing. Of course the grass grows by itself, but what can you do with the grass? One gets tired seeing the grass growing by itself!

Kevala, collect a few beautiful jokes before you leave this body. Listen to my suggestion—I am really serious about it!

Enough for today.

CHAPTER 14

The Forgotten But Not the Lost

The second question

Why does everybody think enlightenment is a joke?

It is! But only a child can ask such a beautiful question – Sarito is only twelve years of age. Enlightenment is a joke because it is not something that you have to achieve, yet you have to make all possible efforts to achieve it. It is already the case: you are born enlightened.

The word "enlightenment" is beautiful. We come from the source, the ultimate source of light. We are small rays of that sun, and howsoever far away we may have gone, our nature remains the same. Nobody can go against his real nature: you can forget about it, but you cannot lose it. Hence, attaining it is not the right expression; it is not attained, it is only remembered. That's why Buddha called his method *sammasati*.

Sammasati means right remembrance of that which is already there. Nanak, Kabir, Raidas, they have all called it *surati*. Surati means remembering the forgotten, but not the lost. Whether you remember or not, it is there — it is there exactly the same. You can keep your eyes closed to it— it is there. You can open your eyes—it is there. You can keep it behind your back—it is there. You can take a one-hundred-and-eighty-degree turn and see it—it is there. It is the same.

George Gurdjieff used to call his method self-remembering. Nothing has to be achieved, nothing at all, but only to be discovered. And the discovery is needed because we go on gathering dust on our mirrors. The mirror is there covered by the dust. Remove the dust, and the mirror starts reflecting the stars, the beyond. Krishnamurti calls it awareness, alertness, attentiveness. These are different expressions for the same phenomenon. They are to remind you that you are not to go anywhere, not to be somebody else. You just have to find out who you are, and the finding is not difficult because it is your nature— just a little reshuffling inside, a little cleaning.

It is said that when Bodhidharma attained enlightenment, he laughed for seven days continuously. His friends, his disciples, thought he had gone mad. They asked him, "Have you gone mad?"

He said, "I *was* mad, now I have become sane. I have gone sane!"

"Then why are you laughing?" they asked.

He said, "I am laughing because I have been searching for thousands of lives for something which was already within me! The seeker was the sought, and I was looking everywhere else—I was looking everywhere except inside."

The famous Sufi woman, Rabiya al-Adabiya, one evening when the sun was setting, was found searching for something just in front of her door on the road. A few people gathered and they said, "Rabiya, what have you lost? We can help you."

She was an old woman and loved by the people, loved because she was beautifully crazy. Rabiya said, "I have lost my needle. I was sewing and I lost my needle. I am searching for it, and there is not much time because the sun is setting. If you want to help me, help quickly, because once the sun has set and darkness has descended, it will be impossible to find the needle."

So they all started a hectic search for the needle. One of them suddenly thought, "The needle is such a small thing and the road is so big, and the sun is going down every moment, the light is disappearing —unless we know the exact spot where it has fallen it will be impossible to find it." So he asked Rabiya, "Will you please tell us where the needle has fallen exactly? Then it will be possible to find it. Otherwise soon there will be darkness, and the road is very big and the needle is very small."

Rabiya started laughing. She said, "Please don't ask that, because I feel embarrassed by the question!"

They all stopped searching. They said, "What is the matter? Why should you feel embarrassed?"

She said, "I feel embarrassed because I lost the needle *inside* the house, but because there is no light there, how can I find it? Outside on the road there is just a little light from the setting sun."

The Forgotten But Not the Lost

They all said, "Now you have gone completely crazy! We had always suspected that you were not sane, but this is an absolute proof!"

Rabiya said, "You think me insane, yet you have been doing the same for lives together—and *you* are sane? Where have you lost yourself, and where are you trying to find it? Where have you lost your bliss, and where are you trying to find it? It is lost in your inner world, and you are searching on the outside!"

Everywhere people are running with great speed. Time is short, the sun is setting; any moment the darkness can descend. Run as fast as you can! Man has been inventing faster and faster ways to reach, but if you ask him, "Where do you want to reach?" he feels embarrassed; he is not really clear where he wants to reach. One thing he is clear about is that he wants to reach there quickly, because life is short and much has to be found. The soul, God, bliss, truth, freedom....so many things have to be found, and his hands are absolutely empty.

Sarito, in that sense enlightenment is certainly a joke. If you understand it, there is no need to seek and search; you can just close your eyes and find it. But this question coming from a small child is beautiful. The grown-up person will not be able to ask such a sane question. The grown-up person will ask, "What is enlightenment? How has it to be found? What are the right methods, ways and means? How should one live? What virtues should be cultivated? What prayers should be said?" And all those questions look very relevant.

Your question does not look very relevant, but it *is* relevant, more relevant than any grown-up person can ever ask. Grown-up people ask questions which look good in the asking, but they are not really interested in asking an authentic question—they are *afraid* of asking the authentic question.

In an old Scottish mansion the resident ghost is floating through the living room. Everybody seems to be scared to death except a little boy who is watching the spectacle with a curious look on his face.

"Hey, Mister Ghost," he says, "have you lost your handkerchief?"

"No," replied the ghost, "that's not a handkerchief, that's my son!"

But only a small boy could have asked, "Hey, Mister Ghost..." All the grown-ups were very much scared; they must have been trembling, avoiding, pretending that they had not seen anything.

One little boy asked the other, "Did that play you saw last night have a happy ending?"

The other one said, "I'll say. Everybody was happy when it was over."

The Christian priest was telling the little boy, "Herb, I want you to remember that we are here to help others."

Herb said, "Sure, but what are the others here for?"

"I never slept with a man until I married your father!" she declared emphatically to her unconventional teenage daughter. "Will you be able to say the same thing to your daughter?"

"Yes, Mother," replied the girl, "but not with such a straight face!"

Mummy and Daddy are talking about the Millers who live next door. "Well, the stork is going to pay them a visit for the fourth time soon," says Daddy.

Their little son laments, "They get one baby after another. And you—what are you doing? Hanging around doing nothing!"

Children are very perceptive! You cannot deceive them.

They were discussing the attraction older men have for young girls.

"My grandfather was like that. Young girls were crazy about him."

"Was he crazy about them too?"

"He certainly was. He used to cut a notch on his cane after every conquest. And that's what killed him."

"How?"

"Well, one day he made the mistake of leaning on his cane!"

Sariyo, you must have heard this comment amongst the small sannyasins in the ashram: "Why does everybody think enlightenment is a joke?" This must be coming from the small boys and girls; they must be thinking, "Enlightenment must be a joke. What is the need for enlightenment?" You need a teddy bear—you can understand that. You need a tricycle—that you can understand. You need a toy gun—that you can understand.

Just a few days ago a new visitor was seen carrying a big gun. The guards became a little bit concerned; he was continuously carrying it and even trying to hide it, but it was too big to hide. Then one woman sannyasin saw him also carrying the gun in the marketplace. The visitor was asked, "Why do you carry this gun?"

He said, "I feel so embarrassed, but what to do? I have brought my little son with me and he loves the gun! Without the gun he goes nowhere, and the gun is so big he cannot carry it himself, so I have to carry it; otherwise he won't go anywhere, and I cannot leave him alone! His mother has not come; I was not aware that I would have to do this thing. Everywhere people are asking me, 'Why are you carrying this gun?' And this is only a toy gun! I feel embarrassed, I try to hide it, but the more I try to hide it the more people become curious—'Why?'"

Children have their own interests and they must be wondering, "Why? What is this enlightenment? And why are so many people interested in it? It must be some kind of joke!"

In fact, it is a cosmic joke. It is God seeking himself. It is a game of hide-and-seek: God hides himself and then tries to find himself! Being alone, what else to do?

When I used to travel in India—for twenty years continuously—many times it happened that I would be in a train compartment with only one passenger. And because I was not interested in talking to the passenger, he would start playing patience— a game of cards you can play alone, you need not have any partner. They would feel a little embarrassed, but I would not pay any attention to them so they would start playing cards.

One day one man said, "You must think that I am crazy playing cards alone."

I said, "I don't think you are crazy. This is my business too!"

He said, "What do you mean? You also play patience?"

I said, "No, but enlightenment is like patience!"

Enlightenment is a dialogue with yourself, it is a monologue. You have to ask the question and you have to give the answer. When you see the futility, you become silent. That's how Buddha became silent! Then one sits under the tree "doing nothing, and the spring comes and the grass grows by itself." And what to do? — when the grass grows you have to cut it and *again* sit silently, and *again* the grass grows so you cut it again. Again and again...!

Just the other day I was talking about Gunakar. This is the third time he has become enlightened, and he will become enlightened many more times. Now he is feeling very sad—after each enlightenment he feels very sad. He is doing something impossible; nobody has done it before. After enlightenment people never feel sad again, but after each enlightenment he feels very sad. In fact, one enlightenment has always proved enough, more than enough! Three times he become enlightened; then he becomes unenlightened again— and then the great sadness.

But he cannot control himself. The urge to become enlightened is so irresistible that within three or four months he will again forget and will become enlightened. To be enlightened may be a joke, but to become unenlightened is not a joke, it is a really serious affair!

So when he came for blessing the other night he could not even look at me. I tried in every way, but he went on looking down, up, here, there, but he wouldn't look at me. I forced his third eye very much, but what can you do? — Germans don't have any third eye! You can go on pushing and pushing, and nothing happens!

The second question

> What part of Moses' teaching in the Sinai desert could bring down the ages such a chain of suffering to the Israelination? Is there any fate for a nation? And from your knowledge, did the Jews have any chain for transferring the Torah from one master to the other?

These two religions, Judaism and Hinduism, are the most ancient religions in the world. Just because they are the most ancient, they are the most rotten too! And out of this rottenness, what else can you expect? The mind of man clings to the old. And religion is not like wine, that the older it is the better; the fresher it is, the better. Religion is not wine, it is just a hot cup of tea, an old, ancient cup of tea... But thousands of flies, and pundits and rabbis will be found in it; there will not be much tea in it at all! And it was bound to happen.

The Hindus and the Jews both became dominated by the pundits, the scholars, theologians, rabbis. They lost track of the enlightened masters. Even though sometimes enlightened people happened in spite of the rotten tradition, they were not accepted, they were rejected.

Hinduism rejected Buddha, and Buddha was the peak of the whole Hindu consciousness—the greatest peak, the Everest. But Hindus rejected him for the simple reason that if he had been accepted that would have meant the death of the whole establishment—the exploitation and oppression by the priests—and they had great vested interests in it.

The same has been true of Judaism. Jesus was the peak, but the Jews rejected Jesus. In that very rejection, they rejected their own flowering. They remained a tree without flowers, in fact even without foliage—just a dead tree with no leaves, with no greenery, with no flowers, with no birds singing, no shade for travelers to sit underneath.

Whenever enlightened masters are rejected by any tradition, that is an indication that the tradition is absolutely dead; it cannot absorb any new, fresh insight. The living tradition is that which is capable of absorbing new insights. And they are always coming—God is not finished yet with creation. The idea that God finished within six days and then rested on the seventh is sheer nonsense. God is not finished yet—he will never be finished. God is not a person but creativity, not a creator but creativity. It goes on and on; God is still working. And there is no holiday for God, because the work itself is holy, the work itself is joy. When the work is not a joy, then you need a holiday; when it is tiring, when you are not in love with it, then you need a holiday. When you love it, it is a holiday, it is relaxation, it is rest. God is still at work, but the priest cannot accept it.

The Hindu priest says that God gave his message in the Vedas and that was the end of it. He gave all that was needed by man; nothing more is needed at all. And the Jews think that the Old Testament is the end of the story. It is only the beginning, not the end. And beginnings cannot be very great, remember, they are bound to be childish.

Remember the difference between childlike and childish: to be childlike is to be a sage, to be childish is not to be a sage. To be childish means to be immature; it needs much improvement, growth, maturity.

Judaism and Hinduism both have remained immature. They had the opportunity to become mature. Buddha could have transformed the whole Hindu world, he could have given it splendor, but he was rejected; the priests would not allow him entry. The Jews would have been the most significant people on the earth if Jesus had been absorbed. But strange are the ways of man, very strange: the Jews have been waiting and waiting for centuries for this same man, Jesus, to come. They were waiting for the Messiah to come, and when he came they rejected him —they rejected him absolutely.

The priesthood is like a cancer to every religion. The priesthood destroys every religious possibility, the very potential; it poisons the very source. That is the first thing to be understood. The priests are businesslike, they are businessmen. They are selling some invisible commodity to the world, and because the commodity is invisible, it is very easy to sell. Because it is invisible you cannot catch them at what they are doing.

I have heard that a New York shop advertised that invisible hairpins had arrived, and there was a great queue of women. Invisible hairpins – who can miss? And they were selling like hotcakes.

A woman went in, she looked in the box—they were invisible hairpins, so what was there to see? — an empty box! She said, "But are they really there?"

And the salesman said, "Lady, they are *invisible* hairpins! In fact, the truth is for three weeks we have been out of stock, but still they are selling! What difference can it make? When the pins are invisible, whether they are in stock or out of stock makes no difference!"

Whether God exists or not, whether there is a heaven or not, whether there is a hell or not does not matter — these are invisible commodities, and priests have been selling these invisible commodities.

People like Jesus or Buddha are very pragmatic, very realistic. They don't sell invisible commodities; they start making a great effort to make God visible on the earth. They themselves are a visible expression of God. Now, the priests cannot tolerate this. What will happen to their invisible commodities? And it is such a vast establishment.

The Jews have been dominated by the rabbis, not by masters. The rabbi is the exact equivalent of a pundit. He knows the scriptures, but he is cunning, clever. He theorizes, he exploits your misery, he consoles you, he gives you comforts...but he is in business. And because the enlightened masters have not been accepted by the Jews, the whole community has become a community of businessmen; it has lost all other qualities.

I have heard the old story...

God wanted to sell the commandments. He asked a great Vedic seer, Yagnavalka, "Would you like to have the commandments?"

Yagnavalka looked at the commandments and he said, "No, because if you prohibit us from killing, our whole religion will be destroyed, because in our *yagnas*, in our worship, in our religious rituals, killing is a must."

You will be surprised to know that today Hindus talk so much about nonviolence, but they are the most ancient of violent people on the earth. Not only that, but they gave violence a religious color. Even cows were slaughtered in their religious rituals, and not only cows, but even men were slaughtered. And still, once in a while, it happens that small children are slaughtered in a religious ceremony, in a religious ritual. And this country calls itself nonviolent!

Yagnavalka said, "No, we don't want the commandments. 'Thou shalt not kill' — then what will happen to our religion?"

God asked the French people. They said, "No, without adultery our whole joy will be lost! How can we exist without adultery? Adultery is the whole game of life that makes it enchanting, meaningful, that gives it some ecstasy, some excitement. No, it is not possible" — and so on and so forth.

God went to all the races, and then finally, as a last resort he asked Moses, "Would you like to have the commandments?"

Moses asked, "How much?"

And God said, "Free of charge."

Then Moses said, "I will have ten!" He never looked to see what those commandments were — if they are free, then why not have ten?

That's how the Ten Commandments came into the hands of the Jews! The Jews became a society basically of businessmen. That created great hatred against the Jews. They became cunning, clever, and people became jealous of them.

You ask me: "What part of Moses' teaching in the Sinai desert could bring down the ages such a chain of suffering to the Israeli nation?"

Moses' basic revolution was not religious, it was political. He was fighting against the slavery imposed by the Egyptians on the Israelis. Hence the color of his revolution was less religious and more political. That's why in Judaism you will not find enlightened masters like Buddha, Lao Tzu or Krishna, but you will find prophets.

The word "prophet" is absolutely irrelevant in the Eastern context. You cannot call Buddha a prophet; he has nothing to do with prophecy. You cannot call Mahavira a prophet, you cannot call Lao Tzu a prophet — the word will not fit — but all the Jewish religious leaders are prophets. The prophet is a special thing that has happened to Judaism. The prophet is something in between the religious master and the political leader — a crossbreed. He is religious *and* political.

Moses' inspiration was basically political. Nothing is wrong with it — he was fighting for freedom, he was fighting against slavery. It is good, but the fight was on the outside; the religious fight is inner. That beginning made Jews very outward, very extrovert. That extroversion made them businesslike. They lost track of the inner world. Yes, once in a while a few people escaped from this pattern—Jesus escaped, but he was crucified. Then other masters learned that if you want to escape it is better to escape silently. Then silent societies existed, silent mystery schools existed in the deserts, in the caves. And Hassidism in particular is the fragrance of the whole Judaic religion. If the whole Judaic religion is destroyed and we can save Hassidism, then all is saved. It is exactly the same: if we can save Sufism and the whole of Mohammedanism disappears from the world, nothing is lost. If we can save Zen then the whole of Buddhism can be forgotten, because that is the very essence of it.

But the Hasids learned that it was better to live inside the conventional mode; it was unnecessary to get crucified. After Jesus they learned one thing: don't proclaim; Jews won't accept it. The extrovert people become desertlike inside, and that creates hatred against them.

A beggar asked a rich Jew for something to eat.

The Jew says, "You look very Jewish and I am in a good mood today, so if you can guess rightly which of my eyes is a glass eye I will give you something."

The beggar looks into the Jew's face and after a short glance says, "Your left one is the glass eye."

"That's right! But, tell me, how did you find out?" asks the Jew.

"It looks human."

Jacob gets off the plane and arrives at customs with three bags and one parrot. The customs officer, opening the first bag, sees that it is full of coffee. "Who's all this coffee for?" he inquires.

"It's for the parrot to eat!" replies Jacob.

The customs officer then opens the second bag which is full of tape recorders, radios and watches. "And who is *this* for?" he demands.

"For the parrot to eat!" responds calm Jacob.

Opening the third bag, the officer stares unbelievingly at a suitcase full of gold and precious jewels. "And these jewels?" he shouts. "Are these for the parrot to eat too?"

"Yes," replies our traveler. "Everything is for the parrot to eat!"

"And if the parrot doesn't eat these things?" says the officer sarcastically.

"If the parrot doesn't eat them? If the parrot doesn't eat them?" repeats an unbelieving Jacob. "Well then, if the parrot doesn't eat, Jacob sells everything!"

Sergeant Kazawinsky of the Polish police force was attending the entrance examination for officer training.

"What are rabies, and how would you treat them?" he was asked.

The Polack was obviously puzzled and thought for a few moments. Then he brightened visibly. "Rabies are Jewish ministers, and I treats them with contempt!"

In a German prisoner-of-war camp the commandant announced over the loudspeakers: "I have some good news for you. Today is sports day. The English will play cricket on the cricket field, the Americans will play baseball on the baseball field, the Indians will play hockey on the hockey field, and the Jews will play hopscotch...in the mine field!"

Adolf, the greatest conqueror of all times, asks Satan for a forty-eight-hour holiday on earth. After some hesitation, his wish is granted. However, he is back in hell after only twenty-four hours.

His comment: "Everything is topsy-turvy on earth. The Jews are into wars and the Germans are into money making!"

But things are changing. The time for a great change has come. The Jews have suffered much, but the basic cause is within themselves. Their rejection of Jesus has been the major part of their suffering. Secondly, they became extroverts, interested only in money and power; they lost their interiority. And any man who loses his inner world becomes shallow, empty, hollow, meaningless.

You ask me: "Is there any fate for a nation?"

No, we create our fate; hence we can change it any moment we decide. We are born in absolute freedom; then it is our choice what to be.

You ask me: "And from your knowledge, did the Jews have any chain for transferring the Torah from one master to the other?"

It has been there, but only in the Hassidic tradition, not in the ordinary formal Jewish religion. The Hasids have been thought to be mad people, but they carry the real essence, and that essence has nothing to do with Jews or Hindus or Mohammedans or Christians or Jainas or Buddhists. It is the same— it is a kind of religiousness. It has been carried from the master to the disciple. But that is not part of the main tradition; that has gone to the side — small labyrinths, but not the main asphalt road. The main Jewish current has been very worldly; it has lost track of all religion. But a few people have dared to go into the jungles on their own, alone, and they are the most beautiful people the world has ever known.

My love is for Hasids, for Sufis, for Zen people, for Tantrikas, for Yogis, for Taoists. These are non-formal people; they don't really belong to any tradition as such, to any church as such, to any race as such, but they are the real people of God.

The last question

There are sannyasins living all over the world who feel a deep connection with you. However, on celebration days there is always that longing to be in your silent presence in Buddha Hall. Can you please send a message to the thousands of sannyasins who will be celebrating in many countries, but not in your physical presence? How about a few special jokes for us?

Remember one thing: that each of my sannyasins carries something of me, each of my sannyasins becomes a part of me, spiritually, physically, in every possible way. My sannyasins are not believers, my sannyasins are in a love affair. It is a *mad* phenomenon! So wherever my sannyasins meet, my presence will be felt. Wherever my sannyasins celebrate, my message is realized, because celebration is my message.

Rejoice! Sing! Dance!

Dance so totally that your egos melt and disappear.

Dance so totally that the dancer is no longer there, but only the dance remains. Then you will find me wherever you are.

And it has now to be a known and recognized fact that my buddhafield is not going to be confined to the small place where I will be living with a few thousand sannyasins. All the small communes, ashrams, centers, all over the world will become little buddhafields. We have to fill the whole earth with buddhafields! We have to create a chain of buddhafields. And it can be done: if you can take some of my joy and some of my love and some of my laughter with you wherever you go, you will be taking the fragrance of the buddhafield there. You will be taking seeds.

Scientists say that in the beginning only one seed must have reached the earth by some coincidence – maybe a collision of stars, the explosion of a star. One seed, and the whole earth slowly, slowly became green. One seed is enough to transform the whole earth into a garden.

The same is true on higher planes too. Just a single seed of love, awareness, joy, is enough to create the buddhafield. So wherever you go, wherever you are, never forget for a moment that you are not far away from me.

Between a master and the disciple the question is not of physical distance at all. You can be sitting here physically, but you may not be in tune with me; then you are not here. You may be thousands of miles away, maybe on the moon, on Mars, it does not make any difference. But if your heart is beating with me, if you are attuned to me, if there is an inner connection, then you are in my physical presence. Neither time makes any difference nor space. The thing that makes the difference is love.

Next time when you celebrate, celebrate with the full recognition that I am there amongst you. Just a recognition is needed and you will find me there.

Jesus is reported to have said, "Wherever four of my disciples are gathered together, I will be there." And he was not so fortunate as I am —his disciples were very ordinary people. I am fortunate in many ways: my disciples are in many ways very creative, talented, very intelligent, exploding in love. So I can say to you that not even four are needed; just a single sannyasin is enough to make my presence felt by others.

So next time you are celebrating, make it a point that I am there, and you will feel it. It only needs a recognition. If the recognition is not there, and even if I suddenly reach your celebration, you will not recognize me at all.

It happened with Jesus...the story is:

When he escaped from the cave in which his body was kept, when he resurrected after three days, obviously he tried to find out where his followers were. He found two followers who had lived with him for years, and he waited for them to recognize him. He walked with them for miles, because they were going to another town. They talked — they talked about Jesus, they talked about the crucifixion, they talked about many things — but those two disciples could not recognize that the man they were talking to was Jesus himself. It was as if a cloud prevented them. The cloud was that they were thinking that he was dead, finished, so there was no question of even asking, thinking, reconsidering who this man was. They recognized him only when they sat in a small hotel to eat their lunch. When Jesus poured the wine and served the bread and the sweets to the disciples, then suddenly a recognition arose in them. This was the way Jesus always used to serve them — the way he poured the wine, the way he gave them the bread and the butter and the sweets. The gestures, the very gestures were so unique to Jesus that suddenly a cloud disappeared and they fell at his feet.

And Jesus said, "Why could you not recognize me? For two hours we walked together and talked about every kind of thing and gossiped, and yet you could not recognize me?"

They said, "There was no question of it, because a cloud was there in our eyes that you are dead. We did not even ask the question to ourselves."

Remember, we take note only of things if we are consciously ready to take note. If you are not consciously ready to take note, somebody may pass by your side and you may not see him at all.

Next time you are celebrating, make it a known fact to all the sannyasins that I am there. And those who are in tune with me, those who really love me, those who are surrendered, those who have known some trust, will immediately feel the presence. The presence can even be felt more there than here, because here you take it for granted that I am present; you need not make any effort. But there you will have to make a conscious effort to feel it. That very effort will make my presence more penetrating.

And these are a few jokes for you to laugh at:

Salesgirl to shopper: "Yes, madam, these bras come in four sizes: small, medium, large and wow!"

The light in the whorehouse was out so Mimi came into the room and did not even look at the body of the man whom she was in bed with. After rolling around on the bed for a while, she stopped, looked at the guy and said, "What is this, man, don't you have one?"

"Oh yes, I do!" answered the guy. "What I am missing is my left leg!"

Two Italian woodcutters were working in the forest. Suddenly one of them missed the tree with his ax and cut off his companion's right leg in one blow.

In between screams and yells the other woodcutter angrily shouts, "If you do that again, I'm-a gonna kick-a the shit-a out of you!"

A Frenchman who recently arrived in New York was invited to a golden wedding anniversary. He didn't understand the celebration and asked his American friend about it.

"Do you see those two old people?" asked his friend. "Well, they have been living together for fifty years and now they are celebrating their golden wedding."

"Ah, ah!" exclaimed the Frenchman. "He live with the lady fifty years, and now he marry her. How noble!"

It was morning, and she was still in her robe. Pausing in the half-open entrance door of her home, she called to the milkman who had just then pulled up to the curb.

"Pardon me, but do you have the time?" she asked.

"Yes," he said, "but not the inclination."

The Polish Police Department send their officers for an examination before giving them promotion. Kazowinsky came back from the examination with his extra stripe and was warmly congratulated by his commanding officer.

"Good work! Tell us all about it!" said the inspector.

"Well," replied Kazowinsky, "we were all close until the final question of the mathematics paper. They asked us to add two and two—I said five!" he announced proudly.

"But Kazowinsky, two and two are four, not five!" said the inspector.
"I know that now," he grinned, "but I was the closest!"

A Polack answered a nationwide quiz program that gave away money even to the dumbest people.

"Okay, Mr. Kozakowsky, for one thousand dollars, tell us, which famous French general was defeated at the battle of Waterloo?"

The Polack looked puzzled.

"We'll give you a clue," smiled the questioner, and opened the door of a large refrigerator. Inside was a bottle of Napoleon brandy. Kozakowsky still looked bewildered and scratched his head.

"Just read the name you see and you win one thousand dollars. Now, what was the name of the general?"

The Polack stared for a moment, then smiled.

"Of course," he said, "it must have been General Electric!"

An Italian frog was traveling to America. On his way he passed a beautiful swamp where he met a big fat American frog. He said, "How-a are you doing-a?"

"Great!" replied the frog. "In swamp, out swamp, lots of food. Far out!"

The Italian leaped on and met another big American frog. "How-a are you doing-a?" he asked.

"Groovy, man, just great!" came the reply. "In swamp, out swamp, lots of food — great!"

The Italian began to feel very happy about his new land. He leaped on and met a tiny, skinny little girl frog.

"What's-a wrong-a here?" he asked. "I have-a met-a two big-a fat-a frogs who said, 'In-a swamp-a, out-a swamp-a, lots-a of food-a!' But what-a has happened to you?"

The tiny frog whispered in answer, "I am Swamp!"
And the last:

"That parapsychology course at the Osho Meditation University is fabulous!" says Swami Francesco. "My ESP talents are developing so fast!"

"That's hard to believe," states his friend, Swami Giovanni, "you'd better prove it."

"For instance, my telepathy," says Francesco. "You just point at any door, and I shall give you remarkable particulars about the person who answers."

"Okay, *that* door," points his friend. "Tell me what will happen."

"Well," meditates Francesco. "I feel that a man whose girlfriend is having her period will open the door...."

"Hello, friends," greets Swami Mariano, entering the room through the same door.

"Does your girlfriend have her period?" asks Giovanni.

"Shit!" answers Mariano, wiping his mouth and chin. "Can you see it?"

Enough for today.

CHAPTER 15

No Question Means the Answer

The first question

I feel too lazy to think of a question. What to do?

It cannot be true that you really feel too lazy; otherwise who has written this question?

A man was lying down on the couch of a very famous psychoanalyst, and he was continuously talking about his failures in life, failures of all kinds in all directions. He was trying to prove that he was an utter failure, the ultimate in failure, that there was nobody in the world who was more of a failure than he was.

The psychoanalyst listened to him silently as long as he could tolerate, and then he said, "Stop all this nonsense! You cannot be such a failure!"

The man said, "Why?"

The psychoanalyst said, "If you were a failure you would not be able to afford my fee! If you can afford my fee for years— and I am the most expensive psychoanalyst in the world— how can you be a failure?"

You can ask such a beautiful question and you think you are lazy? And still you are asking what to do. If you are really lazy you should ask what *not* to do. Lazy you can be, but at least be consistently lazy. Either you are a philosopher or a Polack! In fact, both are synonymous! If you like big names, beautiful words, then think of yourself as a philosopher.

In the past, particularly in the Middle Ages, many mystics used the word 'foolosopher' for philosopher— and they were right. If you want to be down to earth, then the fact is that you are simply a Polack. Philosophers are expected to ask such things...

Centuries after Hamlet had told us what the question is— "To be or not to be?"—Gertrude Stein's deathbed utterance became a familiar quotation. Remember it, Chinmaya, when you are dying! Just before dying she opened her eyes and said, "What is the answer?"

The people who were around her were a little bit puzzled: "How can one suddenly ask, 'What is the answer?' when even the question has not been mentioned?"

Somebody gathered courage and responded to Stein's remark, "But we don't know the question!"

She smiled her beautiful smile and said, "Okay, then what is the question?"

Neither the question is known nor the answer is known, and you need not do anything. If there is no question at all, it is simply far out! Why create trouble for yourself? Why hanker after trouble? If there is no question, you have attained the answer! No question means the answer.

You are not here to ask questions. I am not here to answer your questions. You are here to be ready to destroy all your questions; I am here to go on hammering on your questions so that they are shattered. I will not give you any answer, I will only destroy your questions. And a moment comes when there is no question, no answer, and that is the state of samadhi, that is the state of ultimate consciousness. When words disappear, thoughts disappear, knowledge disappears, ignorance disappears. When only pure consciousness is left just like a mirror reflecting that which is, just like *this* moment...a silent pause... You can hear the traffic noise...it always happens! That's why the mystics say existence is such a harmony! You can hear the birds, you can even hear the silence...this throbbing of the hearts. This is the state which we are searching for— not for questions, not for answers.

The philosopher was at his favorite occupation—lying in the sun. The flies buzzed around and settled thickly on his face, but he was too lazy to shoo them away. Finally a hornet lit among the flies and stung his nose. This was different. He slowly wiped his hand across his face.

"As long as some of you won't behave," he muttered, "all of you will have to get off!"

Questions don't know how to behave. They are all like hornets lit amongst the flies. Your answers are like flies and your questions are like hornets lit amongst the flies. They all have to be wiped off.

The mind has to be utterly emptied.

The empty mind is the buddha mind.

But if you don't want to be a philosopher, if you are not interested in wiping off all the problems, all the questions, then you can be a Polack. That is the same in a more gross way. The philosopher is subtle, the Polack is gross, but they belong to the same ladder. The Polack may be the lowest rung and the philosopher the highest rung, but the ladder is the same.

Frankowski showed up at the practice field to try out for the high school football team.

"What position do you want to play?" asked the coach.

"Quarterback!" answered Frankowski.

The coach handed him a football and said, "Do you think you can pass this ball?"

"Hell," said the Polack, "if I can swallow it, I can pass it too!"

A journalist visiting a local penitentiary in the heart of Poland is being shown around by warden Poltowsky. As they enter the maximum security block, the reporter is surprised to hear a shout from one of the cells, "Twenty-two!" followed by raucous laughter from all the other cells.

Another voice then shouts, "Forty-three!" which is again followed by loud outbursts of laughter.

"What is going on, warden?" asked the bewildered journalist.

"It is quite simple really," replies the warden. "These fellas have been in this block so long that they know each other's jokes. So now when someone wants to tell a joke he simply shouts out the number. Everyone remembers the joke and laughs."

"Quite a good idea really," remarks the reporter, as the number thirty-seven is called out and followed by peals of laughter.

Then there is a loud, "Seventeen!" and then silence. Puzzled by the lack of response, the reporter asks the warden what went wrong.

"Ah, that was Jakowsky in cell eight," sighs the warden, "he told it wrong again!"

An American, a German and a Polack were going on safari. They split up in the morning and met again in the evening. Sitting around the camp fire they started telling of their adventures.

The German says, "I shot two tigers, an elephant and some apes."

The American, says, "Ah, I shot much more: six crows, four tigers and about three elephants."

They both look at the Polack, who's saying nothing at all. "What about you, Polanski?" they ask.

"I shot sixty-seven no-no's," he says.

Although the American and the German had quite a bit of experience in the jungle, they had never heard of such an animal. "What is a no-no?" they ask.

"Well," Polanski replies, "they are about six feet high, black, curly hair, big lips, and when you point your rifle at them they shout, 'No! No!'"

You need not be a philosopher, you need not be a Polack; just be a sannyasin! And to be a sannyasin means not to be bothered about questions and answers. The whole process of sannyas is getting rid of the mind. Mind consists of questions and answers. The moment you get rid of the mind, then only consciousness is left in its purity, with not even a ripple. The lake is so silent, so unperturbed, so still, it starts reflecting the stars, the clouds, the moon, the trees, the flowers, the birds on the wing.

There is a Zen saying that the birds have no desire to be reflected in the lake, the lake has no desire to reflect the birds— but it still happens. The birds are reflected, the lake reflects, although the desire exists neither on the part of the birds nor on the part of the lake. In this desirelessness everything happens, nothing is done.

A sannyasin has to relax to that total state of let-go when everything happens and nothing is done. Much happens, miracles happen, but don't ask me what to do. Ask me only one thing: "How to get out of the old rut of the mind?" And it consists of question and answers; it is a question-and-answer game.

Slip out of the mind like a snake slips out of the old skin. The mind is always old. It belongs to the past; it is not in the present, it has no future. Mind means the past, the dead. Mind is like a rearview mirror in the car. If you go on continuously looking in the rearview mirror, you are bound for a great disaster. The car has to go ahead, and you will be looking in the rearview mirror at the road that you have already passed, at the dust on the road that you have raised. That is not the way you are going, and you are not looking where you are going. Disaster is absolutely certain.

And this is happening in everybody's life. You go on reading the Vedas – that is looking in the rearview mirror. Five thousand years have passed, and still you go on looking at the Vedas, you go on reading the Bible, you go on reciting the Koran, you go on discussing Kanad, Kapil, Aristotle, Plato, Confucius, Ma Tzu...but all this is sheer wastage of time.

Look at the present.

This very moment God is within you and without you.

And if you can live this God in total serenity, in total attunement, at-onement, you would know the ecstasy that I am talking about, the bliss, the benediction.

The second question

> God knows I would never wish to contradict my master, but the other day you went too far! You said that all the enlightened ones have been Italians in one life or other. No doubt about you, or Jesus or Buddha, Lao Tzu or even Nanak, and Ramana...but Krishnamurti? My God! How can you honestly assert that someone so sane and sober as Krishnamurti has ever been an Italian? We hope you apologize.

> In fact, I myself, Jesus, Buddha, Lao Tzu, Nanak and Ramana may not have been Italians at all; hence still the attraction. I love the Italians— that is proof enough I have never been an Italian before! But Krishnamurti?— it is absolutely certain that he has been an Italian, and not only in one life but many lives; otherwise, how can he be so sane and sober? The Italians have done so much damage to him, he has not been able to recover yet—he is still under the impact. He is so much afraid of laughing in case somebody may discover that he has been an Italian! His seriousness is just the other extreme.

> I can understand your question, because Krishnamurti is deadly serious about things; that is one of his flaws. A really totally enlightened person cannot be so serious.

> Seriousness is a disease of the mind. When the mind is no longer

there, seriousness has no ground to stand upon. But Indians have respected seriousness very much; it is a long tradition. And Krishnamurti has been brought up by very serious people, the Theosophists.

That whole bunch of Theosophists was very determined to show the world that they are the only spiritual people. Their whole investment was in proving to the world that they had come to redeem the world of all its problems, illnesses, diseases. They were bound to be serious. When you are a savior you cannot joke around; you have to destroy your sense of humor absolutely. You have to be continuously concerned about the misery and the suffering that people are passing through. And when people are passing through so much suffering, how can you laugh? how can you enjoy? how can you even smile? That will be cruel.

The Theosophists had this idea — a very ancient idea that has clouded many people's beings — that they wanted to redeem the whole world. In fact, it is nobody's business to redeem the whole world — and who has the right to redeem anybody else? If the other person is enjoying his dream, you have no right to wake him up. At least his permission is needed, at least you have to ask him. Unless he wishes, you have to keep off. It is interference — maybe for his own good, but who are you to decide? If somebody chooses hell, then it is his freedom to choose it. You can feel compassion for him, you would have liked him not to choose hell, but what can you do? Who are you?

But these saviors of humanity are bound to be serious people; they are bent upon it. Whether you want it or not, they will force you into paradise! They will not leave you alone. And the Theosophists were preparing for a great event: to declare a world teacher. They had chosen Krishnamurti to be the messiah. Of course they conditioned him in every possible way: they regimented him, disciplined him for so long that the traces of it have not left him yet; the wounds are still there. For twenty-five years continuously he was in this wrong company.

Look into the training of J. Krishnamurti, and it will help you to understand why he is so serious. He was never allowed to mix with ordinary children — to play with them, to laugh, to giggle, to climb the trees, to swim the rivers, to fight, to be beaten. He was never allowed to do anything that every child has a right to do. His childhood was completely crushed. He was only nine years of age when he was taken away from his parents. His mother had died, and his father was a poor clerk, so poor, and he was not economically in a situation to educate his children. He had two children, two boys, Nityananda and Krishnamurti.

Seeing that the Theosophists were interested in the children he was thrilled—a great opportunity was opening up. They would not only teach him in ordinary schools, they were promising that they would educate him at Oxford, and in some very special schools meant only for royalty. They would take him around the world, they would arrange for private tutors, the best possible. What more could the poor father have desired and dreamt of? He willingly gave the children to the Theosophists.

And then a long struggle began between Krishnamurti's father and the Theosophists, because when the father became aware of what they were doing to his children, he was aghast. He could not believe it, that they were being forced like slaves. They had to get up at three o'clock in the morning and read the scriptures—Tibetan, Chinese, Japanese, Sanskrit. And they were almost asleep, repeating them in their sleep. Even in sleep they were not allowed to have a normal sleep; they would be sleeping, and the man who was in charge, Leadbeater, would go on repeating sutras and scriptures softly in their ears.

That was the first experiment in teaching children through hypnosis. Now it is a recognized scientific method, and particularly in Russia where hypno-teaching is becoming very common. Children can be taught with no need even for somebody to sit by their bed. Earphones can be put on, and the tape recorder can go on repeating silently, very whisperlike, so their sleep is not disturbed but still the message can go on penetrating to their unconscious. Even in their sleep they were not allowed the freedom to dream. Even their dreams were controlled.

You will be surprised to know that dreams can be controlled—your dreams can be managed by others. For example, when you are falling asleep, a certain program can be given to you for the whole night so that these will be your dreams. And those dreams can be manipulated from the outside also. For example, when you are falling asleep, there comes a moment, an interval, when you are not awake and you are not yet asleep either—just in between, that boundary line. That boundary line is the most sensitive part of your existence because you are changing the gears from one gear to another gear. Before you change gears you have to pass through the neutral gear, and when you are in a neutral gear anything can be put into your head. That's the whole secret of hypnosis: the neutral gear. That is the time when you are absolutely vulnerable; you cannot defend, you cannot argue.

So Leadbeater, Annie Besant and others would be sitting around when Krishnamurti was falling asleep, waiting for the moment, for indications. And there are very simple methods to know whether the child is in the interval or not. For example, the child can be told, "Go on looking at the roof continuously without blinking your eyes." A moment comes when the eyes become glassy; they are seeing and yet not seeing. That is the time when the neutral gear has come into existence. Wakefulness has gone, sleep has yet to come. It is the evening time; the day is no more, the night is entering. It is the most vulnerable, the most sensitive time. Say anything and it will go directly to the heart of the child. It will condition the child the deepest.

So they were conditioning the child, even managing his dreams, telling him, "You will be dreaming of a great desert. For miles and miles there is nobody— sand and sand and sand, and you go on and on..." And you can help the dream from the outside too. You have put the seed inside; then just a little heat near the feet and the child will start dreaming of the desert, because the heat near the feet will give him the feeling of walking on hot sand. A little heat near the head and he will feel he is under the hot sun, and you have triggered... You have done both the things: you have put the idea in the unconscious, and you have triggered the process from the body. The child is bound to dream about the desert, and of course he will follow the program that you have given.

This way Krishnamurti was conditioned while awake, while asleep. He was moved from one country to another country. He was never allowed to become friendly with anybody; he had no friends. How can he know what laughter is? He was never allowed to fall in love with a woman, with a girl—how can he know what laughter is?

And the people he was with were really a strange group of people. This Leadbeater was a homosexual; he was not interested in women and hence he was very much against women. And he was found in very suspicious postures with Krishnamurti—a small child.

When the father became aware of what was going on, he went to the courts. The case went on for years in the high court of Madras. The father proved in every way that Leadbeater was a homosexual. He produced witnesses who had seen him doing wrong things with his children. But then Leadbeater escaped from India, and before the court could decide that the children should be returned to the father, Annie Besant escaped with the children out of India, and the father could never get the children back.

Nityananda, the elder brother, died because of all the work that was being imposed upon them. When he was suffering from delirium, they thought that he was being influenced by great spiritual masters—Kuthumi, et cetera—that he was being transformed by the spiritual hierarchy. And that is all bullshit! There is no spiritual hierarchy, nothing.

Even Gunakar has started writing about spiritual hierarchy. He has issued letters and messages to all the UN members, and they must think that I am behind it, because my name, my picture is on his letterhead. And Gunakar goes on suggesting to them that there is a spiritual hierarchy working in the world. First he used to call me "Master," now he calls me "Elder Brother." Sooner or later I am waiting for him to write, "Dear Younger Brother." He is rising higher in the hierarchy! Now I am just an elder brother. It will not be a surprise if one day he writes, "My dear son."

Leadbeater was the most cunning of the people who were trying to manipulate these small children in the name of some hierarchy. He was writing books in the name of Krishnamurti. He has written a book *The Past Lives Of Alkayoni*. Alkayoni is the fictitious name for the many, many lives of Krishnamurti. Because in each life there was a different name, Alkayoni is the fictitious name for all these lives, thousands of lives. Leadbeater wrote these books and they were all signed by Krishnamurti. And now Krishnamurti says, "I don't remember at all when I wrote these books, when I even signed. I know nothing about them." They were all written by Leadbeater.

In fact, a child of ten or twelve years cannot have written those books; he cannot have any such stupid ideas—no child can be so stupid. And all this spiritual jargon... And then, finally, Leadbeater and his colleagues started writing a very famous book which became a world-famous spiritual treatise: *At The Feet Of The Master*. That too was published in the name of Krishnamurti, and Krishnamurti simply says he knows nothing about it.

These twenty-five years of all kinds of unnecessary torture, no ordinary life available... He was not allowed to walk in the gardens where other people were. He was not allowed to meet and mix with people, because he was "the world teacher"— how could he mix with ordinary human beings? Naturally he has lost all sense of humor. It is sad — and all because of that idea of the world teacher. He renounced the idea finally, and that is the only good thing that he has ever done in his life. He renounced the idea that "I am a world teacher," but that renunciation was only superficial; it never came through his innermost core. Deep down he continues to be the world teacher still. That's why he becomes very angry if you don't listen to him; he even starts hitting his own head. Even talking to people, if they don't understand him and the way he talks—it is so monotonous, it is so boring, that unless somebody is doing some research on boredom, nobody can be interested, people cannot understand— then he starts beating his head, shouting, becomes enraged. But the whole idea deep down is to redeem the world.

If you don't understand me it doesn't matter, it is your freedom. It is my freedom to talk; it is your freedom to understand or not to understand or to misunderstand. How can I decide for you? I cannot be enraged. Even if you all fall asleep I cannot be enraged. I will have a good laugh! Even the idea of giving so many people a good morning sleep is such a consolation that one is doing some service to people!

You say: "...but Krishnamurti? My God! How can you honestly assert that someone so sane and sober as Krishnamurti has ever been an Italian?"

For me to assert anything honestly or dishonestly makes no difference. Whatsoever is right at the moment, honest or dishonest, right or wrong, true or untrue.... I believe in Gautam Buddha's definition of truth: that which works. If honesty works, perfectly okay. I am a nonserious person; these are also serious things. Honest? — why should I be honest? Things should be taken playfully. What is wrong in being dishonest once in a while, just for a change?

And you say, "...so sane and sober..." If a man is one hundred percent sane, then he is insane. Something of insanity is a basic ingredient of real sanity.

Zorba the Greek says to his boss, "Boss, everything is right in you, only one thing is missing— a little touch of madness."

A man without a little madness is flat—flat like a flat tire! A little bit of madness brings some spice to your life—some color, some intensity, some passion, some dance, some celebration.

Krishnamurti, even if he enters paradise, will remain sane and serious. I don't think he will be welcome there. He will start talking about the same things he has been talking about on the earth for sixty years, and he will beat his head because even the angels are not going to listen to him! Angels don't listen to spiritual discourses. Their whole work is playing their harps, sitting on the clouds and shouting "Alleluia!" They will fit with me perfectly, but can you imagine angels playing "Alleluia!" on their harps and dancing around Krishnamurti? He will commit suicide: All this "Alleluia!" and the whole world has to be redeemed! Everybody is suffering, and these fools... But I can enjoy! I may even start learning how to play on the harp. I have tried a little bit, just in order to be ready at least, so I am not an absolute outsider there!

But if he is so sane and sober, it must be the spaghetti that has gone to his head! Too much spaghetti in the head makes people very sane and sober.

And you say to me, "We hope you apologize."

I have never done that, and I am never going to do it – that is not my way. I never repent, I never apologize—for what? I am doing my thing. If somebody feels angry he can do whatsoever he wants to do. He can shout at me, he can condemn me; there is no problem for me at all. In fact, I enjoy all this. Whenever people become interested—this is a kind of interest, if somebody is offended—I rejoice. A connection has been made—not a very good connection, but a connection is a connection anyway! If it is bad today, tomorrow it can be good.

Mrs. Carbotti went to the doctor complaining of fatigue. After the examination, the doctor decided she needed a rest.

"Can you stop having relations with your husband for about three weeks?" he asked.

"Sure," she replied, "I got two boyfriends who can take care of me for that long!"

That's why I like the Italians —they are so human, so truly human!

Giovanni said to his daughter, "I no like-a that Irish boy taking you out-a. He is-a rough and common, and besides-a, he is-a a big-a dumbell!"

"No, papa," replied the girl, "Tim is the most clever fella I know."

"Why-a you say-a that?"

"We have only been dating nine weeks and already he has cured me of that little illness I used to get every month!"

A vet goes to Giuseppe's farm to artificially inseminate his cows. While there, he gets an urgent call to another farm. He decides to give Giuseppe the syringe and explain how to do it, then rushes off.

A little while later the local parish priest doing his rounds knocks on the farmer's door. Pierino opens the door and the priest asks where his father is.

"He is-a down at-a the cow-shed," replies the little boy, "but it is-a better not-a to go there. It is-a the third-a time that he tries to inseminate the cow and he is-a swearing like hell-a!"

"What, what...what are you saying?" says the priest. "Ah, my God! And does your mother know what he is doing?"

"Of course-a," replies Pierino. "She is-a the one-a who keeps-a the cow's fanny open and shouts, 'Come on-a, Giuseppe, this is-a time you will-a make it!'"

Now these beautiful Italians...who cares about enlightenment?

A teacher was getting acquainted with her fourth-grade pupils by letting them get up and talk about the best thing they did during the summer holidays.

"And you, Johnny?" asked the teacher.

"Well, I played with my train set," reported Johnny.

"What about you, Gloria?"

"Ah, we took a wonderful trip to the mountains for the whole summer," said Gloria.

"And you, Liza?" asked the teacher of Little Black Liza.

"I like to fuck!" reported Liza.

"Ah, Liza, what a terrible thing to say! I want you to go home and not return until you have a note from your mother, informing me that she is aware of what you have said!" demanded the teacher.

Two days passed before Liza finally returns to class.

"Do you have that note I asked you to bring, Liza?" asked the teacher.

"No, teacher, I ain't got no note. I told Momma what I said, then I told Momma what you said, and Momma said that if somebody don't like to fuck they must be a cocksucker, and she don't want to correspond with your kind!"

The third question

Please tell us a few more Murphy sutras and a few Murphy anecdotes too.

The Murphy sutras are really beautiful!

The first sutra: If wives were good, God would have one.

Second: Some people are born silly, some people acquire silliness, and some fall in love.

Third: After man came woman, and she has been after him ever since.

Fourth: Be thrifty when you are young, and when you are old you will be able to afford the things that only the young can enjoy.

Fifth: Never miss an opportunity to make others happy, even if you have to leave them alone.

Sixth: Heredity is something people believe in if they have bright children.

Seventh: When in Rome, do as the Romans do – eat spaghetti.

Eighth: Some men have no solution for any difficulty, but will find a difficulty for any solution.

If you don't believe in this eighth sutra you can ask Asheesh. He is the perfect personification of this sutra! He has no solution for any difficulty, but you give him any solution and he will find the difficulty!

Ninth: There is no time like the present for postponing what you don't want to do.

Tenth: Teamwork is essential—it allows you to blame someone else.

Eleventh: You can make it foolproof, but you can't make it damn foolproof.

Twelfth: The height of futility is to tell a hair-raising story to a bald man.

Thirteenth: What is dumber than a dumb Italian? A dumb Indian.

Fourteenth: Adam was the happiest man on earth. Eve's mother never told her that nice girls did not do it that way.

Fifteenth: You can't get there from here, and besides there is no place else to go.

And a few anecdotes about Murphy...

The first: "I am getting more and more absent minded," said Murphy to a few of his cronies. "Sometimes in the middle of a sentence..."

"That fellow Bobo is so rude: this morning he was snoring in church!"
"Yes, I know," said Murphy. "He woke me up!"

Murphy had recently become the father of triplets, and the priest stopped him on the street to congratulate him.
"Well, Murphy," he said, "so the stork smiled on you."
"Smiled on me!" exclaimed Murphy. "He laughed out loud!"

One friend met Murphy at the station. "Where are you going?" the friend asked.
"To Paris, for my honeymoon," said Murphy.
"Without your wife?"
"Listen, when you go to Munich, do you take beer with you?"

One Sunday morning the preacher was ill and could not come to the church to perform his duties, so Murphy was doing his work. He was urging his congregation to sing.
"Now is the opportunity for all of you gifted with wonderful voices to show your gratitude towards the Lord. And for all of you without good voices, this is the time to get even with him!"

Murphy came home an hour earlier than usual and found his wife stark naked in bed. When he asked why, she explained, "I am protesting because I don't have anything to wear."
Murphy pulled open the closet door. "That's ridiculous," he said, "Look in here. There is a yellow dress, a red dress, a print dress, a pant suit...Hi Chris!...a green dress..."

And the last: The son was sitting at the bedside of the elderly gentleman, Murphy, who was dying. "Where do you want to be buried," the kid asked, "in Forest Lawn or Hillside Memorial Park?"

The old man creaked up on his elbow and answered, "Surprise me!"

Enough for today.

Appendix

1. ABOUT OSHO
Osho defies categorization, reflecting everything from the individual quest for meaning to the most urgent social and political issues facing society today. His books are not written but are transcribed from recordings of extemporaneous talks given over a period of thirty-five years. Osho has been described by the *Sunday Times* in London as one of the "1000 Makers of the 20th Century" and by *Sunday Mid-Day* in India as one of the ten people –along with Gandhi, Nehru and Buddha– who have changed the destiny of India.

Osho has a stated aim of helping to create the conditions for the birth of a new kind of human being, characterized as "Zorba the Buddha"– one whose feet are firmly on the ground, yet whose hands can touch the stars. Running like a thread through all aspects of Osho is a vision that encompasses both the timeless wisdom of the East and the highest potential of Western science and technology.

He is synonymous with a revolutionary contribution to the science of inner transformation and an approach to meditation which specifically addresses the accelerated pace of contemporary life. The unique Osho Active Meditations™ are designed to allow the release of accumulated stress in the body and mind so that it is easier to be still and experience the thought-free state of meditation.

2. OSHO COMMUNE INTERNATIONAL : An Invitation to Experience
Osho Commune International is a meditation resort that has been created so that people can have a direct experience of a new way of living– with more alertness, relaxation, and humor. Located about a hundred miles southeast of Mumbai in Pune, India, the resort offers a variety of programs to the thousands of people who visit each year from more than one hundred countries.

The campus is spread over forty acres in the tree-lined residential area of Koregaon Park. Although accommodation for visitors is not provided, there is a plentiful variety of nearby hotels and private apartments available for stays of a few days up to several months.

The programs at the meditation resort, which take place in an elegant pyramid complex next to the famous Osho Teerth Zen Garden, are designed to provide the tools to allow contemporary people to transform their lives. The whole point is to give people access to a new lifestyle–one of relaxed awareness, which is an approach they can take with them into their everday life. A variety of self-discovery classes, sessions and courses and the Osho meditative processes are offered throughout the year. In the main meditation hall, the daily schedule includes meditation methods that are active and passive, contemporary and traditional. For exercising the body and keeping fit, there is a beautiful outdoor facility where one can experiment with a Zen approach to sports and recreation.

Every evening visitors have the opportunity to participate in a unique two-hour meditation beginning with exuberant dancing, following by a video of Osho speaking, and ending in relaxed silence.

Following this meeting, the nightlife in this multicultural resort is alive with outdoor eating areas serving traditional Indian fare and a choice of international dishes. The plaza café fills with friends and there is often dancing, with a DJ or to live music.

The Commune has its own supply of safe, filtered drinking water and the food served is made with organically grown produce from the Commune's own farm.

An online tour of the meditation resort, as well as travel and program information, can be found at: www.osho.com

The Meditation Program

The range of methods offered in the main meditation hall include:

Osho Dynamic Meditation™ : A technique designed to release tensions and repressed emotions, opening the way to a new vitality and an experience of profound silence.

Osho Kundalini Meditation ™: A technique of shaking free one's dormant energies, and through spontaneous dance and silent sitting, allowing these energies to be redirected inward.

Osho Nadabrahma Meditation ™: A method of harmonizing one's energy flow, based on an ancient Tibetan humming technique.

Osho Nataraj Meditation ™: A method involving the inner alchemy of dancing so totally that the dancer disappears and only the dance remains.

Vipassana Meditation: A technique originating with Gautam Buddha and now updated for the 21st Century, for dissolving mental chatter through the awareness of breath.

No Dimensions Meditation ™: A powerful method for centering ones' energy, based on a Sufi technique.

For detailed information to participate in this meditation resort please contact:

Osho Commune International
17 Koregaon Park, Pune-411001, MS, India
Phone: 020 4019999 Fax: 020 4019990
Email: visitor@osho.net Website:www.osho.com

3. BOOKS BY OSHO IN ENGLISH LANGUAGE

Early Discourses and Writings
A Cup of Tea
Dimensions Beyond The Known
From Sex to Superconsciousness
The Great Challenge
Hidden Mysteries
I Am The Gate
The Inner Journey
Psychology of the Esoteric
Seeds of Wisdom

Meditation
The Voice of Silence
And Now and Here (Vol. 1 & 2)
In Search of the Miraculous (Vol. 1 & 2)
Meditation: The Art of Ecstasy
Meditation: The First and Last Freedom
The Path of Meditation
The Perfect Way
Yaa-Hoo! The Mystic Rose

Buddha and Buddhist Masters
The Book of Wisdom
The Dhammapada: The Way of the Buddha (Vol. 1-12)
The Diamond Sutra
The Discipline of Transcendence (Vol. 1-4)
The Heart Sutra

Indian Mystics
Enlightenment: The Only Revolution (Ashtavakra)
Showering without Clouds (Sahajo)
The Last Morning Star (Daya)
The Song of Ecstasy (Adi Shankara)

Baul Mystics
The Beloved (Vol. 1 & 2)

Kabir
The Divine Melody
Ecstasy: The Forgotten Language
The Fish in the Sea is Not Thirsty
The Great Secret
The Guest
The Path of Love
The Revolution

Jesus and Christian Mystics
Come Follow to You (Vol. 1-4)
I Say Unto You (Vol. 1 & 2)
The Mustard Seed
Theologia Mystica

Jewish Mystics
The Art of Dying
The True Sage

Western Mystics
Guida Spirituale (Desiderata)
The Hidden Harmony (Heraclitus)
The Messiah (Vol. 1 & 2) (Commentaries on Khalil Gibran's the Prophet)
The New Alchemy: To Turn You On (Commentaries on Mabel Collins' Light on the Path)

Philosophia Perennis (Vol. 1 & 2) (The Golden Verses of Pythagoras)
Zarathustra: A God That Can Dance
Zarathustra: The Laughing Prophet (Commentaries on Nietzsche's Thus Spake Zarathustra)

Sufism
Just Like That
Journey to the Heart
The Perfect Master (Vol. 1 & 2)
The Secret
Sufis: The People of the Path (Vol. 1 & 2)
Unio Mystica (Vol. 1 & 2)
The Wisdom of the Sands (Vol. 1&2)

Tantra
Tantra: The Supreme Understanding
The Tantra Experience
The Royal Song of Saraha (same as Tantra Vision, Vol. 1)
The Tantric Transformation
The Royal Song of Saraha (same as Tantra Vision, Vol. 2)
The Book of Secrets: Vigyan Bhairav Tantra

The Upanishads
Behind a Thousand Names (Nirvana Upanishad)
Heartbeat of the Absolute (Is havasya Upanishad)
I am That (Isa Upanishad)
The Message Beyond Words (Kathopanishad)
Philosophia Ultima (Mandukya Upanishad)
The Supreme Doctrine (Kenopanishad)
Finger Pointing to the Moon (Adhyatma Upanishad)
The Art Thou (Sarvasar Upanishad, Kaivalya Upanishad, Adhyatma Upanishad)
The Ultimate Alchemy, Vol. 1 & 2 (Atma Pooja Upanishad Vol. 1 & 2)
Vedanta: Seven Steps to Samadhi (Akshaya Upanishad)
Flight of the Alone to the Alone (Kaivalya Upanishad)

Tao
The Empty Boat
The Secret of Secrets
Tao: The Golden Gate (Vol. 1 & 2)
Tao: The Pathless Path (Vol. 1 & 2)
Tao: The Three Treasures (Vol. 1-4)
When the Shoe Fits

Yoga
The Path of Yoga (previously Yoga : The Alpha and the Omega Vol. 1)
Yoga: The Alpha and the Omega (Vol. 2-10)

Zen and Zen Masters
Ah, This!
Ancient Music in the Pines
And the Flowers Showered
A Bird on the Wing
Bodhidharma: The Greatest Zen Master
Communism and Zen Fire, Zen Wind
Dang Dang Doko Dang
The First Principle
God is Dead: Now Zen is the Only Living Truth
The Grass Grows by Itself
The Great Zen Master Ta Hui
Hsin Hsin Ming: The Book of Nothing
I Celebrate Myself: God is no Where, Life is Now Here
Kyozan: A True Man of Zen
Nirvana: The Last Nightmare
No Mind: The Flowers of Eternity no Water, no Moon
One Seed Makes the Whole Earth Green
Returning to the Source
The Search: Talks on the 10 Bulls of Zen
A Sudden Clash of Thunder
The Sun Rises in the Evening
Take it Easy (Vol. 1 & 2)
This Very Body the Buddha
Walking in Zen, Sitting in Zen
The White Lotus Yakusan: Straight to the Point of Enlightenment
Zen Manifesto: Freedom from Oneself
Zen: The Mystery and the Poetry of the Beyond
Zen: The Path of Paradox (Vol. 1, 2 & 3)
Zen: The Special Transmission

Appendix

Zen Boxed Sets
The World of Zen (5 vols.)
- Live Zen
- This, This, A Thousand Times This
- Zen: The Diamond Thunderbolt
- Zen: The Quantum Leap from Mind to No-Mind
- Zen: The Solitary Bird, Cuckoo of the Forest

Zen: All the Colors of the Rainbow (5 vols.)
- The Buddha: The Emptiness of the Heart
- The Language of Existence
- The Miracle
- The Original Man
- Turning In

Osho: On the Ancient Masters of Zen (7 volumes)*
- Dogen: The Zen Master
- Hyakujo: The Everest of Zen with Basho's haikus
- Isan: No Footprints in the Blue Sky
- Joshu: The Lion's Roar
- Ma Tzu: The Empty Mirror
- Nansen: The point of Departure
- Rinzai: Master of the Irrational

*Each volume is also available individually

Responses to Questions
Be Still and Know
Come, Come, Yet Again Come
The Goose is Out
The Great Pilgrimage: From Here to Here
The Invitation
My Way: The Way of the White Clouds
Nowhere to Go But In
The Razor's Edge
Walk without Feet, Fly without Wings and Think without Mind
The Wild Geese and the Water
Zen: Zest, Zip, Zap and Zing

Talks in America
From Bondage to Freedom
From Darkness to Light
From Death to Deathlessness
From the Flase to the Truth
From Unconsciousness to Consciousness

The World Tour
Beyond Enlightenment (Talks in Bombay)
Beyond Psychology (Talks in Uruguay)
Light on the Path (Talks in the Himalayas)
The Path of the Mystic (Talks in Uruguay)
Sermons in Stones (Talks in Bombay)
Socrates Poisoned Again After 25 Centuries (Talks in Greece)
The Sword and the Lotus (Talks in the Himalayas)
The Transmission of the Lamp (Talks in Uruguay)

Osho's Vision for the World
The Golden Future
The Hidden Splendor
The New Dawn
The Rebel
The Rebellious Spirit

The Mantra Series
Hari Om Tat Sat
Om Mani Padme Hum
Om Shantih Shantih Shantih
Sat-Chit-Anand
Satyam-Shivam-Sundram

Personal Glimpses
Books I Have Loved
Glimpses of a Golden Childhood
Notes of a Madman

Interviews with the World Press
The Last Testament (Vol. 1)

Intimate Talks between Master and Disciple—Darshan Diaries
A Rose is a Rose is a Rose
Be Realistic: Plan for a Miracle
Believing the Impossible Before Breakfast
Beloved of my Heart
Blessed are the Ignorant
Dance your Way to God
Don't Just do Something, Sit There
Far Beyond the Stars
For Madmen Only

The Further Shore
Get Out of your Own Way
God's Got A Thing about You
God is Not for Sale
The Great Nothing
Hallelujah!
Let Go!
The 99 Names of Nothingness
No Book, No Buddha, No Teaching, No Disciple
Nothing to Lose but Your Head
Only Losers can Win in This Game
Open Door
Open Secret
The Shadow of the Whip
The Sound of one Hand Clapping
Ths Sun behind the Sun behind the Sun
The Tongue-Tip Taste of Tao
This is it
Turn On, Tune in and Drop the Lot
What is, is, What Ain't, Ain't Won't you Join The Dance?

Compilations

After Middle Age: A Limitless Sky
At the Feet of the Master
Bhagwan Shree Rajneesh: On Basic Human Rights
Jesus Crucified Again, This Time in Ronald Reagan's America Priests and Politicians: The Mafia of the Soul
Take it Really Seriously

Gift Books of Osho Quotations

A Must for Contemplation before Sleep
A Must for Morning Contemplation
India my Love

Photobooks

Shree Rajneesh: A Man of Many Climates, Seasons and Rainbow through the eye of the camera Impressions... Osho Commune International Photobook

Books about Osho

Bhagwan: The Buddha for the Future by Juliet Forman
Bhagwan Shree Rajnesh: The Most Dangerous Man Since Jesus Christ by Sue Appleton
Bhagwan: The Most Godless Yet the Most Godly Man By Dr. George Meredith
Bhagwan: One Man against the Whole Ugly Past of Humanity by Juliet Forman
Bhagwan: Twelve Days that Shook the World by Juliet Forman
Was Bhagwan Shree Rajneesh Poisoned by Ronald Reagan's America? by Sue Appleton.
Diamond Days with Osho by Ma Prem Shunyo

For any information about Osho Books & Audio/Video Tapes please contact:

Sadhana Foundation

17 Koregaon Park, Pune–411001, MS, India
Phone: 020 4019999 Fax: 020 4019990
E-mail: distrib@osho.net Website:www.osho.com